Trademark Acknowledgments

The following list recognizes the commercial and intellectual property of the trademark holders whose products or technologies are mentioned in this book. Omission from this list is inadvertent:

Acrobat is a trademark of Adobe Systems, Inc.
ActiveX is a trademark of the Microsoft Corporation
Afterburner is a trademark of Macromedia, Inc.
AIX is a trademark of IBM Corporation
Authorware is a trademark of Macromedia, Inc.
Cold Fusion is a trademark of Allaire Corporation
Director is a trademark of Macromedia, Inc.
FileMaker Pro is a trademark of Filemaker, Inc.
FreeHand is a trademark of Macromedia, Inc.
HyperCard is a trademark of Apple Computer, Inc.
Illustrator is a trademark of Adobe Systems, Inc.
Informix is a trademark of Informix Software, Inc.
Internet Explorer is a trademark of the Microsoft Corporation
IRIX is a trademark of Silicon Graphics, Inc.
Java is a trademark of Sun Microsystems. Inc.
Jscript is a trademark of Microsoft Corporation
LiveWire is a trademark of Netscape Communications Corporation
Navigator, Communicator, and Netscape are trademarks of Netscape
       Communications Corporation
Macintosh is a trademark of Apple Computer, Inc.
ODBC is a trademark of the Microsoft Corporation
Oracle is a trademark of Oracle, Inc.
OS/2 is a trademark of IBM Corporation
PhotoShop is a trademark of Adobe Systems, Inc.
QuarkXPress is a trademark of Quark, Inc.
RealAudio is a trademark of RealNetworks, Inc.
Shockwave is a trademark of Macromedia, Inc.
Solaris and SunOS are trademarks of Sun Microsystems, Inc.
SQL Server is a trademark of Sybase, Inc. and Microsoft Corporation
Sybase is a trademark of Sybase, Inc.
UNIX is a registered trademark licensed exclusively through X/Open Company, Ltd.
VBScript and Visual Basic Scripting Edition are trademarks of the Microsoft Corporation
Windows, Windows 95, and Windows NT are trademarks of Microsoft Corporation

Web Site Engineering

Beyond Web Page Design

Thomas A. Powell

with

David L. Jones and Dominique C. Cutts

Prentice Hall PTR
Upper Saddle River, NJ 07458
www.phptr.com

ISBN 013650920-7

90000

9 780136 509202

Editorial/production supervision: *Nicholas Radhuber*
Cover design director: *Jerry Votta*
Cover design: *Design Source*
Acquisitions editor: *Mary Franz*
Marketing manager: *Dan Rush*
Editorial assistant: *Noreen Regina*
Manufacturing manager: *Alexis R. Heydt*

© 1998 by Prentice Hall PTR
Prentice-Hall, Inc.
A Simon & Schuster Company
Upper Saddle River, NJ 07458

Prentice Hall books are widely used by corporations and government
agencies for training, marketing, and resale. The publisher offers
discounts on this book when ordered in bulk quantities.

For more information, contact:
Phone: 800-382-3419   Fax: 201-236-7141
e-mail: corpsales@prenhall.com.
or write:
Corporate Sales Department
Prentice Hall PTR
One Lake Street
Upper Saddle River, NJ 07458

Printed in the United States of America
10   9   8   7   6   5   4   3   2

ISBN: 0-13-650920-7

Prentice-Hall International (UK) Limited, *London*
Prentice-Hall of Australia Pty. Limited, *Sydney*
Prentice-Hall Canada Inc., *Toronto*
Prentice-Hall Hispanoamericana, S.A., *Mexico*
Prentice-Hall of India Private Limited, *New Delhi*
Prentice-Hall of Japan, Inc., *Tokyo*
Simon & Schuster Asia Pte. Ltd., *Singapore*
Editora Prentice-Hall do Brasil, Ltda., *Rio de Janeiro*

Contents

Preface

Web Site design is not graphic design. Far too many books treat Web site development as simply the choice of a usable interface and an appropriate market identity, or the production of correct HTML. This is a simplistic way to describe Web development. Certain classes of sites certainly fall into such generalizations, but what about intranets? What about Web-based applications? What about transactional systems? The list goes on and on. This book attempts to deal with the possibility that there is more to Web sites than visual design and user interface—namely functionality. Sites are not just about content; they are often also about application. Yet with the addition of more sophisticated function beyond simple content navigation comes system design, planning, testing and a whole range of problems. Engineering principles and organization can help bring this potential chaos under control. Now sites are becoming more like software projects and less like art projects. In fact, the battle for control of a Web site is fought daily between the MIS and Marketing departments of many firms around the world— but should it be? This book is not a declaration of the supremacy of the software approach. Neither is it a claim that designers shouldn't run a project. Software Engineering principles are not the law of the land any more than a particular design style is the best way sites should be built. After reading this book it should be obvious that building sites is a complex task. Without people versed in graphic design, usability, server design, and numerous other disciplines, a site will be less successful than it could be. Computer professionals with graduate degrees should not be telling designers their business any more than accomplished visual designers should claim to understand object-oriented coding techniques. Reading this book should teach you that you don't have to be expert in everything to pull a site off. In fact, just being able to bring together a diverse team of people and produce a site is a talent all its own.

Acknowledgments

The ideas in this book are the result of many interesting and enjoyable collaborations. The author owes a debt of gratitude to all those who helped shape this work. First, I would like to thank the two co-authors, David Jones and Dominique Cutts from Powell Internet Consulting, LLC (PINT), who kept the project going last summer when their boss was committed with other projects. Other PINT staffers, including Dan Whitworth, Rob McFarlane, Jimmy Tam, and Tyde Richards also provided a great deal of help. Our clients have also provided a great deal of project experience and input, particularly Berta Creter of Pulse and Kelly Johnson of AMCC. Special thanks for Bill Griswold of the UCSD Computer Science Department for advice on the early ideas of the book. San Diego Sea World deserves special credit for providing nightly fireworks for the enjoyment of all local late night workers. Mary Franz at Prentice Hall deserves a special patience award for dealing with this book's multitude of challenges. All the folks at Prentice Hall helped to make sure to finally get this out the door, particularly Nick Radhuber. Many thanks to the numerous technical reviewers. Your comments helped to shape this book. Lastly, the authors would like to express our thanks to our friends, family, and loved ones who always lend their love and support when needed.

Thomas A. Powell
tpowell@pint.com
January 1998

Introduction: Evolution of Web Site Design

A major problem with discussing the creation of Web pages is that one aspect of the process, like HTML or graphic design, is often confused with the complete process of Web design and publishing. Web design describes the process of creating appealing and usable Web sites. Graphic design is part of Web design, but it is only a part of the process. HTML and more programming-oriented technologies are also part of the process. Web "publishing" is a more appropriate term to describe the overall process of planning and putting together a Web site, particularly when some degree of forethought, skill, and artistry is employed. This is, however, a limited, paper-centered way of viewing Web sites. Traditional Web publishing tends to focus on sites as "brochureware"—literally an online marketing piece with a minor amount of interactivity and technology. This way of thinking about the Web may be appropriate for certain promotional purposes, but as the size and complexity of Web sites grow rapidly, a more rigorous software-centered approach to Web design is required. By applying traditional software engineering practices and combining them with Web publishing ideas, a next-generation hybrid process called *Web Site Engineering* is born.

Web Design

Before discussing Web Site Engineering, it is important to understand Web Design. While many people discuss Web design, there is no clear consensus on what Web design actually is, let alone what constitutes *good* Web design. So, how is good Web page design defined? Often, it is far easier to discuss what it is not (www.webpagesthatsuck.com), but this really doesn't demonstrate how to create good Web sites. Others like to discuss aesthetics and layout (www.highfive.com). This may be appropriate on a superficial level, but beauty is in the eye of the beholder. Appearance isn't everything. Function is equally important. Some like to answer the question about good Web design by providing pure function. If a site is not utilitarian (www.useit.com), it isn't reasonable—but function without motivating form is boring. Some people talk too much about success, citing large numbers of visitors as validation of a site's design. This assumes that the Web is primarily about popularity. Who cares how many visitors come to a page unless they bring some benefit to it? Think about quality and success. If serving the most burgers says anything about making quality hamburgers, then McDonald's makes the world's best hamburger. This kind of misguided logic gets people in trouble on the Web all the time. Think about whether or not the economically successful or even trendy Web pages are well designed. Often they are not, but this *doesn't* necessarily mean the site is a failure. Characterizing good Web design can be difficult.

Most Web discussions lose sight of the big picture. They place too much emphasis on how pages look, and not on their content, purpose, functionality or the user's experience. Graphic design— artistic style, color theory, typography, and other visual concerns—is an important part of the Web process, but it's not the same thing as Web design. Web design also includes information design, which specifies how information should be organized and linked. In this sense, hypertext theory is a part of Web design. To some extent, so is technical writing. However, today Web site design might also include system design. Web pages aren't always static pages, but often consist of programs that *do* something. So, programming is a part of Web design, as are network and server design. Business issues and project management also might be considered realities of Web design. There are many aspects of Web site design, but what is the ultimate purpose? Before presenting our opinion on the purpose of

Web design and why it should be approached in a more structured manner, we should first look at its evolution. This will explain a great deal of the motivations for the Web Site Engineering concept.

The Early Web

Before the arrival of Mosaic, the first graphical Web browser, there was the early Web—and before that, many forms of hypertext. The idea of hypertext is actually an old one. Many credit Vannevar Bush as the grandfather of hypertext. He worked on an idea called Memex as early as the 1930s, though the main article that described his ideas of a modern hypertext system was not published until 1945. In 1965, Ted Nelson coined the actual word "hypertext." Hypertext is vaguely defined as interconnecting pieces of information in a non-sequential, but usually relational, manner for efficient browsing of a body of information. Much research was conducted in the field of hypertext from the mid-60s to the mid-80s. It was not until 1987 that an easy-to-use hypertext system, HyperCard™ by Bill Atkinson of Apple Computer, became widely available. It is interesting to note that much of the rich history and body of research in hypertext, the foundation of the Web, has been forgotten.

In 1989, a team lead by Tim Berners-Lee at the European Center for Particle Research (CERN) in Switzerland proposed an idea for managing a large body of information of use to researchers in high energy physics. The original purpose of this project had a direct influence on the Web and its growth. According to the paper "Information Management: A Proposal," the hypertext system[1] should provide remote access to existing data across a heterogeneous network, and must not require central management. It should also provide private links and capabilities for data analysis and visualization. Bells and whistles, such as support for graphics, were not needed. The proposal also suggested that security and information ownership were not issues in the new system.

---

1. According to the historical documents at the World Wide Web Consortium (www.w3.org), the name World Wide Web was not decided upon until October 1990. Furthermore, the basic technology was not even available until early 1992.

The early Web was built for a research environment that had little need for presentation, security, or programming facilities. There is nothing wrong with this picture of the Web, but it is very different from what people want today: a presentation-heavy environment with support for programming facilities to build client/server systems. In the Pre-Mosaic generation, presentation was not the issue. The Web was about information. Commercialism and appealing to the masses were not a concern. This was a system initially built for a specific purpose and later extended for more generalized use. At the time, Berners-Lee probably never could have believed that the Web would be anything like it is today. He certainly didn't think about designing his system for today's require-ments. Yet, from his idea to solve a difficult information-sharing problem was born a system with profound implications.

First Generation: Mosaic

When Mosaic arrived on the scene in 1993, it was a huge improvement just to see an image embedded in a text document delivered via the Internet. But there was more than pretty pictures and an improved browser interface behind the rapid adoption of Web technology that followed. Thanks to simple tech-nologies like Hypertext Markup Language (HTML), Hypertext Transport Protocol (HTTP) and the Common Gateway Interface (CGI), it was fairly quick and easy to put together a simple Web site. The skills required to build first-generation Web sites included a basic knowledge of HTML, writing, information organization, rudimentary graphic design, some programming, and, typically, knowledge of UNIX. Often, these skills could be found in a single person—usually a UNIX system administrator or programmer with a creative flair, a publisher or writer with a technical background, a librarian, or a self-taught entrepreneur. These pioneer Web builders led to the rise of the common concept of a Webmaster, a literal jack-of-all-trades. For better or worse, the legend of the Webmaster lives on. In reality, the purpose of today's Webmaster is changing as fast as the Web.

First generation Web sites were simple affairs—some text, a few pictures, and maybe some forms for interactivity. The sites often consisted of a few pages, and were very experimental. The technology used to build such early sites included HTML, and, occasionally, simple CGI programs to access backend systems. Two dimensional graphic files, typically in GIF format, or small multimedia files accessed via helper applications were the extent of the graphics used. Sophisticated graphic design was not really possible under Mosaic. Early HTML and browsers did not support background colors, object centering or any degree of screen layout control such as tables or style sheets. Programming fared no better on the early Web. It consisted of simple code, generally written in Perl, that was used as a gateway to legacy Internet services such as Archie. Figure 1-1 shows a generic first generation Web site, while Figure 1-2 shows the technologies that were involved in such pages.

Figure 1–1. First Generation Web Page.

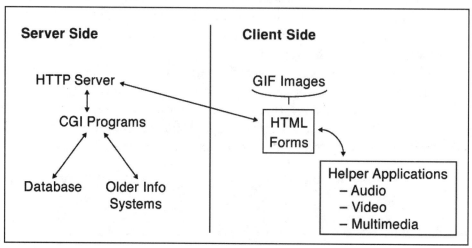

Figure 1–2. First-Generation Web Technology.

Initially, companies allocated little or no budget to the construction of a Web site. Typically, the site was often the pet project of a system administrator or marketing manager with a little spare time. Because many of these sites were the first Web sites representing their particular industry, they often received significant media attention regardless of the merits of their content or design. The race was on to stick your flag in the sand and proclaim that you had colonized the Internet. Because of this, the first Web sites often were not initially well thought out. They often were constantly under construction, or abandoned entirely. Because of the potential promotional benefit of Web sites, however, advertising and corporate communications professionals quickly took notice of the Web.

Second Generation: Early Netscape

With the introduction of the first beta of Netscape Navigator™ (then known as Mosaic Netscape, from a company originally called Mosaic Communications Corporation) in the fall of 1994, the dynamics of the Web suddenly changed. The initial version of the Netscape browser introduced new HTML features such as centering, text flow around graphics, and a choice of backgrounds. Compared to the standards-based default gray or white background and nonaligned text and pictures, Netscape's features were a huge improvement. Consequently, managers, advertisers, marketers, and even most technical professionals almost always picked Netscape. Once Netscape introduced its first proprietary tag, the first battle of the standards war was lost. The browser market quickly decided what features should be included on the Web from that moment in time. When Netscape added new HTML elements for centering, building tables, and setting background and color, the general graphic presentation of the Web improved and began to evolve. A generic second-generation printlike page is shown in Figure 1-3.

Figure 1–3. Second Generation Web Page.

Along with Netscape, the old media players entered into the Web in force starting in 1995 and 1996. Commerce on the Web began to become more important. Armed with new HTML layout facilities, graphic designers began to assert their role on the Web. At this point, the technical and creative ends of the Web began to diverge. As marketing departments moved in to mold their corporate Web sites, the more technical Webmasters were pushed aside in favor of designers who could design within (or around) the technical limitations of the Web. The spotlight was now on the graphic designers to create so-called "killer" Web sites. This influx of graphic designers certainly improved the look and feel of the Web, but often at the expense of the technical aspects of the site. Many second-generation sites were more about appearances than about functionality, let alone a well-defined purpose.

The second generation wasn't all about overdesigned Web brochures. Some people started to figure out how the Web could really communicate. People didn't read Web sites—they "visited" them. Furthermore, people didn't just visit Web sites randomly. They were there for a purpose. Web sites were about doing something. If the "doing" was reading a brochure, so be it, as long as it was the brochure the visitor wanted to read. However, doing something was a little difficult because the Web lacked much of the programming technology needed to add functionality. Figure 1-4 shows the basic technologies involved in second-generation Web sites.

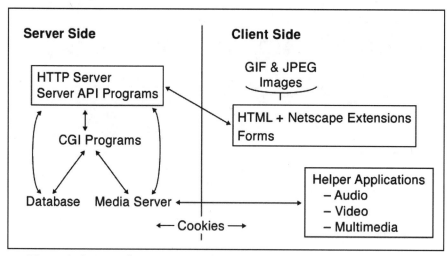

Figure 1–4. Second-Generation Web Technology.

Server-side programming in the form of CGI programs increased dramatically in complexity. One significant hurdle facing programmed Web pages was the lack of state preservation provided by Web servers and protocols like HTTP. The problem was that it was difficult to preserve state or to "remember information" across pages or site visits. The eventual introduction of cookies helped address this lack of state problem, but to this day state preservation issues make Web programming less than ideal. While programming was on the rise, the Web was still mostly a print-oriented medium. The designers promoted this approach, since print is what they knew and the current tools didn't support much else. With the introduction of the 3.0 versions of Netscape Navigator and Microsoft's Internet Explorer™, it became obvious that the next generation was heading towards a programmed Web.

Third-Generation: Mature Netscape and Internet Explorer

With the rise of second- and third-generation browsers, the Web began another significant shift. Viewers were no longer impressed by visually well-designed sites that provided limited interactivity. Computer users were already accustomed to the presentation, content, and interactivity of a CD-ROM, and began to expect the same of the Web. Such expectations were totally unreasonable given many users' relatively slow modem connections. With the increasing availability of bandwidth and the development of technology to deal with the bandwidth crunch, this is slowly changing. The browser vendors introduced even more facilities for layout, including proprietary HTML tags, navigation devices such as frames, and style sheets. Many of the programming technologies like plug-ins or Java™ initially focused on presentation-oriented services like animation or video. Figure 1-5 shows an example of a generic third-generation Web site.

Figure 1–5. Third-Generation Web Page.

In addition to their improved look-and-feel, Web sites had grown significantly more complex. Many new technologies became available in the third generation. These include Java, JavaScript, and ActiveX™, as well as refined server-side approaches as shown in Figure 1-6.

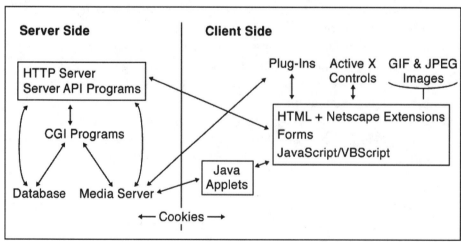

Figure 1–6. Third-Generation Web Technology.

Armed with development tools, corporations began to use the Web to provide valuable services to users online. Innovators like FedEx (www.fedex.com) showed how useful a Web page could be by allowing people to schedule package pick-ups and track delivery. Purpose-driven sites can now be found in many industries. For example, Southwest Airlines (www.iflyswa.com) provides online travel services, including full booking. MovieLink (www.movielink.com) dispenses movie information services and ticket sales. Mapquest (www.mapquest.com) offers local mapping services, and many vendors, such as Dell (www.dell.com), sell a wide variety of products online. People often overlook the numerous purpose-driven Web sites that exist both within corporate networks and between corporations and their partners. Corporate intranet and external Web sites can be linked to automate the hiring process, for example. Inventory systems can be made accessible to key corporate customers. Suddenly, the Web has moved away from *being* and into *doing*. However, this shift from a printed page paradigm to a program paradigm comes with a price.

By the third generation, it was no longer possible for one person to master all aspects of the Web. The design of the Web, as well as the visual design tools, has matured to the point that classically-trained designers can now build interfaces. Programming is also much more complex. A simple Perl program won't provide the robustness necessary for a large firm to run a sophisticated transaction-based ordering system. Besides the database skills, programming skills, graphic design knowledge, business knowledge, and other talents required by a modern Webmaster, the sheer scope of some Web sites begs for a team-based approach to Web site construction. The days of the Webmaster are over. Today it is the *Webmanager* who manages a diverse mix of people to pull off a Web site.

At this point you might ask what generation you are in. When did the second generation begin or end? Is there a fourth generation? Exact dates are not necessary in this discussion. This brief history, based on how we remember things, is simply meant to illustrate why Web Engineering is an inevitable requirement for some Web sites. However, Web Engineering is not for everyone. Many of the Web sites of the past, as well as their ideas, continue to live on.

Generations Don't Matter, Purpose Does

While generations may help categorize Web technology and trends, Web sites do not have to belong to a particular generation. A first- or second-generation Web site might be valid in many situations, since not every Web site has the same purpose or the same development requirements. A one-page advertisement site similar to a yellow pages ad does not require the rigorous planning of a complex order entry system capable of handling thousands of transactions per day. Before determining *how* to do something, it is obvious that *what* to do should be given serious consideration. The first question to ask is: What is the purpose of the site? Yet, clear purpose and goals don't always drive Web sites. Quite often the goals for a Web project are vague, yet the need for the site seems paramount. Many corporate Web site projects have been fueled by "FUD"—fear, uncertainty, and doubt. With all the hype surrounding the Web, many companies believe it is important to get online or add a new technology before the competition. If the competition is already online or uses a hot new feature, a Web site project may appear to be even more crucial to corporate success. This is a dangerous state to be in. Even if budget is not an issue, the benefit of the site will eventually be questioned. Web professionals may find their jobs at risk when projects and benefits are not clearly defined.

There are many common purposes for Web sites. These include marketing, promotion, commerce, entertainment, technical support, investor relations, employee recruitment, personal satisfaction, research and artistic expression. A corporate Web site may include demands for marketing, public relations, investor relations, technical support, commerce, and human resource services. Determining a purpose usually isn't hard, as this book will later discuss, but a purpose must be well defined early on. Who is the site's intended audience? What is its goal? What is the scope of the information and function to be provided? How much should be spent? How long will it take to implement? And how will the success or failure of the project be determined? This process is often called Web design, or Web publishing. Yet the current ideas behind Web publishing are often too document- or print-centered to meet the requirements of many modern Web sites.

Document-Centered Web Page Design

The field of information design (or document design) is concerned with understanding how to create documents that combine words and pictures to help people understand the content and to satisfy their reasons for using the content. The well-designed document enables a reader to use the document successfully to accomplish some goal, such as understanding the content. In advertising, document design is often more about meeting the needs and goals of the designer, such as convincing the reader to buy something. Document design should address the balance between what the viewer wants and what the creator wants.

In many situations, Web sites can be very similar to print, and don't have to do much of anything beyond providing information for people to access. The site designer should consider many of the elements of document design so that the information is presented clearly and accurately and the visuals provide benefit rather than decoration. The key balance in good document design is between the content, presentation, and structure. Too much focus on any particular aspect of document design as well as Web design may result in a less than acceptable site.

Focusing on the technology or even the content, and then decorating a Web page, leads to the dreaded "Christmas Tree" design. Christmas Tree design describes pages put together in HTML and then spruced up with various ornaments like colored balls, a rainbow color bar, and animated clip art. In this sense, visuals are mere decoration with little benefit for the site. On the other hand, focusing too much on the visual often leads to online brochures laden with full screen images and long downloads. While layout control is nearly absolute, the resulting files are huge. Text on a page can't be changed without a graphic designer, let alone indexed by a Web search engine. Visual Web design may produce attractive pages, but it tends to relegate Web sites to nice digital brochures. Document design suggests that visual design and content organization must proceed hand in hand. So should Web site design. But remember that Web sites are not just documents. What happens when logic, in the form of programmed pages, is added into the mix? Certainly the issues change.

While the idea of document design seems correct when applied to the Web, it misses one key element: most documents are used to perform a function, but they do not actually do the function. For example, a paper-based tax estimation form can't automatically calculate a person's taxes. A Web version of the same document can. So Web design is not always just about putting together information. More accurately, the goal of a Web design is to come up with a usable and appealing visual design for a software system in the form of a Web site, which helps a user fulfill some goal. In other words, the objective is to develop a site that can be delivered to the user in a satisfactory manner, be interpreted correctly by the user, and help induce the desired outcome. Web design should be concerned not only with the aesthetic qualities of a Web site, but with the overall user's experience in the context of a specific task or problem. The focus is on how something can be done, not just on how it looks. In a sense, a Web site is no more than a tool. The designer creates it for some purpose to be used by the viewer. Hopefully the site works properly and the viewer enjoys the site and uses it properly.

Software-Centered Web Site Development

Web sites are becoming more like programs and less like static documents. Many modern Web sites must perform some function: implement an order entry system, provide a technical facility, or provide access to a legacy database or some backend system. Web technology itself also suggests the paradigm shift. The document object model (DOM) referred to as Dynamic HTML (DHTML) already allows documents to be programmed and manipulated right down to the single character level. Other programming technologies like Java, JavaScript, VBScript™, ActiveX, and server-side technologies like CGI, NSAPI, ISAPI abound. Programming brings new challenges. As static documents strike a balance between presentation, organization, and content, a programmed site must also deal with the implications of added logic. Yet, far too often the issues are all mixed up. For example, HTML tags are often used to create presentation, complex programming technologies like Java are selected for inappropriate tasks like animation, text is put in image form, and so on. Mixing page presentation and structure is hardly a problem when considering that now, logic, as well as style and structure, can be mixed up into one giant Web page mess. To make matters worse, the actual delivery of Web pages may ruin even the most well-implemented Web page. When a site is delivered from a server to a customer, client issues, server issues, database issues, and network issues may influence the user's perception of the Web site. In short— things can go wrong everywhere. The problems are distinct, and yet part of the whole that the user sees is shown in Figure 1-7. To minimize the possibility of failure, a rigorous approach to site development should be adopted.

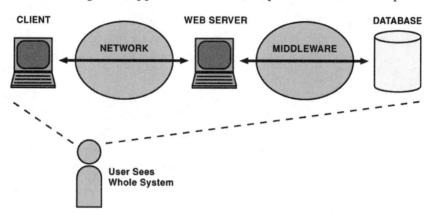

Figure 1–7. Web Model.

Just as in the 1960s when a "software crisis"[2] developed, a Web crisis is rapidly developing because of the increase in complexity of sites in conjunction with the current Web culture and ad hoc methodology used to build many sites. Many people would easily dismiss this statement as reactionary and point to client/server techniques as the savior of the Web development process. But is client/server technology well understood by all programmers? Furthermore, the people who build Web sites are not always schooled in basic programming techniques. Lastly, is the Web exactly the same as the client/server environment? How often in a software application is the interface the overriding aspect of the project? Now think about that same question in terms of the Web. Today many Web sites are 90 percent or more interface,

---

2. The "software crisis" of the 1960s refers to the problems of the software development field, which resulted when third-generation hardware made very large applications possible. The "Web crisis" is similar in that previously difficult-to-create networked applications are now becoming possible to build.

with a little logic. This will change, but to what degree? Despite its document-centered and interface slant, Web development isn't completely foreign to the notions of traditional software development. Turning to known methods of software development may be the best way to deal with potentially difficult Web projects. There are many approaches and ideas in software engineering that might be applied to the Web. For example, academics might like to use a formal transformation model where a paper specification is transformed into a program in a stepwise fashion. However, many of these ideas resist direct application. For example, in formal transformation there is no agreed-upon way to specify Web sites. Furthermore, if there is such a heavy emphasis on interface, does this transformation method even apply? Other approaches, such as the traditional waterfall model, spiral model, or prototyping methods—including exploratory programming and rapid application development—might make more sense. Looking at the Web today, it seems that some of these ideas have taken root. In fact it appears that the rapid application development style is the leading method for building Web sites today; in our opinion use of this approach is premature and may be harmful.

Initial Failure of Web RAD

A very persuasive idea in the software development industry, particularly in the client/server arena, is the idea of Rapid Application Development (RAD). RAD is actually widely practiced on the Web, but in a form that often causes more harm than good. The key to RAD is the idea of prototype-driven design. On the Web, this would mean creating a Web site and then revising the site in numerous iterations with input from the users, until the final design falls out. In this sense, RAD means building the wrong site multiple times until the right site falls out of the process. Yet how far is the rapidly developed Web site from what the users actually want? Furthermore, will there be repercussions if an inferior site is launched for public use? Looking at all the sites with "under construction" signs on them, RAD appears very popular on the Web, but we believe it is not a safe approach to building Web sites, particularly complex ones.

RAD grew from the maturity of the software engineering discipline. Before RAD, a variety of structured design paradigms helped developers understand the systems they were developing. How can we create a RAD-based tool or philosophy for an environment that is still in its infancy? RAD will work, and it will certainly have its place on the Web. The problem is that it is too soon for Web RAD. Many Web page developers are barely schooled in software development, let alone structured software development. Ask yourself if HTML, let alone the scripts of many Web site files, exhibits strict coding standards. Naming conventions, organization, and coding rules are not widely promoted on the Web. Using RAD tools and techniques in such an environment may simply speed up the production of poorly designed or impossible-to-maintain Web sites.

No further evidence of the Web's lack of software development maturity is required than a look at testing methods. Vague references to "testing your site under other browsers" is the typical depth of discussion, with absolutely no discussion of test plans and matrices, test types, or regression testing. Even if browser testing were the only aspect to Web testing, just how many versions of browsers are there? There are literally hundreds. The relative payoff of making the site work under the Commodore 64 browser (there is one), for example, is generally minor. It makes more sense to test under major browsers like Netscape, but how many Netscape versions are there? A quick survey reveals Netscape ports for Macintosh, Windows 3.1, Windows 95/NT, OS/2, and numerous flavors of UNIX. The browser itself has gone through four major releases at the time of this writing (versions 1.X, 2.X, 3.X, 4.X), and there are various beta releases still floating around. "So what?" you ask. The problem is that these browsers act differently. Serious programming bugs exist under different versions of the browser, so ad hoc "looks right so it must be right" tests by example could spell disaster for complex programmed Web sites.

The bottom line is that programming-intensive or interactive Web sites are far more complex than they may appear at first glance. Print design approaches, and even RAD, makes sense for some sites. For large-scale or complex Web sites, a more structured approach is appropriate given the current Web development climate.

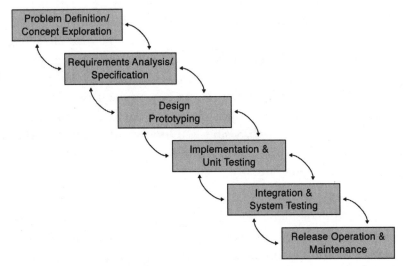

Figure 1–8. The Waterfall Model.

A Model for Web Development: Modified Waterfall and Spiral

The model that we believe is the most appropriate for Web development today is a form of the waterfall model. The waterfall model, occasionally called the software life cycle, is a very structured approach to creating a program.

The basic phases of the waterfall model are shown in Figure 1-8. Note that the process may repeat steps and continue over again.

1. Problem Definition and Concept Exploration
2. Requirements Analysis Specification
3. Design Prototyping
4. Implementation and Unit Testing
5. Integration and System Testing
6. Operation and Maintenance

The first step in this model is to figure out what to do. What should the Web site do? What will it need in order to accomplish its goals? Should the site even be built at all? The next step is to design the site. What will the site look like? How much will it cost? How will it be organized? How will it be implemented? The actual implementation of the site follows the design process, and may include building pages in HTML, implementing a database, designing graphics, and programming business logic in a variety of programming languages. Integration and testing follow to make sure the various components that make up the Web site work as designed. Lastly, the site is released and maintained. In many ways this process really doesn't differ too much from a publishing process, except for the heavy emphasis on planning and testing. However, the Web is not an appropriate environment for a pure waterfall approach to development.

The waterfall approach may be slow and require a heavy degree of planning and documentation. In the fast-moving "post it today" environment of the Web, changes are ongoing and things often can't wait. The waterfall method tends to support the development of software that is published in distinct releases, while Web sites are often growing continuously and specifications often change with the wind. A faster waterfall approach that allows rapid minor changes to the site within a larger general phased effort is more appropriate for the Web. Given the risky nature of Web projects, a great deal of risk analysis should precede the adoption of a waterfall methodology. Once a site is solid, then future changes can be managed using less formal methods, possibly following the spiral model of software development. Regardless of what process models are adopted for future development, everything should be performed in a structured manner. Rapid application development should be kept in check. A simple rule to apply minor site bug fixes or add new pages at regular intervals might go a long way to providing checks and balances for changes made to a large-scale Web site. It might also provide some hope that, if problems arise, the system can be rolled back to a working environment. Meanwhile, long-term changes or large site changes could be planned behind the scenes in a very formal manner. With this approach, developers can leverage the forethought of the waterfall model to build and grow the site as a whole, and then use rapid development ideas managed by the spiral model to experiment with changes to portions of the site. Hopefully, by blending the two approaches, sites can be built that generally work, but leave room to correct for the rapidly changing environment of the Web. Chapter 2 will begin to explore the idea of software engineering process models for the Web; the rest of the book will examine the individual stages of the process in detail.

Readers unconvinced that such formal methods are necessary to build Web sites should consider that many large corporate Web sites have been through more than three or four complete revisions in just two years. When users or vice presidents complain about look and feel, or new technologies come out, whole sites are often thrown away in favor of a brand new site. In many of these cases, there has been an enormous expenditure of money just to see what the Web will do, or to explore some new technology like Java or Macromedia Shockwave™. Throwing away and rebuilding sites is expensive, and the industry is only a few years old. Reuse and site maintenance is not well considered, but it will be, particularly as the purpose of a firm's site (as well as its budget) becomes more focused. Incremental changes to Web sites and an evolution of the project should occur. However, change must be managed—otherwise sites will certainly degrade and costs will skyrocket. Many of these potential problems could be avoided, and long-term costs lowered, if a more rigorous approach were applied to the development of pages. For example, compare the long-term cost of developing four iterations of a simple static HTML site to a single dynamic database-driven site. Software development process can help, but the application of software engineering ideas to the Web may not be easy.

Why the Web is Different

Web development is not exactly like software development. First of all, it is unfamiliar territory for many people. Even seasoned Web veterans have, at most, three and a half years of Web experience. Second, many Web developers are not formally trained in computer science or engineering. The Web exemplifies a greater bond between art and science than generally encountered in software development, except possibly in the development of games or some CD-ROMs. This bond may make managing a Web project a more difficult, though not an impossible, process. Third, Web development often has far more aggressive release demands than traditional software, making it difficult to apply the same level of formal planning or testing to Web sites as used in software development. Fourth, Web development tools are not very mature, so developers often have to build their own systems or do things by hand. Fifth, the Internet is a difficult environment to publish under because it is highly unpredictable; users may blame Internet issues on the site. Finally, the culture of the Web is still somewhat hype-driven, and still tends to favor visual creativity over program correctness. Any one of these environmental issues may derail a Web project, as discussed in Chapter 10. These are just a few of the many nuances to Web development. The rest of this book discusses the previously mentioned issues, as well as others, in more detail. There are, however, three aspects of Web site development that should be introduced before going further. These include the realization that not all Web sites are the same, the content requirements of Web sites, and the visual emphasis of most Web sites.

The software development community realizes that there are unique aspects to developing a program for commercial release (such as a game) versus developing a business application to be used within a corporation. Web sites as applications are no different. There are many forms of Web sites, and just as many applications. In general, there are three major categories. First there are those sites that are built for the public (Internet Web sites). Second, there are those sites that are for internal use within an organization (intranet sites). Finally, there are those called extranets, which bridge the gap between private and public Web sites, such as a site that provides access to a unique community of customers. Each of these forms of a Web site may have different concerns. On a public Internet Web site, there is really not a guaranteed set of users who may access the site. Many people may access the site all at once and at very unpredictable times. A variety of browsers may be used. People may come from different backgrounds, each with different potential interpretations of the site. An intranet site may be easier to deal with since the potential number of visitors may be understood, as well as the actual visitors themselves—including what kind of browsers and computers they use. In intranet development (and extranet development to some degree), the developer has some knowledge of the environment and customers; on the Internet, this is rarely the case.

Within the general categories of Web sites, there are numerous forms of sites, including human resources, sales, marketing, technical support, and entertainment. Regardless of their purpose, Web sites share many basic ideas. There are, however, always application-specific nuances that are useful to understand. While building an online catalog is the same in the general sense, there are many different requirements between a cataloging system for magnetic parts and one for running shoes. Treating all Web sites as generic programs shows little understanding of the medium. Just as there are application programming niche markets, there are niche markets in Web development.

One aspect of Web sites that is different from some forms of software is its focus on content and presentation. Many Web sites are very document-centered and focus on helping users access information. While this is not very different from many client/server systems, Web development projects often include the actual development of the content itself. This is not necessarily a requirement for many software systems, which simply help users manage or access content developed at another time or by other people. However, CD-ROM projects may also have the problem of developing content as well as access logic. This combination of content and programming isn't a completely foreign idea, though it may cause people within an organization who don't normally work with each other to have to work hand in hand (for example, the art department and MIS). Another aspect of Web sites that requires closer inspection is the emphasis on the presentation. The importance of visual appeal is obvious given the public nature of sites. Many Web sites serve marketing functions where look and feel is paramount. The creative demands of look and feel can potentially cause the best-laid Web development plans to go awry. Imagine building a large-scale sophisticated Web site and having the vice president veto the site just before release because he or she doesn't like the positioning and organization of buttons. Unfortunately, this happens much too frequently. A site may be judged solely by its look and feel. There might be a very complex information system that helps people easily find the products they are looking for, but the site languishes because it doesn't look exciting enough. Web design firms are initially compared on the basis of the visual nature of their sites.

Programmed sites have to balance the creative demands of the Web with the robustness and functionality of modern software. Who cares about the way something looks if it doesn't work well? Well-designed sites shouldn't require the user to choose which browser they are using, pick their bandwidth level, or resize their window. Things are taken care of. But to control a user's experience properly requires careful planning; engineering a site like software may be in order. However, Web design is not exactly like software engineering. Many sites may not ever need such ideas, but when programming is required, designers should take advantage of the principles that the software engineering industry has established.

Summary

Much of the Web is moving quickly from a printed page paradigm to a program paradigm, but this shift brings a potential Web crisis. The rapid and often ad hoc development of Web sites creates a great deal of waste and may result in failed projects. A rigorous approach to site development is needed, but what approach makes sense? Web site development could learn a great deal from the accumulated knowledge of software engineering. But simply applying software engineering principles or saying that Web site development is exactly the same as client-server development doesn't take into account the creative aspects of the Web or acknowledge many of the real problems facing Web professionals today. "Web Site Engineering" is the term we have given to our attempt to marry the ideas of software engineering with Web publishing. What constitutes Web Engineering will certainly change over time, but hopefully some of the ideas presented will serve as a base for development or at least inspire people to adopt a more structured approach to site design.

Recommended Reading

Creating Killer Interactive Web Sites, Adjacency, Hayden Books, 1997

Designing and Writing Online Documentation, 2nd Edition, Horton, W., John Wiley & Sons, Inc., 1994.

Designing Large Scale Web Sites: A Visual Design Methodology, Sano, D., John Wiley & Sons, Inc., 1996.

Designing Visual Interfaces, Mullet, K., and Sano, D., SunSoft Press, 1995.

Dynamics in Document Design, Schriver, K.A., John Wiley & Sons, Inc., 1997.

Chapter 2

Software Engineering Principles and the Web

Web sites are becoming more like software. Like building software, building Web sites is a complex process. A single Web site may have to fulfill many roles ranging from document delivery to business process automation. Sites are often built to suit the needs of diverse groups including potential customers or departments in an organization. The many requirements for sites, the number of concerned parties, and the pace at which sites must be developed make Web site development a challenging endeavor. Software Engineering methods can be applied to Web site development to help bring the chaotic process under control and minimize the risk of a failed project. Just as in software development, Web-oriented methods and tools will not provide a single "silver bullet" [(1) Brooks 87] which slays the monster-sized problems facing many projects. Rather, applying a methodology will help minimize problems and provide a framework to manage the project.

Web Sites as Software

Software is a computer program, or a set of computer programs plus associated materials like documentation, which is used to perform some task [(2) Sommerville 92]. Can Web sites be considered software? In many cases, they can. Simple Web sites may be nothing more than a collection of documents that is retrieved from a remote file server. Once functionality—collecting user information with a form, providing database query capabilities, generating pages dynamically, or even providing an online game—is added to the site, the site is no longer a collection of static pages. It can actually be thought of as a program. Not all of a Web site may be deemed software; many parts may be considered more documentlike.

Range of Complexity

The continuum of Web sites ranges from purely static Web sites (sometimes called brochureware) to full-fledged Web-based software applications. A graphic representation of the progression of sites from document to software is shown in Figure 2-1.

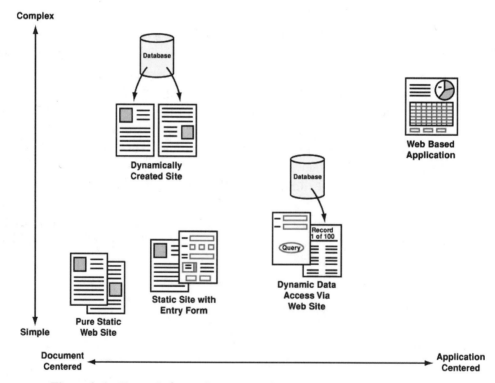

Figure 2–1. Sites as Software Continuum.

Static Web Sites

In its most basic form, a Web site is little more than a collection of static documents created in HTML and tied together with links. The only software aspect of the site is the interactivity provided by links or any graphic user interface built to move from page to page. In a purely static site, much of the emphasis is placed on the information provided and the presentation of that information.

Static with Form-Based Interactivity

Limited interactivity is often added to sites via fill-in forms. Forms are generally used to collect information from the user, including comments or requests for information. In this case, 90 percent or more of the site's purpose may be pure document delivery, with a limited emphasis placed on comment forms and other data collection mechanisms. The division between what is document and what is software is generally clear. In this instance, a formal Web engineering process may be unnecessary.

Sites with Dynamic Data Access

Many people have discovered the possibility of using a Web site to provide a front end for accessing a database. Via a Web page, users can search a catalog or perform queries on the contents of a database. Data returned from these user actions is displayed in the form of an HTML document. Like sites with interactive forms, the division between the dynamically generated aspect of the site and the static aspect of the site may be very distinct. While Web Engineering principles may be unnecessary for the static parts of the site, applying an established methodology can facilitate the development of the more programmed aspects of the site.

Dynamically Generated Sites

One problem with Web sites is that they often have to meet many needs at once. Marketers want to provide customized pages and content based on user preferences in order to foster a one-to-one marketing relationship. Technologists also want to build custom pages dynamically to account for the differences between user browsing environments. To meet these needs, sites must migrate away from static documents that exist in a flat file system to dynamically created documents with content often generated from a database. While the resulting pages may be static and provide no interactivity, the method used to create pages is similar to the method used to build screens in a software application. A fully dynamically-generated site is, at its heart, a software application; the rigors of Web Engineering will help ensure that it operates properly.

Web-Based Software Applications

At the end of the "Web sites as software" continuum is the Web- or intranet-based application. Such an application could be an inventory tracking system in the form of a Web page or a sales force automation tool. Web sites that facilitate business processes beyond providing information have more in common with traditional client/server applications than with static Web sites. Because of the emphasis on function, Web Engineering principles are mandatory to insure that the resulting product works well and can be maintained.

Diversity of Purpose

Just as there are different degrees of complexity for Web sites, there are many different purposes that a Web site might serve. Some Web sites are built for marketing needs, some to automate a business process, some to provide access to information, and some strictly for entertainment or personal enjoyment. Thinking about all Web sites in the same way oversimplifies Web site development. Nevertheless, this way of thinking is common today. Note that the sites built by some Web developers are very diverse. The same company may build Web sites for a major studio's upcoming movie, a tuna fish vendor, an injury attorney, and an internal group for a steel manufacturing company. Software also comes in many forms. A game, a screen saver, a combinatorial chemistry application for drug discovery, and a mission-critical electronic funds transfer system all can be described abstractly as software, but the differences among them are huge. It should be obvious that the purpose, goal, presentation, and complexity of a video game are far different from those of a client/server system used internally within a manufacturing plant. Game developers like Nintendo tend not to bid on nor build banking systems, so it seems interesting that Web sites are often treated the same by firms looking to outsource them or build them, regardless of industry. This will probably change in the future as Web sites become more complex and specific field or industry knowledge is required to develop a site.

As Web sites vary, so do their development needs. For example, publicly accessible Web sites are like mass-marketed software in their concerns. Just as a CD-ROM product may compete for shelf space, a public Web site may have to compete for user attention. Presentation, promotion, and marketing may be extremely important in determining the success or failure of a public Web site. An internal Web site may be less concerned with presentation and more concerned with correctness and functionality. A site for consumers may be very concerned about download speed, performance on low-end systems and preservation of brand identity, while a business-to-business site may be concerned about security and database access. While there may be differences between sites, few people can argue the need for quality.

The Signs of a Well-Engineered Web Site

Regardless of their purpose, all well-implemented Web sites exhibit similar characteristics, just as good software does. Quality software should be maintainable, reliable, efficient, and provide the appropriate user interface [(2) Sommerville 92]. Web sites should also work properly and reliably, download or execute efficiently, and provide the appropriate presentation. There are numerous aspects to the well-engineered Web site; developers should always strive to meet these goals.

Correct

A site is correct if it performs properly and is functionally and cosmetically error free. In a purely theoretical sense, correctness is hard to define; a site may be correct, but a user may not perceive it as such. No matter how it is defined, many sites do not emphasize correctness when they contain obvious problems like broken links, scripts that don't work, or incomplete navigation. Correctness is often difficult to pin down on the Web because of the technologies used. For example, HTML is often misused, but browsers will read incorrect

HTML anyway and attempt to present something. Correctness is never absolute but can be ensured with testing, another aspect of a well-engineered site.

Testable

Since Web sites often are not well specified, it can be difficult to do adequate testing. Testing comes on many levels ranging from functionality testing to usability testing. The key to a functionally testable site is defining what the site should do and then developing a battery of tests to prove that it does what it was designed for. Particularly for interactive sites, the allowed data types and expected results should be specified beforehand and then proved to be acceptable. However, thorough site testing generally goes beyond functionality, and should also address usability and user acceptance as discussed in Chapter 8.

Maintainable

Studies show that software maintenance costs far outweigh initial development costs. In some cases it may even account for close to three quarters of the total software system's lifetime costs [(3) Lientz and Swanson, 1980]. This is the same for Web sites. A well-designed Web site should be maintainable; that is, it should be easy to make changes to the site. Web site maintainability not only should provide the possibility of adding or removing sections or functionality, but also should provide ways to do it with ease. Sites can be developed with site maintenance tools that allow information and process to be controlled in an automated fashion. These ideas are discussed further in Chapter 9.

Portable and Scalable

A well-developed Web site should be portable; this means that it performs across platforms and is cross-browser safe. For informational sites, this may mean simply that the site renders properly in different browsers. However, portability extends beyond the client side. Truly portable sites should be easy to move from server to server with few changes required. Links should be relative and content well-organized. Any application programs used, such as CGI programs, should also be portable. Portability for Web sites is important in that it allows the site to be replicated easily for mirroring and other forms of distribution. In this sense, a truly portable site implies that the site is *scalable*, that it can be quickly extended to handle more users. While this is generally a function of the network and server architecture used, if the site is not portable it may be difficult to replicate the site. Thus, the site wouldn't necessarily be scalable.

Reusable

An important aspect of software is that the components used to build it are reusable. Web sites can benefit from this principle of software engineering. A well-developed site should not have to be completely overhauled every six months or year. Currently, many Web sites go through dramatic overhauls rather than evolving in the way that complex software does. While images and visuals may change and not be reusable, the core infrastructure of the site, such as the database elements, scripts, and content, can be reused as the site evolves. The cost savings for software reuse can be significant. Likewise, creating Web site components that are reusable can save time and money.

Robust and Reliable

Web sites should be robust and reliable. This requirement refers to the quality of the visual and technical implementation as well as to the delivery of the site to the end user. For example, developers often focus greatly on the visual or programming nature of the site but spend little time on the network issues, such as bandwidth availability and server responsiveness. However, if these issues are not well considered, the site may not be robust. It also may be unreliable, failing at inopportune moments or not working consistently. Unlike Web site development, in traditional software engineering, robustness and reliability are relegated strictly to the software itself. The physical medium of the Web, as discussed in Chapter 3, is intertwined with the site and must be considered as well.

Efficient

Efficiency is another important principle of software engineering. The efficiency or performance of a Web site (including the amount of data delivered and the quality of the programming elements) is determined not only by the quality of the implementation, but by the server and network issues over which developers may have limited control (Chapter 3). From the user's perspective, the efficiency of a site is often more related to its delivery. Consequently, it is important to optimize those aspects of the delivery medium that are within the developer's control.

Readable

For maintenance purposes, all files used to make a Web site should be readable. Readability refers to the understandability of source files. Readable files provide adequate comments, use judicious white space and logical formatting, and choose meaningful names so that future developers can understand the code. The use of HTML and scripting coding standards as discussed in Chapter 7 is the best way to improve the readability of Web site source files.

Well Documented

Web sites should be well documented. This has many meanings. First, any programming code or HTML markup should be commented so that future maintainers can modify the content. This makes the site more maintainable. However, well-documented sites go beyond simple code comments. Design documents, flowcharts, change history, project history, and other support documents should be developed and made available for future developers. Well-documented sites should also provide documentation in the form of help files or other forms of information to help endusers use the site. As a site becomes more than a browsable information repository, instructions and help systems become mandatory, just as they are in traditional software applications. At the time of this writing, few sites provide adequate help information for users.

Appropriately Presented

Very important to Web sites, probably more so than with traditional software, is the choice of the most appropriate presentation and user interface. Many sites are driven by marketing goals. If a site doesn't invoke the appropriate mood in the user, help establish a brand, or help users find the information they are looking for, the site is bound to fail. While a quality Web site will generally exhibit a quality presentation, too much emphasis on look-and-feel

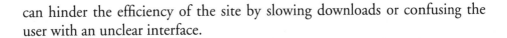
can hinder the efficiency of the site by slowing downloads or confusing the user with an unclear interface.

Current Practices in Web Development

Engineering describes the methods that are applied to help build quality software. Given the goals of a well-engineered Web site, how is the developer to meet these expectations? Software is the term given to the application of software engineering and other principles to help build quality Web sites. Unfortunately, there is no single correct approach to site building. Today, building Web sites is not well understood, a trend that probably will continue for some time. This should come as no surprise given that there are only a few years of direct Web development experience from which to draw. Of course, developers often bring experience from print publishing, technical writing, or software development projects that can be applied to Web projects. While imported techniques help, current Web development practices, good and bad, vary widely. Formal development methods are still not as common as they should be. The current practice is to implement first and ask questions later. The lack of formality is often a direct response to overwhelming pressure from management to develop a Web site very quickly. The gross mismanagement of sites combined with a rapid rise in complexity leads to the current Web crisis.

The Web Under Construction

Evidence of the Web crisis is everywhere. Unlike software projects of the past, the dirty laundry of many failed Web projects may be aired for all to see. The number of sites and pages that appear to be permanently under development is staggering. A search engine query for the phrase "Under Construction" during the summer of 1997 revealed over one million occurrences. Unfortunately, the yellow and black signs and animated jackhammers don't seem to go away. Time stamps and headers reveal sites that have been dead for up to three years. Like online ghost towns, the abandoned sites are cluttered with old content, old style HTML, broken scripts, and broken links to sites that no longer exist. Why these projects fail is not always known. Some sites deteriorate simply because the builders get bored or move on. Others stop development because management withdraws funding, and still others because the site just isn't deemed useful to the company. The number of projects that are not completed or have failed due to lack of acceptance or funding is enormous. These observations are not meant to be pessimistic about the state of site development. While there are many success stories, failures are commonplace. Applying a methodology to development can help mitigate the chance of failure.

Web Site Costing Problems

Nothing is more telling about the immaturity of the Web site development process than the wildly varying budgets allocated to projects. There seems to be very little consensus as to what Web sites actually cost. Surveys show that Web project development costs range from "almost free" up to millions of dollars. Surveys suggest that for the same site, Web design quotes differ by a factor of 10 [(4) NetMarketing, 1996]. Of course, price fluctuations reflect the range of developers as well as the potential scope of projects, but there is still some serious misunderstanding about what is required to build Web sites and how Web site services should be evaluated.

Because people often don't understand Web sites, they tend to oversimplify things. "How much does a Web site cost?" is the most common initial question asked during a client meeting. Web site development costs can't be determined unless the scope of the site is clear. The desire to "productize" the site for the customer leads some developers to offer plans where the client gets a certain number of pages, graphics, and scripts for a set cost. While such pricing schemes appear to simplify things greatly, they often lead to trouble. Invariably, the need for changes arises. The client wants special features, they want to put 100 pages of text into their 10 allocated Web pages, they want script—basically, they want customized development.

Cost also varies due to Web misconceptions and market factors. Many purchasers of Web sites believe that all site development is easy. If this is true then why should any money be spent on it? With WYSIWYG design tools and slick demos, it appears that a nice looking Web site is a drag and drop away. Some vendors even have people thinking that the programmed aspects of site development, like database integration, are no harder than a few wizard clicks. This begs the question of the design of the database, the business logic behind it, and many other issues that the wizard won't consider. The market for Web sites is also very new. Some companies really don't need Web sites, and are unwilling to risk a great deal of money. Others feel that the Web site will change the nature of the firm's business and are willing to invest large sums in development. Developers may feel forced to reduce or raise costs based upon the attitude the client has towards the site. Budgets are often too low because of the perceived ease of development, or too high because of perceived value. Schedules are usually too aggressive because of the desire to launch sites as quickly as possible. Even more so than software cost estimation, Web site estimation is an imprecise science at best. The current lack of experience with the medium seems to be part of the cause of these widely ranging values.

Ad hoc Web Process

The Web crisis is exemplified by the ad hoc Web processes being used to develop sites. Typically, the process for building Web sites is "implement, test, and release." This is similar to the "code and test" process for software development. Most software engineering professionals agree that such limited methods are only good for small projects, generally employing only one programmer, and particularly ones where future maintenance is not expected to be great. These ad hoc approaches tend to create convoluted programming code, often called "spaghetti code," which is very difficult to maintain. Casual inspection of the scripting code and HTML markup used on many corporate Web sites shows that spaghetti code with a side dish of "tossed salad markup" is a main entrée for today's Web developer.

Planning can help offset some of the problems with Web development. When building a Web site, there is always some planning involved. Unfortunately, planning is often limited to a few brief meetings, a collection of marketing materials, and a flow chart. The amount of time spent planning sites is negligible compared to implementation. There are a few developers who suffer from "analysis paralysis"; they plan so much that they impede the development of the site. The amount of planning required depends greatly on the size and significance of the site, but no amount of planning will address every problem. The likelihood of failure on the Web is increased by the inexperience common to site builders and their only vague familiarity with the medium (see Chapter 3 for more information on the medium). This is likely to continue for the foreseeable future, given the number of sites that need to be built. However, just as software engineering methods emerged from years of experience, including many failures, so will Web site development methods.

The problems of the ad hoc Web development process are obvious. Notice how many sites are released with broken links, browser incompatibilities, typographical errors, scripts that don't work, and other problems. In general, testing receives even less focus than planning. The Web's "implement, briefly test, release" process turns it into the world's fastest rapid application development environment with only one development step— implement. Notice that many Web tools almost encourage a design-on-the-fly approach. Some want the user to decorate or design the interface and then tie in the functionality, while others help generate HTML markup quickly and then worry about the presentation. Neither approach is correct; both show the immature processes used to build Web applications. No one doubts that reducing time to release is crucial, particularly in Web development. However, releasing shoddy sites may backfire if the user becomes frustrated because he or she is basically debugging the site. Ad hoc development processes don't work for software. With the growing complexity of Web development, they don't work for the Web either.

The Need for Process

Building Web sites is hard. To help reduce the difficulty in building sites we need a *process model* that describes the phases of Web site development. Each step then can be carefully performed by a developer, applying methods along the way that tell the developer how to do things and ensure the step is carried out properly. Tools may also be employed during the process to support the completion of the step and aid in the building of the site. An example of a process model step would be the planning phase. An example of a method might be the use of a particular design exercise or document standard to help narrow down the requirements for the site. As with software, there are inherent aspects to the Web that make it a difficult environment to work in regardless of the process used.

Complexity

First, like software, Web sites can be very *complex*. A large challenge is the number of functions a site may be expected to perform. Even with adequate decomposition of the various functions of a site, the technology used to implement sites is changing very rapidly, making it difficult to keep up. Lastly, the medium of the Web, including the browser, network, and server, has many subtle aspects that can introduce many problems external to the programming. A development model for the Web should help deal with complexity.

Changeability

The second aspect of software and Web sites that makes them both difficult is the need for continual *change*. Software becomes less and less useful unless it is changed over time. Consequently, software should be designed with change in mind [(5) Belady and Lehman 76]. Since software does change and maintenance is very expensive, planning for change will hopefully help minimize the cost of future changes. Web sites certainly change, and it is widely held that sites quickly become useless if they are not updated. Unfortunately, change introduces further complexity into sites, and may actually lead to structural degradation in the site. Any process model adopted should deal with change, not only in the software but in the project itself, since change also may occur during the middle of the process. This is very common for the Web and software where the goals of the project change midway or a new technology is adopted as the project goes along.

Invisibility

The third aspect that makes Web site and software development difficult is its *invisibility*. Managing Web development projects is often difficult because they are not as tangible as a building or bridge; instead they are somewhat invisible. Managers and clients want to see what is going on in a Web project, not wait until the end when the graphics are in place. They need to see results and feedback as the project progresses, or it will be difficult to deal with problems before they occur.

Unrealistic Schedules

Lastly, Web sites are difficult to build because they often have *unrealistic development schedules*. Unachievable schedules are the direct result of the perceived competitive advantage of launching a site right away. Because of the need for speed, many developers are hesitant to use any sort of formal process that may slow down the site's progress. Yet experts tend to agree that developing software quickly is not easy and a process is still very important to deliver a quality product quickly [(6) McConnell, 96]. A Web development process must take into account the need for speed and must not burden the developer with excessive formal requirements.

Web sites, like many software projects, are risky ventures. In addition to the problems that arise unexpectedly, projects often fail because developers are unfamiliar with the nature of the Web and specifications and requirements are poorly detailed. Implementing a formal software process should help reduce risk. By managing risk, the development process moves from "fire-fighting" and "crisis management" to a proactive decision-making process that attempts to account for and avoid problems before they arise. The best approach to minimize risk in software development has been to develop incrementally rather than all at once. By making small changes and evaluating the result, the overall risk in the project can be reduced. The ad hoc development style of coding the site and then fixing the problems is the most risky development approach because it deals with problems only after they have happened and the penalty for the problems has been incurred. If the site is not mission-critical, such an approach might be tolerable; otherwise, it puts a developer's job at risk. Any Web development process should attempt to minimize the risk of developing sites.

Process Models

An ideal process model for the Web would help developers address the complexity of a Web site, minimize the risk of development, deal with the likelihood of change, and deliver the site quickly, while providing feedback for management as the project goes along. Additionally, the process also would be easy to apply. A pretty tall order, particularly considering that there is not necessarily any one software engineering process model that makes sense in all cases. Since many Web developers are probably not schooled in software engineering, we will briefly present some of the more popular software engineering process models and suggest what we feel is the best approach as discussed throughout the rest of the book. Note that there are more software engineering process models, such as formal transformation, than those presented here. We have attempted to present only those that we feel are viable for most Web development projects.

Waterfall Model

Probably the oldest process model, beyond the ad hoc code and test model, is called the waterfall model. The waterfall model describes the lifetime of a soft-

The Waterfall Model

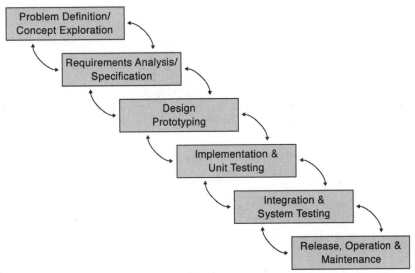

Figure 2–2. Example Stages in Pure Waterfall Model.

ware project as a set of distinct stages that proceed one after another. While the number of steps and their names will vary, typically the process includes a planning phase, a design phase, an implementation phase, a testing phase, and a maintenance phase. An example of the waterfall model is shown in Figure 2-2.

In the pure waterfall, the next step should not proceed until the previous step is finished. While it may be possible to return to previous steps, it is often difficult and may come with some penalty. The good thing about the pure waterfall method is that it makes developers plan everything up front. That is also its biggest weakness. Often there is uncertainty in a project as to what is required and how the project can be implemented. Such is the case with many Web sites, particularly when developers have not built many Web sites previously. In such cases, detailed planning may not help that much. Time may be spent creating detailed plans that will inevitably be changed as knowledge is gained. Another problem with the waterfall model is that each step is supposed to be distinct. In reality, Web development steps overlap or have to be repeated. The pure waterfall does not support concurrent steps well or returning to past steps. It may even impede development. In short, the main problems with the waterfall process are that they don't deal with change well and tends to be inflexible. Waterfall continues to be popular and forms of it are continually promoted in Web design texts. One of the reasons the waterfall continues to be popular is that from a management point of view it is very easy to understand. The steps are easily monitored, and can serve as project milestones.

Modified Waterfall

Given the popularity of the waterfall model, much work has gone into trying to modify it in order to address some of its limitations. One idea might be to introduce some concurrency in the steps so that phases are not discrete but overlap each other a little bit. Another approach is to use the waterfall up to the design phase and then attempt to iterate implementation of smaller subprojects within the main waterfall process. An approach that we term the whirlpool method, given that there are often small whirlpools in a river before

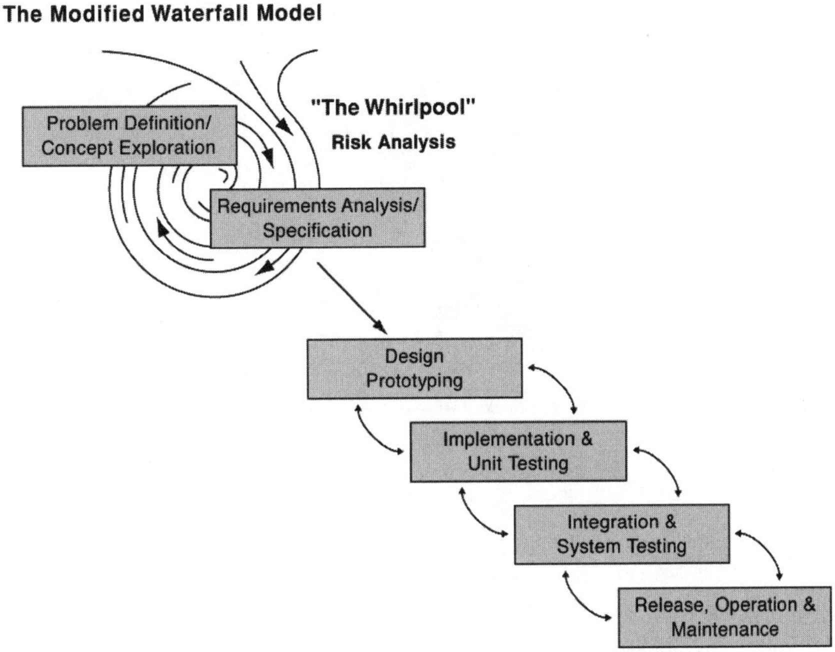

The Modified Waterfall Model

Figure 2–3. Modified Waterfall with a Whirlpool for Risk Analysis.

a waterfall, suggests that the planning stages of the project iterate a few times to reduce risk by trying to throw out the noncritical aspects of the project.

For some Web projects, particularly first time Web site development projects, the whirlpool method is a good approach to building a site. A diagram of the whirlpool-modified waterfall is shown in Figure 2-3.

Evolutionary Prototyping and Joint Application Development

One software development approach that may be viable for some Web projects is called Evolutionary Prototyping. Rather than creating a prototype simply to prove an idea and then throwing it away, evolutionary prototyping incrementally modifies the prototype until it provides all required features. It is then released as the final product. The process often involves direct feedback

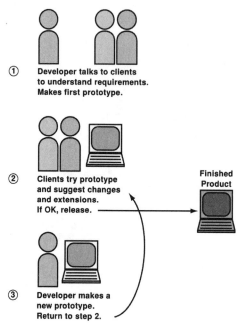

Figure 2–4. Overview of the JAD Process.

from the customer or end user, who looks at the prototype and suggests possible improvements or new features. In many circles, this is called Joint Application Development (JAD) because the developer and the user share in the development of the product. Figure 2-4 illustrates the JAD process.

Many aspects of this process model seem inviting, particularly the incremental development method versus the more "big bang" style of the waterfall which releases the product at the end with little feedback. However, JAD has serious drawbacks for some forms of Web development. JAD makes a lot of sense for intranet application development when communication between internal company departments is mandatory.

However, when building a site for the public, letting the users see an unfinished product may introduce problems. Furthermore, users outside the corporation probably will not understand the process and may get the developer off track, since they often do not share the ownership of the site equally. Another problem of JAD style projects is that they often are not well suited to outsourcing development; it is difficult to determine when they are going to end as the process of incrementally adding to the prototypes may go on a long time. Contracting for such development is next to impossible since it requires vague cost estimates based on a probable number of iterations for a still-unspecified product. While the incremental and risk reducing nature of JAD is intriguing, it is probably best for more experienced Web developers.

Spiral Model

The spiral model [(7) Boehm 88] attempts to put flexibility into the waterfall model. The basic idea of the spiral model is to incrementally develop the site by breaking development up into many subprojects. One of the main points of the process is to attempt to reduce or at least manage risks by focusing on the most critical aspects of the system first. The idea is to define and implement the most important features first, and with the knowledge attained from doing this, to go back and implement the next most important features in small subprojects. As illustrated in Figure 2-5, the concept is to spiral multiple times, starting tightly at first and expanding the project on each loop.

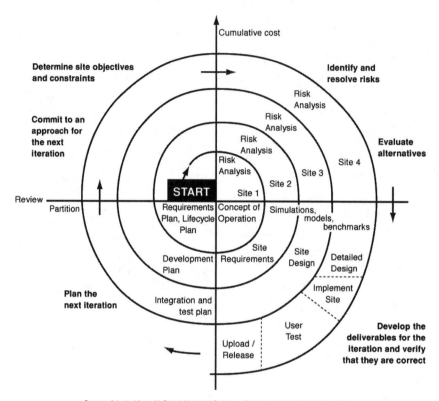

Source: Adapted from "A Spiral Model of Software Development and Enhancement" (Boehm 1988)

Figure 2–5. Spiral Model.

The spiral model seems to make a great deal of sense for the Web. However, it is complicated and difficult to manage. Compared to the waterfall model, it is difficult to tell when stages are beginning and ending. In practice, the spiral model is particularly useful during the planning stages because it helps reduce risk by encouraging people to think about what is really important. For a first time site developer, however, it might not be appropriate. The modified waterfall that introduces risk reduction makes sense for getting a site running initially. Further site development work could proceed with the spiral method. Maintenance work, in particular, is a good choice for the spiral model. However, it is often difficult to get going in the spiral model, particularly when an existing site is being taken over. In such cases, creating a plan to make a major overhaul using a modified waterfall with heavy risk analysis can provide the "running start" necessary to later use the spiral method. Another big reason for not jumping into spiral right away for Web sites has to do with budgeting and outsourcing issues. Projects based on the spiral model often spiral budgetwise as functionality is added. For initial site development, management may prefer to invest a set amount of money and see what happens. With the spiral model, it is difficult to predict how much things may cost. It is also difficult to hire outside developers since fixed-price contracting will not make sense for the same reasons as with JAD. In our opinion, Web developers should move away from the waterfall towards the spiral just as software developers have, but only after they have experience-developing a few Web sites using methods like the modified waterfall. Remember, while many software developers may be familiar with development, many Web developers are new to the industry. It is better to gain a thorough foundation before attempting to employ difficult development methods.

Beyond Process

A process model alone is not all that is necessary to implement a Web site. Equally important to the success of a Web project are issues related to the people on the project, the politics and everyday management of projects, and an awareness and acceptance of rapidly evolving Web technologies.

People

Web sites are built by people for people. People are often the biggest obstacle facing the development of a site. No amount of technology or process expertise will save a project plagued by people issues. A lack of communication between parties involved in a project is probably the biggest people problem. If developers don't understand what users or clients really want, the project will probably fail. It is a two-way street; clients and users have to communicate what they want to developers as well as understand the issues that developers may bring up. Another problem that people may bring to a project is unrealistic expectations. As discussed earlier, currently there are a great number of unrealistic expectations as far as what Web sites can do, how cheaply they can be built, and how quickly. The only way to avoid these problems is through education and experience. Lack of "buy-in" from management or users in a Web project is also a common problem. If management doesn't believe in the project, they may cancel it at the first sign of trouble. If users don't believe in the site, they may never use it once it is done. Buy-in is essential for successful projects. In addition, the normal politics that come with an important project as well as a plain lack of understanding of the Web as a medium are also obstacles. The final problem will pass, but users, developers, or managers with little Web familiarity can be huge distractions in a Web project and may steer the project off course. The importance of people can't be overstated in real life Web development. Whether it is by selecting the best developers to work on a project or just by making sure that everyone communicates and gets along well, good people management can help to minimize any other problems which may arise.

Real-Life Process Problems

On paper, the spiral and modified waterfall method look straightforward enough, but in practice things don't always go as planned. Particularly on Web projects, schedules may change at a moment's notice and are often highly unrealistic. Schedules can slip because people don't realize what is required of them. During the planning stage, sites often specify all the wonderful things that would be nice to have, but when it comes down to collecting the information needed to build the site, there is the realization that it takes time. Lack of content is often the biggest obstacle to finishing a site on time. Another problem with site development has to do with approval delay. No matter what process model is chosen, there needs to be approval before moving on to the next stage. Implementing a particular site only to have the CEO veto it on delivery will certainly put a site over budget. Approval delays slow the pace of projects and cause them to go over schedule. Another problem with projects is "feature creep." When features are added in after the specification date, typically some degree of rework is required. A strict interpretation of a process model will alleviate feature creep by saving additions for later project phases or spirals; however, the reality of site development often requires that features be added out of step.

Technology Problems

One big problem with Web site development is technology. Some Web development technologies like HTML, Java, and JavaScript are very much works in progress. Computer languages like C do not change significantly, but both Java and JavaScript have gone through at least three major revisions in a few years. There have even been significant changes in HTML. In addition, the release of new browser versions is frequent. Having to deal with technology changes as the project progresses is inevitable given current advances in Web technology. Often a hot new technology or development tool will be released and the project may quickly move to embrace it; such change may seriously impact the success of the site. Many sites never seem to reach a steady release state because they are always being upgraded to utilize the latest new Web feature.

Web Engineering Is Not Software Engineering

While Web sites can be considered software, Web engineering is not simply software engineering. Web sites have a few aspects that make them different from software. First, Web sites will continue to be document-oriented. There is no reason that fully static sites will go away just because Java or other Web programming technologies become commonplace. Static, document-oriented sites do not have the same requirements as complex, dynamic Web projects. Relatively simple sites may not need all the formality of Web Engineering. Second, Web sites will continue to be very focused on look and feel. Many sites are driven by marketing goals, and there is no evidence that this will cease in the near future. The emphasis on the creative acceptability of the Web site introduces a wrinkle in software engineering that is generally not well considered, except possibly by game or CD-ROM developers. Third, Web sites will continue to be more content-driven. Often Web projects include the actual development of the content presented. Software projects in general, except possibly CD-ROM or multimedia development, do not combine the development of the software with the collection of the data to manipulate or present. Content creation has many issues that will certainly fall outside the process models presented. Lastly, the medium of the Web is not as well understood as the software medium. While many developers may feel that Web application development is nothing more than glorified client/server, the Web is generally more unpredictable. It has structural problems, such as outside influences and user perceptions that make development difficult. This is probably the most significant difference between Web development and software development. Chapter 3 is devoted to presenting many of the medium issues.

Summary

Like developing software, developing Web sites is difficult and the chance for failure is high. In this sense there is risk involved, risk that should be minimized. Current Web site development approaches provide little help in completing a complex project and minimizing the risks faced. In the past, software developers faced similar problems and adopted software engineering methods to improve the process of developing applications. Since Web sites are becoming more like software and less like printed materials, applying some of the lessons of software development to Web development can be beneficial. Two software development models, the modified waterfall and the spiral model, seem particularly well suited to Web development and can be adopted as a fundamental approach. However, Web sites are different from software, particularly as related to the delivery medium and the types of individuals building Web sites. While Web and Software Engineering models are still somewhat separate, they will inevitably converge as the Web becomes the main medium of software.

References

1. Brooks, F. P., "No Silver Bullet: Essence and Accidents of Software Engineering," *Computer*, 10–18, April 1987.

2. Sommerville, I.., *Software Engineering*, 4th edition, Addison-Wesley, p. 2, 1992.

3. Lientz, B. and Swanson, E., *Software Maintenance Management: A Study of the Maintenance of Computer Application Software in 487 Data Processing Organizations*, Addison-Wesley, Reading Mass., 1980.

4. NetMarketing Web Pricing Index, 1996 (http://www.netb2b.com).

5. Belady, L.A. and Lehman, M.M., "A Model of Large Program Development," *IBM Systems Journal*, 15 (3), 1976.

6. McConnell, S., *Rapid Development*, Microsoft Press, 1996

7. Bohem, B.W. "A Spiral Model of Software Development and Enhancement," *Computer*, 21 (5), 61-72, May 1988.

Recommended Reading

Application (Re)Engineering: Building Web-Based Applications and Dealing with Legacies, Amjad, U., Prentice Hall, 1997.

Information Overload, Jerrold, M. Grochow, Yourdon Press/Prentice Hall, 1997.

Tog on Software Design, Tognazzini, B., Addison-Wesley, 1996.

Chapter 3

The Medium of the Web

Before starting a Web project, all participants should have a working knowledge of the medium. This means understanding what the Web is, what it is used for, how the Internet or an internal network functions, how Web sites are served, and what the various Web protocols actually do. Despite this common-sense approach, Web developers are often primarily concerned with building a Web site as rapidly as possible. Consequently, they spend a great deal of money or effort without having a good sense of the variety of Web site types and the medium through which they are delivered. This is analogous to being a printer who doesn't understand the physical properties of paper and ink.

Networked Communication

The communication between a user with a Web browser and a Web site follows the traditional client/server model shown in Figure 3-1.

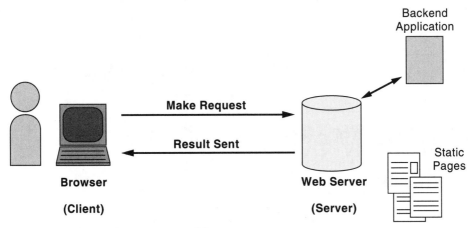

Figure 3–1. Client/Server Model.

In the case of the Web application, the client—a Web browser—makes a request for a Web page or object from a Web server. Then the server—in this case a Web server—reads the request and determines if it should fulfill that request. The whole interchange between the Web browser and the server takes place over a network. Often, the network is the Internet—a wide-scale, public TCP/IP network with varying qualities of service. A Web site exposed on the Internet with no restrictions on who can visit can be called an *external Web site* or a *public Web site*.

In other cases, the network of communication between the user and the Web site is a private network within an organization. An *intranet* is the name given to the use of Web and Internet technologies on such private corporate networks, whether it is a local area network (LAN) or wide area network (WAN). The medium of an intranet is much different from a public Web site: intranet sites run on private, and generally more predictable and secure, networks.

Finally, there is a combination of the completely public Internet and the private intranet, known as an *extranet*. Extranets attempt to combine the privacy and predictability of intranets with the more open nature of the Internet. A corporate extranet describes the idea of a company opening up a portion of its internal or external Web site to an exclusive group, typically composed of customers, trading partners, distributors and other interested parties. Given the potentially sensitive nature of the information on extranets, communication is typically secured with passwords, digital certificates, or encryption. It may take place over a virtual private network built within the Internet. A virtual private network is a private network, often using special routers or security, set up within a public network such as the Internet to provide much of the privacy and functionality of a private network without the cost. These network environments represent three different aspects of the Web, and each have different issues. A public Web site may be very concerned with presentation and image, while an intranet site may be more focused on functionality. An extranet site would have the additional concern of security. The networked environment that Web communication takes place within can be considered the medium of the Web.

Overview of a Web Session

The process of a Web browser or other user agent, such as a Web indexing robot, requesting a document is simple.

As shown in Figure 3-2, the first step is for a user to request a document from a Web server by entering the document's address in the form of a URL (Uniform Resource Locator) like the familiar http://www.yahoo.com/. A URL is the address of an object; it specifies where and how to retrieve or activate that object. Once the document to be retrieved has been specified, the location of that document must be determined by looking at the address of the server to which the request should be made.

Every computer on the Internet is identified by a unique numeric address called an IP address. An example of an IP address is 192.102.249.3, which corresponds to a machine located at an Internet Service Provider based in San Diego. The IP address identifies the machine so that information can be routed to it. While computers and network devices like routers can handle numeric values like IP addresses, it is difficult for most people to remember these values. For this reason, computers are generally referenced by their alphanumeric or *domain* names. A domain name is something like www.ucsd.edu. Domain names are easier to remember, and provide some meaning.

53

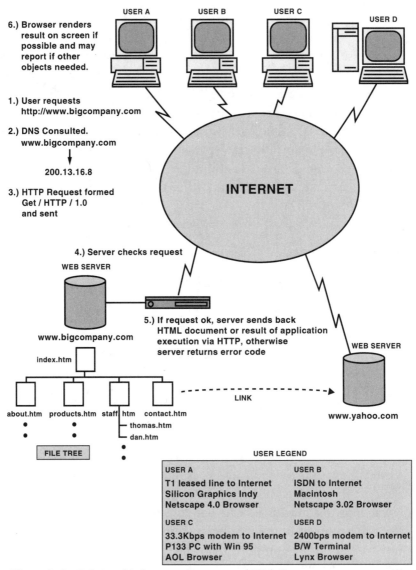

Figure 3–2. Relationship between Browser and Web Server.

In the previous example: *www* is the name of a machine that provides web services, *ucsd* is a university in San Diego, and *edu* indicates that it is an educational organization. Because there is a mapping from a name to a numeric value, or the other way around, the address must be translated.

When domain name addresses are entered into a browser, a domain name server (DNS) is responsible for resolving the name into a numeric value. This is called a *domain name resolution*. This name resolution process may take some time. It may even fail because a machine handling domain name service is unavailable, the lookup service is down, or an error was made while typing the address. The fragile nature of the domain name service has been exposed on numerous occasions when regional Internet Service Providers and Inter-NIC—the organization that used to manage Internet naming—have lost name service for prolonged periods. A great deal of effort is being made to improve these basic facilities that are integral to the operation of the Web. If all works properly, the machine will be found so that a request for a document can be made.

Once the machine has been located, a request can be sent to the server. The discussion between the Web browser and the server is handled by the Hyper-Text Transport Protocol (HTTP). HTTP defines the language the user agent employs when talking to a server, as well as the format of the responses to be made by the server. It is not, as its name suggests, really much of a transport protocol. The actual transportation of data across a network is handled by an underlying protocol like TCP/IP, not by an application level protocol like HTTP. This is a very important distinction.

HTTP is a very simple protocol. A request for http://www.ucsd.edu/ would result in an HTTP request like "GET / HTTP/1.0." This request simply says, "get the root level document, using HTTP version 1.0. " A valid request should return a document or the output of a program specified by the location in the request. In some special cases, such as a request for the root directory of a site, if the location in question is not directly specified, the Web server may return a default document for the request. An example client HTTP request and a server response is shown in Figure 3-3.

Client Request: GET / HTTP 1.0

Server Response:

HTTP/1.1 200 OK

Date: Thu, 23 Oct 1997 21:45:53 GMT

Server: CONNECTnet[welp3]/1.1

Last-Modified: Thu, 07 Aug 1997 00:49:14 GMT

Content-Length: 10395

Accept-Ranges: bytes

Connection: close

Content-Type: text/html

<HTML>

HTML content follows

Figure 3–3. HTTP Request-Response Dialog Between Client and Server.

Once an HTTP request is transmitted to the Web server, the server will attempt to process it. Some of the header information that the client transmits to the server may be very useful in determining the type of client making the request. It may also allow the server to attempt to distinguish between users as discussed later in the chapter. If the server is running, it will first look at the request and determine if it is valid. Even if the request is valid, there may be some restrictions that keep the server from fulfilling the request. Is the browser from a known safe address that is "permitted" to talk to this server? Is the request properly formatted? Does the file being requested even exist on the server? If the file requested does not exist, the server will respond with an error announcement like the ubiquitous "404: Not Found" message. If the request is valid, the server will attempt to fulfill the request by finding the file (or executing a program) and sending the result back to the browser with the appropriate header information that indicates the nature of the data.

Like the client request headers, server responses also include extra information such as the status of the request, the time it was performed, the data returned, and so on. The most important part of this supplementary information is the content indicator, which comes in the form of a MIME (Multipurpose Internet Mail Extensions) header. For example, when a Web server sends back HTML data, it sends it back with a MIME content-type of text/html. Regardless of how the file is named, if the browser sees a MIME heading of this sort, it will treat the data received as HTML. The browser looks at the MIME type of incoming data it receives and determines what to do with it by referencing an internal table that maps MIME types to actions. A portion of this table under Netscape 4 is shown in Figure 3-4.

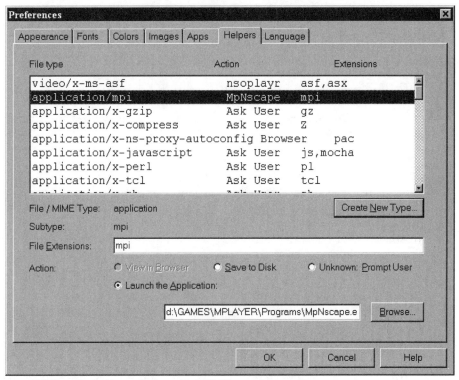

Figure 3–4. Example Browser MIME-type Mappings.

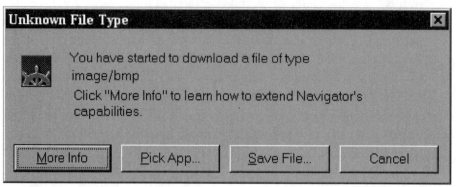

Figure 3–5. Browser Action Query.

MIME is discussed in more depth later in the chapter.

In the case of a Web page consisting of HTML markup, the browser normally reads the information sent and renders the page in the browser window. Other data, like video, might launch a helper application or plug-in to view the information. Completely unknown MIME types might cause the browser to prompt the user to save the data, display it in some helper, or delete it. An example of this sort of browser request is shown in Figure 3-5.

As the browser reads the returned data, it may find that there is more information, such as images, to request from a Web server. If this is the case, the process is repeated, though the early steps may be much more rapid since the location of the server has already been established.

In summary, the Web uses a client/server model. The browser (client) requests pages from a Web server over a network like the Internet. The interchange is handled by HTTP. The actual transmission of data is handled by TCP/IP. The addressing of data objects to request takes the form of a Uniform Resource Locator (URL), which relies heavily on domain name services. Once a request is processed, the resulting information is transmitted with a MIME content-type indicator so a browser can interpret it. Though most pages are created using the HTML markup language, MIME allows other technologies to be included as well.

Components of the Web Medium

Given the previous discussion, it should be evident that the medium of the Web has three well-defined areas to examine: the client side, the server side, and the network in between. A fourth aspect of the Web medium involves external forces. External forces include the perceptions of the users, perceptions of the developers, and even third-party influences that may result in traffic on intermediary networks or beliefs regarding the acceptability of a site. The external aspects of the Web medium are open to the widest degree of interpretation and will be considered at the end of the chapter. An overview of the medium of the Web including some specific examples of client, server, and network details is shown in Figure 3-6.

Each aspect of the Web medium will now be examined in detail, starting with the client side. The discussion will continue with an overview of network considerations, followed by server issues, which are the most controllable aspect of the medium from the developer's perspective. The discussion will conclude by tying it all together, showing that the Web is often shaped by external forces.

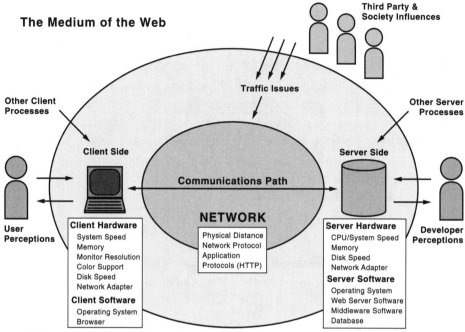

Figure 3–6. The Medium of the Web.

Client Side Considerations

When a user accesses a Web page, numerous factors affect his or her perception of the Web page. Many of these factors are related to the local environment, beyond such basic issues as the bandwidth available to the machine. One major factor is the local hardware that the browser is running on. Even casual observation shows that a Web browser running on a high-end PC or Macintosh (100Mhz or higher) will render pages faster than the same browser on a less powerful system, even given the same network bandwidth. *Bandwidth* is the term used to describe the maximum amount of data that can be transmitted given unit of time. While performance is often overwhelmed by available bandwidth, performance differences based upon local computing power may be particularly significant—especially when pages rely on client side computing technologies like Java. For now we will focus on non-bandwidth oriented performance issues that will be addressed later in the chapter.

System performance is not only related to microprocessor variety or clock speed. While a high-end Intel Pentium PC will certainly outperform a 386-based machine for most tasks, other factors such as available memory, disk speed, bus speed, and speed capabilities of peripherals like video or network cards will certainly affect the perceived performance of a system. Consider the path that the Web page information takes once it reaches the user's system. First, information must move from the network or modem to the client system. Once into the system, information must be passed along a bus to disk or memory and eventually be processed by the browser software. If the information has to be read from disk because it has been previously cached by the browser, or because the operating system has swapped out the application to disk, the system's hard disk can become a constraint. Hard disk speeds vary significantly and may affect the performance of page rendering. Lastly, the browser software itself loads the page and attempts to display it on screen. The speed at which the browser is able to decode information and display content varies greatly from browser to browser. Lastly, the pages must be displayed on screen, meaning that the video subsystem and the monitor itself must be accessed. The speed of this whole process is affected by all the components together, as well as by other factors, such as other programs that may be running on the local system. The complete Web page path from network or modem connection to screen is shown in Figure 3-7.

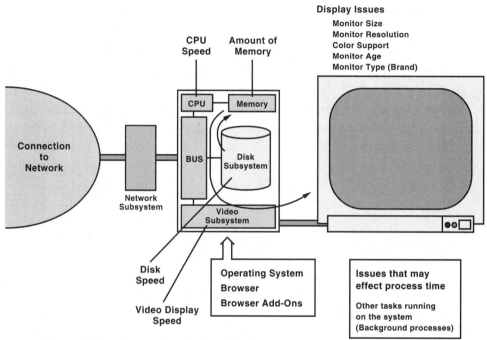

Figure 3–7. Client Side Path for Web Pages.

It may be easy to describe the factors that go into rendering a Web page on a user's system, but generally, these factors are not under a Web developer's direct control. Even on an intranet where systems may be specified ahead of time, there may be differences in the type of equipment used by the various users on the network unless the entire network is designed around the application. A worse case would be a general interest public Web site with a wide audience of viewers, such as a news site. Potential visitors to such a mass appeal site may have systems ranging from black and white terminals to high-end graphics workstations and everything in between. Depending on the technology and visuals used to build the Web page or application, there may be a minimum client software and hardware requirement to ensure correct functionality, proper display, or adequate performance of the Web site. Yet, how are users kept from accessing the site if they do not meet the minimum requirements? Some sites force users to self-evaluate their configuration, as illustrated by the statements in Figure 3-8.

This site is best enjoyed using Netscape Navigator.

You must resize your browser window this wide to use this site.

Click here for high-bandwidth site.

Shockwave users click here.

Minimum Screen Resolution 800x600 for optimal viewing.

Figure 3–8. Selection of Common Web User Self-Profiling Ideas.

While asking questions seems harmless enough, users will make mistakes. A demonstration site developed with a Macromedia Shockwave and a non-Shockwave version was released with an entry page where users were prompted to select which version of the site they wanted. Despite the Shockwave-only button, numerous non-Shockwave users entered the site the wrong way; some then complained because from their perspective the site didn't work. Some developers might claim this is the users' fault, and that they should have known which version to pick, but this is unreasonable. Imagine a Windows software package delivered with a dialog box like the one shown in Figure 3-9.

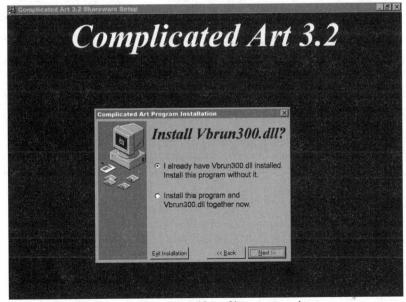

Figure 3–9. Windows Application Self-Profiling Approach.

The dialog asks a simple question. One button prompts the user to install the software application by itself if he or she already has the Vbrun300.dll. Another button installs the Vbrun300.dll and the application. Does the user have Vbrun300.dll? Does the user even know what it is? While many people may know that this is the Visual Basic run-time dynamic load library, many people surely do not. The situation is the same in the Shockwave example. Remember that users may not have configured their systems and may have no idea what is set up and what is not. Furthermore, users generally won't be as familiar with Web technologies as developers. Asking users to evaluate their systems is often asking for trouble.

Client Profiling

Since Web developers will probably not have a great deal of control over the end user's system configuration, a profile of the potential client can be useful. *Client profiling* is simply the idea of trying to determine as much as possible about the client's system and then designing the site or modifying the site to meet a particular configuration. Note that client profiling is part of evaluating the site's intended audience, which is one of the early phases of the Web Site Engineering process. A simple approach to client profiling would be to attempt to profile the user ahead of time. This is most easily accomplished for a relatively controlled environment project, such as an intranet site. What platforms are currently used on the network? What browsers are used? What screen resolutions are supported? For public sites or sites with a marketing focus, other questions might be important. Has the user been to the site before? What language does the user speak? What are his or her likes and dislikes? Some of these issues are obviously beyond the scope of an engineering-oriented book, but in the best case, what would we like to know about the user? In general, it is possible to divide up desirable client information into three basic categories: technology support, display issues, and user considerations.

Technology Support

The visitor's technology support should be thoroughly considered if a site is going to use anything beyond standard HTML. Even if HTML is the only technology used, developers may still want to try to determine the browsers

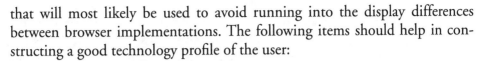

that will most likely be used to avoid running into the display differences between browser implementations. The following items should help in constructing a good technology profile of the user:

- ❑ Operating system type and version
- ❑ Hardware type
- ❑ Browser type and version
- ❑ Client-side programming support
  - ▸ JavaScript / VBScript / ECMAScript support and version
  - ▸ Java support and version
  - ▸ ActiveX support and installed controls
  - ▸ Plug-in support and installed plug-ins
- ❑ Connection Speed
- ❑ HTML
  - ▸ Version supported
  - ▸ Frames support
  - ▸ Proprietary elements
- ❑ Cascading Style Sheets
  - ▸ Feature support
- ❑ Screen resolution and color depth
- ❑ Document Object Model (DOM)
  - ▸ Object support
  - ▸ Event model
- ❑ XML
  - ▸ Generic support
  - ▸ Specific language or document-type support (e.g., CDF, OSD)

After gathering this information, a baseline capability can be determined, such as requiring Netscape 2.X or greater or Microsoft 3.X or greater with Java-Script on and a minimum display resolution of 800x600 with 16-bit color support. Given this profile, it should not simply be listed on the entry page of the Web site. Instead, technology should be used to detect conformance to the accepted profile. Profile conformance can be accomplished by sensing the browser being used and then utilizing some client-side programming to detect if features are available. Though few sites do this, it isn't terribly difficult. The first goal is to detect the browser type or more generically, the user agent, making the request. This can be accomplished with a simple server-side program that simply looks at the USER_AGENT header in the HTTP request packet. Table 3-1 provides a sampling of USER_AGENT values reported by various browsers. More common browsers tend to use the same format of Mozilla/version-number (extra-info) that indicates with which version of Netscape the browser is compatible. However, as shown by the selection of "other browsers," there are many that don't base themselves off Netscape. There are even occasional forged, removed strings, or small privacy protests embedded in USER_AGENT information.

TABLE 3-1. Sampling of User Agent Codes

General Browser Type	Sample USER_AGENT Strings
Microsoft Internet Explorer 4.0	Mozilla/4.0 (compatible; MSIE 4.0; Windows NT)
Microsoft Internet Explorer 3.0	Mozilla/3.0 (compatible; MSIE 3.01; Mac_PowerPC)
Microsoft Internet Explorer 2.0	Mozilla/1.22 (compatible; MSIE 2.0; Windows 95)
Netscape Navigator 4.0	Mozilla/4.03 [en] (WinNT; I ;Nav)
Netscape Navigator 3.0	Mozilla/3.01 (Macintosh; I; PPC)
Netscape Navigator 2.0	Mozilla/2.02 (WinNT; I)
Netscape Navigator 1.0	Mozilla/1.1N (Macintosh; I; PPC)
WebTV	Mozilla/1.22 WebTV/1.0 (compatible; MSIE 2.0)
	Mozilla/3.0 WebTV/1.2 (compatible; MSIE 2.0)
Selected Other Browsers	AIR_Mosaic(16bit)/v3.06.04.01
	AmigaVoyager/2.70 (AmigaOS 3.x)
	ArcWeb/1.77 (Acorn RISC OS; StrongARM)
	Cyberdog/2.0 (Macintosh; 68k)
	Emacs-W3/3.0.82 URL/p3.0.82 (sparc-sun-solaris2.5; TTY)
	Enhanced_Mosaic/2.01 Win32 MKS/2
	IBrowse/1.1 (AmigaOS 3.1)
	Lynx/2.1 libwww/2.14
	MacWeb/2.0 libwww/2.17
	NetCruiser/V2.1.1
	NetManage Chameleon WebSurfer/5.0

The user agent header information may also provide information about the operating system used and, potentially, the platform. Note in Table 3-1 how Netscape indicates if a Macintosh uses a PowerPC or 68000 processor. Header information may also indicate the language being used or at least the character set accepted. Furthermore, looking at the domain name of the requesting browser may also give a clue to foreign language use.

Browsers

During technology profiling, the importance of knowing much about browser capabilities, inconsistencies, and bugs becomes clear. Remember, not all users will be savvy enough to distinguish a properly coded site falling prey to a browser bug versus a miscoded site. For example, a recent version of Netscape contained a bug that printed out each line of a page separately if a particular style sheet rule was used. Experienced Web developers encounter problems like this frequently, and many feel that browser problems are becoming more, rather than less, common as Web technology becomes more complex. Because of the potential for misinterpretation, Web page designers should be intimately familiar with all the browser versions related to their site's target audience as well as the capabilities of these browsers. Sites like Browserwatch (www.browserwatch.com), BrowserCaps (www.browsercaps.com) and Browsers.com (www.browsers.com) are essential reading for those developers wanting to keep up with the multitude of browsers available.

Knowing everything about all browsers that someone might use is pointless. While there are two primary Web browsers in use at the time of this writing, Netscape's Navigator and Microsoft's Internet Explorer, there are more than 100 other browsers in existence. These range from browsers built for legacy mainframe environments to embedded browsers in consumer electronics like WebTV to browsers for older home user systems such as the Amiga. Each of these browsers may render pages differently from another, and may include or omit certain key technologies like Java or JavaScript. Even from just a visual perspective of a page, note the vast differences in browser display capability shown in Figure 3-10.

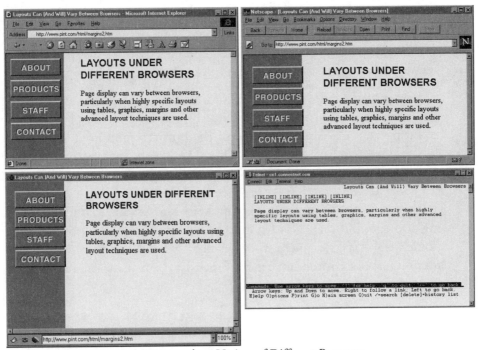

Figure 3–10. Same Page under a Variety of Different Browsers.

Overly optimistic designers may rely on the availability of certain technologies or screen renderings, only to find that users don't see the same effect. As discussed earlier, client profiling can help deal with the multitude of possible user environments. The complexity of building a site that conforms to multiple environments leads some page designers to force the use of one particular browser or another, often resulting in slogans like "Netscape Now!" posted all over their Web site. Yet even if it was possible to control the user's environment so that only one browser was allowed, there are still many issues to consider. How many different versions of a browser are there? Consider Netscape. At the time of this writing there are currently four major generations: Netscape 1.X, 2.X, 3.X, 4.X and a fifth on the way. Now consider all the possible beta versions. Finally consider on how many systems Netscape operates: Macintosh, Windows 3.1, Windows 95/NT, OS/2, and a variety of UNIX systems. Unfortunately, not everything always functions the same across these systems. Margins, JavaScript bugs, and even HTML support vary from version to version and from platform to platform. After adding Internet Explorer to the mix with 2.X, 3.X, and 4.X versions in circulation, there are literally dozens of environments to consider. The differences, even among the same vendor's browser versions, may be subtle, but are disastrous for page designers.

For example, under earlier versions of Netscape, up to version 3.0, there was a problem with margin precision. Depending on the platform, the left and top margin between the edge of the browser window and the first pixel available for layout varied greatly. On a Macintosh, there was an 8-pixel margin on both the top and left. On the PC, there was a 10-pixel margin on the left and a 16-pixel margin on the top. On UNIX, there was a 20-pixel margin on the left and a 22-pixel top margin. With such widely varying margins, laying a foreground image on top of a background could only be accomplished imprecisely. Page designers who did not acknowledge these problems often found their designs did not render properly across platforms as shown by the example in Figure 3-11.

Some users take the standards approach to avoid such problems. Coding Web pages to a particular standard and validating that the page conforms to a standard does not guarantee how a particular browser may render a given page. For example, Netscape and Microsoft both conform to distinct style sheet specifications but the renderings of the same page aren't always identical. Page designers should accept that browsers are different in many ways ranging from layout to speed of page rendering. While standards are important for an accessible Web, the market forces browser vendors to introduce such differences in their products in order to differentiate them. One can only hope that the differences are limited to slight cosmetic dissimilarities only or features that degrade gracefully under other browsers. Because of these differences, designers looking to provide an optimal experience for viewers should test the site thoroughly as discussed in Chapter 8.

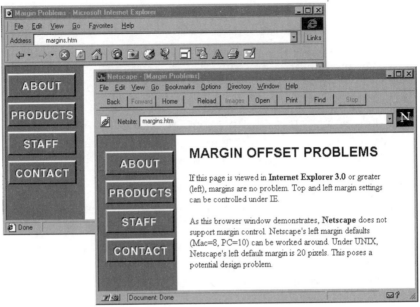

Figure 3–11. Margin Problem Under Older Netscape Browsers.

Implementing Browser and Technology Profiling

Once the browser version and its capabilities have been determined, it is then necessary to determine the technology supported by the browser. In general, browsers can be separated into two categories, those with client/side programming capability using Java or JavaScript and those without. Without JavaScript or Java, it will be difficult to determine much about the user, unless he or she provides the information.

One way to sort users into JavaScript and non-JavaScript categories is to write a small script that runs and automatically redirects the user to a JavaScript enabled page. Then, in the new page, detect the version of JavaScript they are running. Browsers running JavaScript will be redirected to a page that supports the technology, while browsers without JavaScript support will simply load the contents of the first page. If the JavaScript capable page is loaded, profiling can continue using client/side scripting; otherwise, the user can't be profiled and will have to be questioned about their ability to view the site. If profiling continues, various display attributes such as screen resolution, color depth, and available window size can be queried via JavaScript methods in 4.0 generation browsers. Older browsers like Internet Explorer 3.0 may provide an alternative way to determine such user characteristics through the user agent string. Even if the browser is running an older version of JavaScript, such as that supported under the 3.0 generation browsers, it is still possible to gather this information via a Java applet. The applet could then communicate this information back to the script as a variable. Under the 3.0 and 4.0 generation browsers, it is also possible to query for installed plug-ins using JavaScript.

Finally, connection speed can be determined in one of two ways. First, a Java applet could be used to communicate back to a server-side application and calculate round trip transmission time. Second, a set amount of data could be transmitted to the client and a timer could be set to determine how long the data transmission takes. Of course, available bandwidth is not constant so numerous samplings may be necessary for accurate answers; the point here is simply to calculate bandwidth with the precision necessary to determine if a user has a slow connection like a modem or a faster connection through a leased line or cable modem. As discussed in the previous section, the other aspects of technology such as HTML and style sheet support really can't be sensed for; developers will have to know generally which user agents support which features.

Display Issues

Because of the visual nature of the Web, much of the concern with client profiling has to do with trying to understand the user's display environment. Display environments vary greatly from user to user. Some users may have a large monitor with high resolution and true color support. Other users may have a small monitor with limited color support. Designers tend to create their graphic decoration and navigation around their own environments or a particular baseline platform determined ahead of time. The baseline idea attempts to isolate the lowest common denominator, which is often determined to be a PC with 640x480 resolution and 256-color support. While designing around such a baseline may insure that everyone can view the page, it does not ensure that everyone views it optimally. A common statement made by novice Web viewers with high-resolution monitors is "everything is so small." Using profiling, it may be possible to determine the user's display environment and deliver a presentation that fits that environment. This shouldn't seem like an unreasonable expectation considering that many software packages concerned with presentation, particularly games, will reconfigure themselves based on the user's viewing environment.

What issues should be considered when trying to develop optimally displaying sites? The first issue would be the physical dimension of images. Because there are so many different screen sizes and resolutions, the available design area within the browser window before scrolling is necessary and varies greatly. (For navigation purposes, scrolling is considered to hinder usability.) Under a 640x480 environment, the typical safe region is somewhere in the range of 535 to 595 pixels across and 260 to 295 pixels up and down. This depends on whether the user has resized his or her browser window, and whether printing is an issue. If the resolution of the monitor is set at 1280x1024, the safe range may be from around 535 to 1200 pixels across and 260 to 900 pixels or more up and down. The 535 pixel dimension should be consistent regardless of screen resolution to insure proper printing of the page. Printers may truncate any content beyond the right margin of a page. This leads to the question of the final delivery medium. If the user is intended to consume the Web-presented information on-screen, this is a much different medium than if the main goal is for the user to print the information. Information on screen generally must be larger for easy readability whereas printed materials may be much denser. The point is simply to understand that screen resolution and available design area may vary depending on final destination. Since the environment can usually be detected as discussed in the previous sections, it may be possible to build pages dynamically. Depending on the user's viewing environment, multiple sizes of the same image can be used to customize the page.

Another important display issue to consider is color. Different viewers will have different color support. Some users may have very sophisticated graphics cards and be able to view thousands or millions of colors. Other users may be limited to 256 colors, 16 colors, or even gray-scale. Even across systems with similar degrees of color support, the actual colors may vary. Systems, particularly PCs and Macs, are known not to share exactly the same 256 colors, so images should be created only with the colors that the systems have in common. These 216 shared colors are called the "browser safe color palette"; many sites (www.lynda.com) describe how images can be developed to conform to such a palette. While these approaches may be appropriate to create images that do not *dither* or speckle when viewed on platforms lacking a particular color, due to color approximation, the safe palette may be too limited for some situations. In cases where using unsafe colors is appropriate, it might be nice to have a safe and unsafe image and detect which one to use based on the bit depth of the viewing client. With newer browsers, it is possible to detect color support and then dynamically use the appropriately colored image.

Color and image clarity can be more complicated than just image size and color. One problem that print designers have long struggled with is the exact reproduction of colors across monitors. Different monitors will display things differently due to things like brand, monitor age, and a variable called gamma. Gamma can be loosely thought of as screen brightness. For a more technical discussion of Gamma, see http://www.inforamp.net/~poynton/Poynton-color.html. The point to remember here is simply that Macintosh, Windows, and UNIX systems as well as the monitors that are used exhibit different gamma levels, so images prepared on a Macintosh may look a little off on a PC and vice versa. This is particularly true if there is not a heavy degree of contrast between foreground and background or many similar shades of color are used. The best ways to avoid this are to use an image format that corrects for gamma variations such as PNG (Portable Network Graphic format), to have multiple versions of a file that substitute depending on viewing environment, or to design images around an average gamma value. Developers who believe dealing with gamma issues is too much trouble should stay away from light on light or dark on dark style designs and avoid requiring exact reproduction of images.

The last display consideration is font support. Users do not have the same fonts installed on their systems. The default fonts installed on Windows and Macintosh systems are not particularly common except for the somewhat basic choices of Times and Helvetica on the Macintosh, which correspond to Times New Roman and Arial under Windows. Even when the fonts can be found, Windows screen fonts are known to display slightly larger than their Mac counterparts; thus, exact text layout may vary. Of course, Web viewers may override any font rules made under HTML or style sheets by adjusting their settings, which may make text reflow in less than satisfactory ways. The only way to absolutely guarantee text layout is to convert text into bitmapped images, but this results in large files and sacrifices and many of the benefits of pure text like simple modification, indexing, cut and paste capability, and fast download speeds. With the introduction of Cascading Style Sheets (CSS1) and downloadable fonts with the third- and fourth-generation browsers, text layout should improve. However, the technology is not foolproof. Browser support will still have to be determined ahead of time to guarantee optimal layout.

After considering fonts, it is important to consider the actual characters supported in the font. For languages written in other languages or alphabets, issues such as text direction, installed character sets, and other localization issues become important. However, sensing that a user supports the Kanji character set in his or her browser and is coming from a Japanese domain name, doesn't automatically indicate the user wants to see a page rendered in Japanese. What happens if the user is a native English speaker who is just browsing a site from a remote location while on a trip? Obviously, some profiling techniques would take the approach of saving and maintaining user information and preferences using technologies such as cookies or server-side databases; but, if this approach is used, there should be a mechanism in place to recall and verify the validity and applicability of preferences on subsequent visits. These ideas introduce the issues of client profiling that account for user preferences and control.

User Considerations

While client profiling is an important way to offset the effects of the Web medium, it may conflict with the user's desire for control and customization. A rule of the Web that should be obvious by now is that all users are not alike. The needs and desires of a user vary just as much as the demographic break-down like gender, age, and ethnicity. For example, users who have never been to a particular Web site may want to orient themselves, to find out what the company does, and to understand how to navigate the site. However, users who have visited a site many times may not want such general information and may be extremely task-oriented. Presenting the same information to all users is bound to leave some with a less than optimal visiting experience. Preferences also vary. Some users with slow connections may want to browse without a great many images, and others with faster connections may be willing to wait for a rich presentation. Sites should provide for this.

The key issue is one of control. Should the user be in control of the Web site experience, or should the designer? The general answer is that both should be in control. A user will have a goal, stated or not, when he or she visits a site. The goal may be simply to look around or be entertained. In other cases, the goal may be more specific, such as to download a particular software driver or to print out a price list. The Web designer's job is to help the user accomplish these goals by designing, organizing, and implementing the site in such a way that accomplishing the task is straightforward and elicits a positive user experience. Part of doing this may be to profile the user and attempt to program around those aspects of the Web medium that get in the way, such as browser support and bandwidth. If the interface is so seamless and intuitive that the user doesn't notice it, there is generally never a problem. However, what about when the user is inhibited by the interface provided or something goes wrong because a particular technology or presentation decision made during the profiling stage results in a bad experience? Should the user be able to break out of the experience? The answer is an overwhelming "yes." Otherwise, the user may leave the site without accomplishing his or her goal, and even form a negative opinion about the site or its developer. Users are just as much a part of the medium as browser technology. While it may be impossible to control users or their experiences perfectly, as will be discussed at the end of the chapter, such external influences can at least be minimized with a little planning.

Network Considerations

The network between the client and the server may be difficult or impossible to control regardless of profiling. Unfortunately, the user's experience will be shaped significantly by this part of the Web medium. Users complain greatly about the performance of Web pages. It is true that, at times, Web sites perform at speeds that are less than acceptable. Web designers may attempt to improve this situation by creating smaller graphics that can be transmitted more quickly, but this doesn't always result in sites that are delivered more quickly. The reasons for this include both network and server performance. Avoiding the server for the moment, there are three aspects to network performance: bandwidth, latency, and link utilization.

When talking about the network component of Web page delivery, the first point of discussion is invariably bandwidth. *Bandwidth* is the term used to describe the maximum amount of data that can be transmitted during a given unit of time A modem may provide bandwidth of 28.8 kilobits (Kb) per second—also known as the *baud rate*—while a leased line like a T1 may have a transmission rate of 1.544 megabits per second. Users of a local area network viewing an intranet may expect speeds ranging from a few megabits per second up to 100Mbps or higher. Yet the speed of page delivery is not determined solely by the speed of the user's connection to the network. The actual speed is affected by latency, link utilization, and by the rule of the weakest link. As data travels across a collection of networks, the speed of the slowest link dictates the maximum end-to-end connection speed. So while the user generally has the slowest link, it is possible that other links between the user and the final destination may affect the download rate. The key issue here is to understand the path that the information takes to get back and forth between the server and the client.

Latency is the term used to describe the amount of time that is required for a single data packet to travel the entire link that connects two systems on a network. In general, latency can be attributed to distance. The farther away the server the user is connecting to is from the user's location, the slower it will usually be to access it. This is common sense, considering the physical laws by which networks abide. Even when using light to transmit information, there is a measurable delay in sending information from one side of the planet to another. Since communication signals degrade, they may have to be amplified occasionally, as well as switched or routed if they need to move from one link to another. Because of this, latency may also increase due to delays introduced by networking equipment that passes data along the network path. The only way to fight latency is to decrease distance between the source and destination. One way to accomplish this is through the use of a mirror site that maintains an exact copy of the primary Web site. Visitors can then select from different sites and pick the one closest to them. Unfortunately, physical closeness and network closeness may have nothing to do with each other. For example, when accessing a Web site just across town, the network path literally may have to cross the country to an interchange point between providers. While Internet Service Providers realize that the more interchange points they have, the better the connectivity, not all providers, particularly the small ones, are in the position to afford to maintain a peering relationship with every network directly. Because of network distance as well as intermittent network traffic patterns, alternate site selection should be handled automatically. A networking device that calculates the shortest path, rather than having the user select it, should be used.

Besides bandwidth and latency, network performance is affected by network utilization. Network links are generally shared, so the amount of traffic on a particular link will have a significant impact on the available bandwidth for any given user and, therefore, the perceived performance of a link. The more people and traffic on a particular network link, the slower things go. When selecting the fastest available route to a particular location, from an American user's point of view, it may be faster to select a site in Europe as opposed to one in the United States, depending on the time of day or the day of the week. Again, having users be aware of time zones and traffic patterns as they browse the Web is unreasonable. Such questions should be answered automatically.

Web developers have very little control over network issues. Consider the Web designer who has done everything right. His or her Web page is well designed, the graphics load quickly, the server is powerful and a well-connected Internet Service Provider or Web hosting vendor has been chosen. However, a few users keep sending messages complaining about performance problems with the site. Analysis of the situation might reveal that the complaining user accesses the Internet through a poorly connected or overloaded Internet provider, or that the network connections between the user and the server are saturated. The only thing that a page designer can do in the case of a public Web site is to try to avoid being the limiting factor. Unfortunately, because of latency, there will always be users somewhere in the world who perceive the site as slow because they are far away from it. The only way to avoid the single point source nature of Web sites is to mirror them, but this may not be cost-effective for all sites. In the case of Web sites designed for more private networks, like an intranet, the responsiveness of the network component of the medium may be more controllable; it may even be possible for the developer to suggest network upgrades to improve site performance. However, even if some of the physical aspects of the network can be controlled, protocol issues still may creep in.

■ Packet Switching and TCP/IP

The Internet, as well as intranets, are packet-switched networks. On a packet-switched network, data is broken up into small pieces called packets that are sent across a network to their destination. Once the packets have been routed to their final destination, they are then reassembled into the original message. The benefit of this idea is that packet-switched networks can provide a great deal of reliability as packets may be routed around bad or saturated links. Secondly, packet-switched networks tend to scale better than circuit-switched networks, such as the voice telephone network, since the number of users is limited only by performance expectations. More users just mean a slower connection, whereas on a circuit-switched network, there is a maximum number of users (thus the occasional "all circuits are busy" message).

However, packet-switched networks do come with drawbacks. First, they must deal with all the issues of data coming out of order, getting lost, and so on. The TCP/IP network protocols deal with these problems. TCP/IP is actually a suite of protocols that includes two main protocols: TCP (Transmission Control Protocol) and IP (Internet Protocol). TCP does exactly what its name indicates: it controls the transmission of data. TCP is generally responsible for disassembling and reassembling data for delivery, acknowledging receipt of data, resending data if no acknowledgment is received, and checking the integrity of sent data. The IP protocol, which handles the addressing scheme on the Internet, provides for the addressing and routing of data packets.

The implications of packet-switched networks are significant, even when protocols like TCP/IP are used. First and foremost, since a packet-switched network in conjunction with TCP/IP doesn't guarantee delivery time, sending time-sensitive information like real-time voice or video over the Internet is less than ideal. This may come as a shock to people who expect the Internet to eventually be as foolproof as a circuit-switched network. While it may be possible to invent protocols to reserve bandwidth or literally reserve—or stream and just live with packet loss—network availability for delivery of time-sensitive data like voice, video or high-twitch response video games, there is a profound implication here. Wouldn't users always want to reserve maximum bandwidth unless there was something to keep them from doing so? Observations of human nature suggest that without pricing based on required network resources, the network would provide no better responsiveness than it does today even with bandwidth reservation protocols. In fact, users may try to commit for extra bandwidth even when they don't need it, thus reserving network capacity that isn't utilized. Real-time data and Web sites generally don't mix well.

The second implication of a packet-switched network follows directly and has to do with congestion avoidance. Because users may try to use the available bandwidth, the TCP/IP protocol uses a slow-start mechanism designed to ensure that a particular connection doesn't attempt to grab more bandwidth than is currently available. During slow start, the data rate starts low and is gradually increased until the maximum data rate is achieved. If the link becomes congested, the protocol may back off from the desired rate in an attempt to decrease congestion. Congestion avoidance mechanisms in TCP/IP have an interesting effect on Web pages. Web site developers tend to be very concerned about optimizing images to the smallest size, but there is a point of diminishing return here. When dealing with a page filled with many small images, network utilization may be relatively low because of TCP's slow start. This leads to an interesting question. Does a page with one big image load faster than a page with ten small images when the byte count is the same, or even slightly smaller, for the ten small images? From a stopwatch perspective, the large image beats the ten small ones without trouble. Users see network effects like this all the time as they download large files on the Internet because download rates start slowly and increase to a maximum speed. Without getting up to full speed, elapsed time may be higher for many small files. The key to improving Web performance in this case may be to limit the number of connections that have to be made by the browser to the server. Does this mean making one big image for a page? Not necessarily. Usability studies suggest that the user should be kept busy and given information to interact with as quickly as possible. Bundling all of a page's information and sending it as one big file could introduce a significant wait time before the user is able to interact with the page, thus defeating the stopwatch benefit. While the implications of TCP's slow start seem significant, the reason it slows Web pages has more to do with the connectionless nature of the application-level protocol HTTP and how Web pages are built rather some oversight of the protocol designer.

HTTP

The HyperText Transport Protocol (HTTP) is the basic underlying application-level protocol used to coordinate the transmission of data to and from a Web server. HTTP provides a simple, fast way to specify the interaction between the Web client and the server. While the common belief is that HTTP is the protocol that delivers Web pages, the protocol actually defines how a client must ask for data from the server and how the server responds when it returns it. HTTP does not specify how the data is actually transferred; this is left up to lower-level network protocols such as TCP, as discussed in the previous section.

The simplicity of HTTP is often its biggest drawback. Version 1.0 of HTTP has numerous disadvantages, including a lack of adequate support for proxies and network caches. A proxy server is used to provide indirect access to an unsecured network like the Internet for users behind a corporate firewall. Network caches and proxy servers can also be used to improve network performance by fetching copies of Web content to a disk local on a network. The bandwidth and security facilities provided by network proxies and caches are becoming more common as the Internet scales, and protocols like HTTP must be augmented to handle them. However, the most significant problem with HTTP 1.0 is that it may have significant performance problems due to the opening and closing of many connections. When combined with the slow start mechanism in TCP, this may reduce the effective link utilization and slow Web page access. Consider a Web page with five images in it. In order to fetch this Web page, it may take six or seven individual requests to pull down all the files. These may include one request for the HTML text, five for the images, and perhaps even a redirect request for a partially formed URL. Imagine that each HTTP request has a little overhead with it. When this is combined with the TCP slow start, the inefficiency of the protocol becomes obvious.

HTTP Keep-alive has been developed to keep a connection open between the browser and the server. Thus, multiple files can be transferred during one connection, avoiding the startup delays. However, this doesn't necessarily alleviate the slow start nature of the link because the data may still be relatively small. Browser vendors also attempt to deal with the HTTP performance problem by requesting multiple files at the same time. While this technique is simple enough, it does result in network bursts that could present problems when servers are overloaded.

The other major problem with HTTP is that it is stateless. After a Web server has finished fulfilling a client request, the server retains no "memory" of the request that just took place, except as a log entry that records the request. An example of this "lack of memory" is when a user partially fills in a form on a Web page, leaves the site, and then comes back to find the form cleared. The state problem is one of the biggest challenges to building complex applications on the Web. Not having to preserve state is what keeps HTTP relatively simple. However, as discussed in Chapter 7, lack of state is what makes programming Web applications difficult. Newer versions of the HTTP protocol such as HTTP 1.1 and HTTP-NG propose many changes to the protocol to improve performance, and may eventually address state issues; however, some feel that using another application level protocol like WebNFS may actually be a better approach than trying to extend HTTP.

Network Addressing Issues

Besides TCP and HTTP, there are other protocols and network issues that may need to be considered. For example, the Domain Name Service (DNS) has a huge effect on the perceived performance of Web pages. Since all Web requests are in the form of URLs that generally use alphanumeric domain names, the host names must first be resolved to their corresponding IP address. The length of time it takes to do this translation varies; users may be required to try to load a page multiple times before the address is finally resolved. At times, the name service will be unavailable on a regional or even national level. The fragile nature of the name system shows how heavily the perception of the Web is influenced by the Internet's infrastructure and a great deal of work is being done to improve the reliability of the service.

Even using URLs has some implications that should be understood. A potential problem with URLs is that they define location rather than meaning. URLs specify *where* something is on the Web, not *what* it is or anything about it. URLs specify where to go, not what to get. URLs blur the line between what a document is and where it is actually located. This may not seem to be a big deal, but it is. This issue becomes obvious when the problems with URLs are enumerated.

The first problem with URLs is that they are not persistent. Documents move around, servers change names, and documents might eventually be deleted. This is the nature of the Web, and why the "404 Not Found" message is so common. When users hit a broken link, they might be at a loss to determine what happened to the document in question and locate its new home. Wouldn't it be nice if, no matter what happened, there was a unique identifier that would indicate where to get a copy of the information? Although worldwide name-based access would be extremely difficult to do, such universal accessibility is important to strive for.

Another problem with URLs is that they tend to be long and messy. People often have to transcribe addresses. The URL http://www.xyz.com/products/mainline/specsheets/prod1.htm is quite a lot to write on a piece of literature. Marketing firms are already scrambling for short domain names and site structures that use shorter URLs like http://www.xyz.com/prod1. These days, the http, colon, and slashes are often assumed, for better or worse.

The main problem with URLs is that by specifying location rather than meaning, they create an artificial bottleneck and extreme reliance on DNS services. For example, the text of the HTML specification is a useful document and it certainly has an address at the W3C Web site. But does it live other places on the Internet? It is probably mirrored in a variety of locations. What happens if the W3C server is unreachable, or domain name services fail to resolve the host? In this case, the resource is unreachable. URLs create a point source for information. Rather than trying to find a particular document wherever it might be on the Internet, we try to go to a particular location. Rather than talking about where something is, we should try to talk about *what* it is.

■ Potential Web Address Forms

Internet documents should be defined by name, not location. This makes sense when thinking about how information is organized outside the Internet. Nobody talks about which library carries a particular book, or what shelf it is on. The relevant information is the title of the book, its author and maybe even some other information. But what happens if there are two or more books with the same title or another author with the same name? This is actually quite common. Generally, a book should have a unique identifier, such as an ISBN number, that, when combined with other descriptive information like the author, publisher, and publication date, uniquely describes the book. This naming scheme allows people to specify a particular book and then search for its location.

The Web, however, is not as ordered as a library. On the Web, people name their documents whatever they like, and search robots organize their indexes however they like. Categorizing things is difficult. The only unique item for documents is the URL, which simply says where the document lives. But how many URLs does the HTML specification have? There could be many places where this document can be found. Even worse than a document with multiple locations, what happens when the content at the location changes? Perhaps a particular URL address points to information about dogs one day and cats the next. This is how the Web really is. However, a great deal of research is being done to address some of the shortcomings of the Web and its addressing schemes.

A new set of addressing ideas, including URNs, URCs, and URIs, are emerging to remedy some of the Web's shortcomings. A URN (Uniform Resource Name) can locate a resource by giving it a unique symbolic name rather than a unique address. Network services analogous to the current DNS services will transparently translate a URN into the URL (server IP address, directory path and file name) needed to actually locate a resource. This translation could be used to select the closest server in order to improve document delivery speed, or to try various backup servers in the event that a server is unavailable. The benefit of the abstraction provided by URNs should be obvious from this simple idea alone.

To better understand the idea behind URNs, think about the idea of domain names, like www.xyz.com. These names are already translated into numeric IP addresses like 192.102.249.3 all the time. This mapping provides us with the ability to change a machine's numeric address or location without seriously disrupting access to it, since the name stays the same. Furthermore, numeric addresses provide no meaning to a user, while domain names provide some indication of the entity in question. It seems obvious that the level of abstraction provided by a system like DNS would logically make sense for Web documents. Rather than typing in some cumbersome URL, a URN would be issued that would be translated to an underlying URL. Some experts worry that using a resolving system to translate URNs to URLs is inherently flawed and will not scale well. As the DNS system is fragile, there is cause for concern. Another problem with this idea is that, in reality, URNs will probably not be something easy to remember like urn: booktitle. They may be something more like urn:isbn: 0-12-518408-5.

A Uniform Resource Characteristic or Citation (URC) describes a set of attribute/value pairs that describe some aspect of an information resource. In some sense, URCs are like the metadata items associated with a Web document, which are used to describe information about that document. The form of a URC is still under discussion, but it is obvious that many of the ideas of URCs are already in use.

Taken together, a URL, URN, and a collection of URCs describe an information resource. For example, the document "XYZ Corporate Summary" might have a unique URN, such as urn://corpid:55127.

Note: The syntax of the URN above is fictional. It simply shows that URNs probably won't have easily remembered names, and that there might be many naming schemes like ISBN numbers or corporate tax IDs. In the example presented here we use a fake corporate ID system like a DUNS entry.

The "XYZ Corporate Summary" would also have a set of citations that describe the rating of the file, the author, the publisher, and so on. Lastly, the document would have a location or locations on the Web where the document lives. These could be http://www.xyz.com/about/corp.htm or http://www.xyz.com.jp/about/corp.htm. Taken all together, a particular information resource has been identified. The collection of information, which is used to specifically identify this document, is termed a URI for Uniform Resource Identifier.

While many of the ideas covered here are still being discussed, some systems, such as Persistent URLS or Purls (www.purl.org) and Handles (www.handle.net), already implement many of the features of URNs and URCs as described by the World Wide Web Consortium (www.w3.org). Other metadata initiatives including these can be thought of as true URIs when compared to the URLs used today. However, URLs are likely to remain the most common way to describe information on the Web for the near future. Because of this, the system will have to be extended to deal with new types of information and access methods. The point of this discussion is simply to show that addressing is very important to the perception of the Web and the future of addresses is far from set. Web addressing will probably change over time and designers should understand the benefits of embracing some of these ideas early.

▮ Other Protocols

Another protocol that is important to the discussion between a Web browser and a Web server is the MIME (Multipurpose Internet Mail Extensions) type that is used to indicate the type of data being delivered. The MIME type of delivered content is indicated by the value of the content-type header in the server response. However, since browsers can post or upload data, MIME types may also be present in client requests. The general format of the data type is: content-type: type/subtype. Type can be image, audio, text, video, application, multipart, message, and extension-token. The subtype gives the specifics of the content. Some samples include text/html, application/x-director, application/x-pdf, video/quicktime, video/x-msvideo, image/gif, and audio/x-wav. Beyond these basic headers, you may also include information such as the character encoding language. For more information about MIME types, see RFC 1521 at ds.internic.net or the list of registered MIME types at ftp://ftp.isi.edu/in-notes/iana/assignments/media-types/. MIME types are important because with them, Web servers can deliver arbitrary data types, not just HTML pages. Yet, when extended to its logical conclusion, doesn't this idea make Web servers seem little more than fairly simplistic, and often slow file servers? The answer is yes, so attention should be paid to engineering the best possible server.

Server Side Considerations

The server side of the Web equation is the part over which the developer has the most control. The components that affect the delivery of Web pages from the server side include the server network connection, server hardware—particularly disk and processor speed—and server software including the Web server, middleware, and database used. Since servers don't display data locally, the main data paths are from the network to the memory to the disk and back again. If the site must access a backend system like a database, there may be multiple network or disk visits. An example of a server-side data path is shown in Figure 3-12.

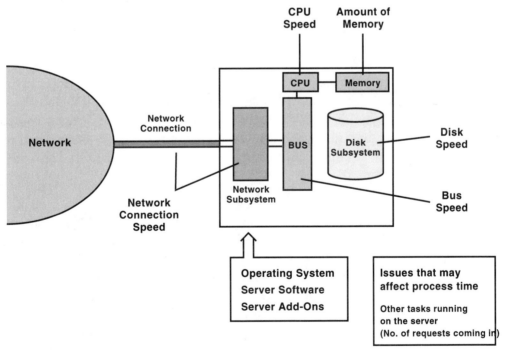

Figure 3–12.   Server Side Components.

It should be evident from the data path that a Web server can also slow the process of retrieving the Web page. On the hardware front, developers tend to host Web pages from UNIX machines or NT systems (for historical, cost, and performance reasons). It is possible to serve pages from almost any system—even a simple home Macintosh or PC—but the hardware and operating system can introduce significant performance problems, particularly under loaded conditions. The type of hardware used should be designed to meet a specified performance criterion. While processor speed seems important, memory and disk capabilities may be more important for Web servers. The importance of the disk should be obvious, since a majority of the Web server's activity will consist of copying files from disk out to network. There are issues about the type of disk access technology employed, such as the use of fast disk technologies like SCSI and RAID devices, as well as disk configuration considerations to provide features such as striping and mirroring. Memory is important since the server may have to support many simultaneous requests. If the site supports a great deal of interactivity through server-side programs or database access, processor and memory availability may be more significant than for simple Web sites. This discussion should indicate that trivializing the role of the server in the process may be disastrous. Imagine a developer designing a database-driven site with a database design that doesn't scale to meet the site's access requirements. Regardless of the quality of the images, content, network link, and so on, the site would probably eventually be less than well accepted because of performance lags.

Engineering the server to meet performance requirements is critical. On an intranet, it may be possible to determine the maximum simultaneous numbers of users and engineer a system that achieves an acceptable response rate given a particular average number of users. On the Internet, such careful planning may not be possible because the number of users may fluctuate. It is possible that the site may encounter a "flash crowd" where a large number of users suddenly access the site at one time. Think of the IRS's site and the major rush of users trying to access the site around the time taxes are due. For most sites, there is no way or need to account for the possibility of such extreme situations. Instead, an initial baseline should be determined and then the performance of the site improved based upon its usage. Generally, bandwidth will not be as significant a problem as server responsiveness and developers may have to opt to use a cluster of Web servers with distributed content and functionality rather than trying to develop a single super server.

Beyond selecting the most "powerful" hardware and operating system to host a Web site, developers must also consider the type of Web software used. Not all Web server packages are created equal. All may exhibit different responsiveness on equivalent hardware. Many Webmasters prefer powerful high-performance solutions like Apache (www.apache.org). Others are willing to give up certain features, and even performance, for the ease of administration, better network integration, or the development environment offered. While server design and performance certainly affect the medium or the Web, the capabilities of the server often extend to a particular development platform or environment that is provided as part of the server software functionality. This can include support of varying technologies including middleware, database connectivity, and other features such as integrated source control and document management systems. The development aspects of Web servers are discussed in detail in Chapter 7. Whatever the case, Web designers should understand that the end user's perception of download speed is affected by server choice. For more information about Web server software, see the Serverwatch Web page (serverwatch.iworld.com).

Other Medium Considerations

The medium of the Web extends beyond the client, server, and network. Users bring in their own perceptions about how Web sites should work. Users may expect the site for a large company to respond quickly and exhibit good design equivalent to the quality of the firm's other public points of contact. Users also come with past experiences of how they believe things should work. For example, users may be conditioned to click on blue or underlined text, read URLs to understand their location within a site, click on graphics which appear three dimensional, and so on. Likewise, developers will bring in their own perceptions about how a Web site should work and will design their sites accordingly. Unfortunately, if developers ignore users' expectations or other aspects of the Web medium, the site may not be well received regardless of the visual design or technical implementation. As shown in Figure 3-5, the communication path ends with people; on one end is the developer, on the other end the user. The site serves as the communication path between the two parties. Just as in a conversation, if one party dominates, the conversation may not be enjoyable. The developer can't easily expect to control the user's experience, and the user can't expect to get by in a site without the help of the developer.

Beyond the influences of the user and developer, third parties may influence a Web site. Other people on a network may generate traffic unrelated to the Web site, which could slow things down for users of the site. Sites that are on shared servers may encounter a performance bottleneck when a Web hosting company over-commits its Web servers. This can result in significant delays, broken images, or even blank pages with "Document contains no data" messages. Even a responsive shared Web server can be damaged when one of the hosted sites suddenly generates massive traffic because of a mention in a magazine. Sometimes Web server hardware does more than just serve Web pages and these other running processes may interfere with performance, just as running multiple applications on the client may slow local rendering. The influences of others, beyond the targeted user, can be significant. A simple negative comment about the design of a site that reaches a decision maker can have impact. So can performance problems resulting from excessive traffic on shared network links. Obviously, these issues occur unpredictably; developers should acknowledge them but not lose sleep over such uncontrollable events.

Summary

The medium of the Web consists of client-side technology and display issues, network delivery issues, and server-side performance issues. External forces such as network traffic and user or developer perceptions can also affect the perceived quality of a Web site experience. Before building Web sites, developers should familiarize themselves with as many Web sites as possible and think about the ramifications of each of the components of the Web medium. Many of the potential technology, performance, and presentation problems with Web sites actually can be engineered around if the developer understands the medium and plans accordingly. However, developers should be wary of exerting too much control over a user's Web experience unless they make sure that the user does not feel limited. The medium of the Web already has many subtleties. There is often an unwritten contract between a site's developer and its users. Before diving into implementation, consider the medium as well as user's expectations. This can serve as a useful jumping off point for exploring the feasibility of the site, which is the first step of the Web Site Engineering process.

Recommended Reading

Applied Data Communications, Goldman, J.E., John Wiley & Sons, Inc., 1995.

Internetworking with TCP/IP: Principles, Protocols, and Architecture 3rd Edition, Comer, D., Prentice Hall, 1995.

The Internet Book 2nd Edition, Comer, D., Prentice Hall, 1997.

Web Server Technology, Yeager, N.J., and McGrath, R.E., Morgan Kaufmann Publishers, Inc., 1996.

Chapter 4

Problem Definition and Exploration

Software applications are generally built to fulfill a specific purpose, such as providing entertainment, generating graphs, or word processing. A word processor rarely performs double duty as a first person perspective shooting game.[1] Web sites, however, often lack a clear purpose. They may even have many conflicting purposes. The main problem is that Web sites are often built without ever clearly defining the problem they are trying to solve. Furthermore, the Internet's hype-driven environment might lead people to create sites or build intranets "just because"—because the competition has one, because the CEO thinks the company needs one, or because of an overwhelming fear of being left behind in the Web revolution. Before deciding which technology, design, and content will be used in a Web site or on an intranet, the purposes and goals for the site must be clearly established. Without a clear idea of the site's purpose, the project may never get started. Even if it does, it may be working toward the wrong goals.

Understanding the Problem

Developing a problem definition doesn't need to be difficult. There are a variety of general questions that can help stimulate ideas and help develop a problem definition. If the upcoming project is a modification to or upgrade

---

1. There are applications that attempt to do many things, but such application generally take the form of a suite of smaller individual applications.

of an existing site, consider the history of the Web site. Understand who has been involved in creating and maintaining it, and its original purpose.[2] While the problem may have changed from then to now, the old problem may be a good starting point for developing a new problem definition for the site. However, don't limit the discussion to the existing site or existing ideas of what is feasible. After the problem definition is documented, perform concept exploration and feasibility analysis to determine the real goals for the site and how they might be achieved.

Education

A fundamental understanding of the medium must be in place in order to do the research to develop the problem definition. As discussed in Chapter 3, a person who attempts to build a Web site without understanding the medium is like a printer who doesn't understand the ramifications of using different types of paper. In addition, familiarity with the Web and a general idea of the capabilities of a Web site are important. Visiting different Web sites and forming an opinion of what is appealing and useful and what is not can be helpful.

Asking "Why?" Questions

In Web site design, addressing the problem should be the main purpose of the site. The preliminary stages of a Web site project are often marked by statements like "We need a Web site," "Our site isn't sophisticated enough." "We need an intranet," or "We can do video with this new technology." To get away from such statements and back to the real issues, ask specific *"why"* questions. Why should video be used? Why should the site be fancier or use a new technology? Why is a site even needed in the first place? Asking why until the reasons become more specific can save a project from disaster later on. Consider the "We need video" statement. The right questions might reveal the belief that having online video will demonstrate that the company is techni-

---

2. Don't confuse looking at the old project for ideas with blame placement and criticism of past work. Sites evolve. Problems change. What appears to be nonsense now may have been appropriate in the past. Pointing out people's past failures during the problem definition phase is guaranteed to create ill will within a project team.

cally progressive. In this case, the real problem to solve could be stated as "the site should show that the company is technically progressive." Now that the problem has been isolated, its solution can be discussed during a concept exploration and feasibility phase. It may turn out that using video is far too expensive, or does not solve the real problem. Driving the site development based on a haphazard solution for a vague problem could result in difficulties further along in the project. Asking "why?" is a good way to start uncovering the problems that a Web site should solve. Problems aren't necessarily bad, particularly if they can be solved.

What Is the Main Motivation for the Site?

Identify which of the following functions a site should fulfill: providing entertainment; advertising; serving as a news source, reference, or marketing tool; providing customer support; recruiting potential employees; functioning as an intranet; or fulfilling some other need. A successful site should not attempt to fill too many roles. Imagine a software product that was a word processing application, encyclopedia, and video game all in one. It probably wouldn't do any of its functions very well. There are many possible motivations for a Web site. Perhaps the company publishes employee benefits information twice a year, and finds it very time-consuming and expensive to print and distribute the literature to thousands of its employees. An intranet could serve as another means of dispersing this same information to employees, as well as account for any changes in a timely manner. Perhaps there is a serious problem finding qualified technical employees, and the Web site could be used as a job recruitment application. The Web site might also serve as support for a large print advertising campaign.

Just as a corporate Web site may have multiple purposes, intranets can be developed to provide many services within a company, such as sales force automation, internal publishing, and purchasing and requisition functions. Trying to accomplish all these goals while thinking about a single site as one cohesive unit can be difficult. Approaching the project in a modular fashion can help deal with those issues, since the site can be broken down into smaller *microsites*, similar to programming modules, each with a distinct goal. The overall motivation for the site does not *have* to be terribly profound or complex. It might simply provide a corporate shell for all the subsites. Identifying the main motivations for the site, and perhaps the subpurposes of the smaller sites, is the first step in deciding whether to move forward. From a user's perspective, the distinctions between various sections of a site, or even between different sites, may be blurry. Often times users may focus on a particular task that encompasses visiting many sites and doing many things at once. Because sites are not as distinct as software in this sense, decomposition may be challenging, and the user may not decompose tasks and sites the same way as the developer.

Why Is the Site Needed?

There is no wrong answer to this question. It is, however, important to consider whether the reasons for having a site are valid, or if they are triggered by FUD (fear, uncertainty and doubt) or hype. What are the motivating factors for the site? "Because the competition has one" may (or may not) be a good reason to establish a Web site. If none of a company's customers are on the Web, how practical is this reason from a business point of view? If the competition has a nice Web presence, but it is not affordable to create one that is comparable, just "having something up there" may be counterproductive. On the other hand, if the competition has had a significant return on investment from their Web site, it may be worth pursuing. A simple online presence can provide a profile of a company. More complex sites can serve as another means of communication between the company and its customers, or provide a conduit for commerce. Significant benefits can be realized when the medium of the Web is leveraged to its full potential. The Web can be conducive to providing large volumes of information that might otherwise be expensive to distribute. It is good for providing immediate access to frequently changing information in a self-service fashion that puts the user in charge.

Intranets can provide many services to a company at a cost savings. Companies can publish internal documents ranging from company policies to price lists and product data sheets on a Web server that is accessible to all users on the network. Additionally, easy-to-use and standardized Web-based interfaces can be used to access applications such as order-entry and inventory systems on mainframes. Such applications are improvements over terminal emulation software that uses cryptic commands to access antiquated systems. When compared to traditional client/server applications, the cross-platform nature of the Web allows targeting of browsers on different platforms within a company. The return on investment from using intranets can be significant. Consider the cost and time-saving benefits of Web-based publishing versus paper distribution or the ability to provide different services to many users within a company using intranet applications.

When Web sites are planned, more fundamental issues, such as the need for a company document management system, may arise. Stay on course; these may be separate problems. A clear idea of why the site is needed will help determine what functionality to include later.

Who Is the Site For?

This is a very important question. Just as a company would not develop a software product without researching the target market, a Web site must have a well-defined target audience to be successful. In order to develop a problem definition that addresses the needs of the users, it is necessary to identify that user audience. Contrary to what many people believe, this does not necessarily mean a big audience. Even if the company has only 10 primary customers on the Web, the site may serve as a valuable way to communicate with these customers. The other tens of millions of people on the Web are irrelevant. Far too often, the focus is placed on the multitudes of people the site might *reach*. *Reach* is an interesting term that describes the maximum possibility of who might visit the Web site. While this might be millions of people, does an electronic component manufacturer really need to reach a 12-year-old boy in New Zealand? While it is great to talk about general users, most sites outside mass media or large consumer-oriented companies will have a very focused audience.

In general, the target audience of an external Web site must be identified in broad terms. Is the primary target a general consumer, home user, general business, business manager, engineer, or student? What is the age range of the target audience? Are they currently on the Web? If they are, do they use it for the desired purpose? This is an important question. Maybe the site is for a local appliance repair company. Part of the target audience would certainly include homemakers in the local area. But how many of these individuals are on the Web? Would they look to the Web to find a local repair shop? In most cases, addressing the target audience issue will not eliminate the need for the site. It may, however, help clarify the purpose.

On an intranet, the audience of users may be known or assumed, removing some of the guesswork that can be necessary to determine an external Web site audience. However, there are issues with audiences on intranets such as which browsers are being used and whether features such as ActiveX are supported. These factors will affect the development standards. Typically, there is a better audience feedback loop on intranets; site managers must interact with the audience. This often involves a user-interview process to determine needs and desires, as will be discussed below.

More specific audience questions might include the following: How many people will access the site, and how? Will they use a modem or a leased line? When will the site be accessed—at night, or during the day? Where will the users come from? In what language will they prefer to access information? What browsers will they use?

While all these questions can help identify an audience, don't get too hung up on the details. At this point, just keep the basics in mind. For example, most home users have modem access speeds in the ranges of 14.4 Kbps, 28.8 Kbps, 33.6 Kbps, etc. An audience of engineers at a large electronics firm may have access through a T1 leased line. With such different audiences, the available network bandwidth is an important consideration that will affect what type of content and design to choose for the site. However, projects can get off track by focusing too early on details. For example, a belief that a few people might access the site with an old Prodigy browser and the design ramifications of such a belief may prevent the discussion from addressing more fundamental issues. There is no way to control all the possibilities and special cases in an audience; try to solve the problem for the majority. Trying to address very specific audience issues at this point just wastes time.

As in software engineering, a compromise may be needed to direct the project toward a platform common to the intended audience. Modern commercial software isn't designed to run on every platform ever shipped, so why is this expected for Web sites? This is not to say that users should be locked out of sites. A Web site probably should be designed around a lowest common denominator (LCD). However, the LCD for one site targeted toward engineers may be far different from one designed for the general public. Though it may be possible to say that an "average" Internet user is a male, primarily Caucasian or Asian, and between the ages of 20 and 40,[3] this doesn't mean that the site's audience has to fit this average. Imagine a site geared toward senior citizens. There is certainly an audience on the Web; it just may be an issue of extent. The key point is to identify the audience's members, size, and requirements.

There is no generic audience for all sites. When considering functionality, the specific users must be considered at all times. The site should be built for them. Too often, Web sites are created according to the designer's needs, with little consideration to those of the user.

Ask the End User

Interviewing users may be necessary in order to develop the problem definition. For an external Web site, a market study may be helpful in determining the desires of the users. If the project is an overhaul of an existing site, a survey can be posted on the Web site to gather user feedback. A more direct approach is to interview the end users. Through this process, many of the requirements of the potential solution may come out. Question and answer sessions can be used to isolate the needs of users who know some of the functions that generally can be achieved with a Web site, but need help in determining the specifics. With an intranet, each department should specify what it would like to achieve with the site. If a consulting firm is used for development, they may need to learn and understand the business practices and needs of their client to assist in developing the problem definition.

Writing the Problem Definition

After pondering these questions, it should be possible to write a problem definition. A problem definition is not a mission statement. Don't try to create one short sentence about the site. But, don't create a monstrous, overly-detailed document, either. A problem definition should be one or two pages

---

3. This is a gross generalization and only used to illustrate a point.

long. Management may have to read it to decide if the site is worth pursuing. The problem should be in "user language"—terms understood by all parties that need a solution to their problem. It should also be written from their perspective. Resist the impulse to propose solutions at this point. That comes later in the process. If the problem definition becomes solution-oriented, revisit the "why" questions.

Figure 4-1 shows an example problem definition.

Big Company, Inc.

Web Site Problem Exploration

Summary: This document summarizes some of the current problems facing the company. It is believed that a Web site may be instrumental in solving some of these problems.

- Currently the firm spends a great deal of money sending out data books and product guides via mail. The current costs for printing and shipping one data book is approximately $20 per request.

- People are constantly requesting the list of distributors. A great deal of time is being spent distributing the list and keeping it up to date manually.

- The firm needs to increase sales, particularly overseas where sales are flat.

- The image of the firm is outdated and does not reflect the world-class stature of the company. The current Web site does nothing to dispel this belief.

- Investors and other parties have expressed an interest in obtaining more timely financial information.

- Currently there is very little press coverage for the company.

Conclusion: It is believed that a Web site may be able to address some of these needs. For example, a Web site may be able to reach foreign customers better than traditional means and the cost savings by providing most product data sheets online may be significant when compared to current paper-based methods.

Figure 4–1. Sample Problem Definition.

While a "wish list"—an exhaustive list of all the features and functionality desired for the Web site—may get the process started, including all these desires in the problem definition is not suggested. However, a brief comparison of the wish list with the problem definition may quickly determine the practicality of the ideas.

Concept Exploration and Feasibility—The Whirlpool Approach

Once the problem definition is established and documented, it is possible to address each aspect of the problem and evaluate the feasibility of a solution. Each point in a problem definition must be considered in the context of the Web and what makes sense in this environment. The goal of the concept exploration and feasibility phase is to determine the real goals for the Web site. Inherent in this process is the consideration of features and functionality. To better understand this phase, using an analogy of a whirlpool can be helpful. Getting from the problem definition to the purpose and goals resembles a whirlpool where all of the issues are in a state of flux as they are explored and analyzed. Eventually, the extraneous issues are filtered out, and when everything settles, the important issues are evident. If the understanding of the issues is not thorough enough to clearly identify the objectives for the Web site, it may be necessary to reenter the "whirlpool." Figure 4-2 illustrates this analogy.

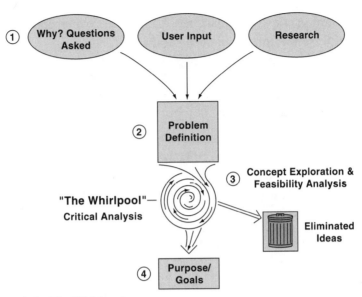

Figure 4–2. The Whirlpool.

Software engineering studies have documented a relationship between the cost to fix a defect or implement an omitted feature and the point in the development cycle when the defect is discovered. The repercussions, temporal and financial, increase dramatically as the project progresses. Furthermore, software developers who spend more time planning and less time programming finish their projects faster [(2) Card, McGarry, and Page 1987; (1) Card 1987]. Though the final functionality of the site and the details will be addressed in the Requirements Specification, it is impossible at this point to determine whether it is feasible to solve a problem with the Web site without considering actual features and functionality. The issues involved in using the Web as a medium must be well understood (as discussed in Chapter 3). Consequently, it may be necessary to consult an expert who thoroughly understands the medium and its possibilities. Practical issues must be addressed at this point. For both software and Web site development, not all ideas that are generated in this phase will be implemented. Possible reasons not to include a feature are shown in Figure 4-3. Concept exploration and feasibility analysis are used to eliminate the unnecessary ideas presented in the problem definition and make the real issues more salient. Each problem and the practicality of its solution must be considered from different perspectives, including cost benefit, technical implementation and its relation to the ultimate goal. In this way, the viable goals for the Web site become evident.

❏ It is unnecessary in relation to the goal of the site as a whole.

❏ It is technically not feasible in light of other, more important goals.

❏ It is economically impractical.

❏ It would significantly increase the project time-line.

❏ Though it is a desirable feature, its implementation makes more sense in a subsequent iteration of the site's development.

Figure 4–3. Reasons Not to Include a Feature.

In the previous discussion of the problem definition, one of the examples involved distributing documentation via the Web is a way to save money. This seems like a good idea, but what about the details? In what format should the information be provided? Should the content be converted to HTML, or provided in some other format such as Adobe Acrobat's Portable Document Format (PDF)? While HTML would seem the obvious choice, it may actually be very expensive depending on the volume of the content, its form, and its life span. If the document changes significantly each month, it may not be worth it to redo the HTML each time a new version comes out unless it could be created automatically from a database. If the document will be accurate for ten years, it may not be prudent to format it in HTML, which is currently in a state of flux. Is it important that the layout of the documentation is accurately preserved? If so, providing the document as a PDF may be a better solution, though there are certainly issues to be considered here as well. Requiring users to obtain the Acrobat Reader software to view the document may be troublesome to them. The proprietary nature of the format may have serious drawbacks. Perhaps providing the documents as downloadable Microsoft Word documents provides the best alternative. As with many issues in a problem definition, there is not always a "right" answer for every situation; it depends on many factors.

A Few Examples of Hard & Soft Measurements

Soft Measurements	Hard Measurements
• Overall company business up by 107%*	• 100 visitors per day
• Business perception improved	• Call volume of Technical Support
• X$ of business deals closed because of Site*	• X products sold via Web site per month
• Improved productivity	• X leads generated by site per day

* Looks hard but they are not since they can't easily be correlated with the Web site

Figure 4–4. Examples of Hard and Soft Measurements.

It may be inappropriate or impractical to provide solutions for certain aspects of the problem definition. Consider the statement, "We need to increase sales." Some might immediately jump to the conclusion that electronic commerce is the perfect solution. However, let's examine the issues involved. First, the company should consider whether it has the capability to fulfill orders. Furthermore, it must be prepared to deal with the people who might respond. These issues may seem far afield from technical or engineering issues, but unfortunately management is often so unfamiliar with the Web that a Web development team may have to raise such obvious considerations. Is it economically practical for a salsa company in San Diego to fill an order from a potential customer in Iceland who only wants one jar of salsa? Are the permits in place to ship the salsa? What about taxes? Language issues? Currency exchange? Aside from the logistics of filling orders and the financial implications, the cost of developing an online purchasing system could be significant even if off-the-shelf software is used. This kind of careful analysis can prevent the mistake of implementing solutions that are not viable. Though electronic commerce via the Web is possible, diligent examination of all the issues for the specific situation may reveal its impracticality. Individuals responsible for evaluating technical feasibility must think beyond what is possible and consider what makes sense from a business standpoint. Perhaps the motivation behind developing an intranet is to enable the centralization of a contacts database. While this could be achieved by building a custom Web-based intranet system, using off-the-shelf software may be far more efficient. The "buy or build" question is an important one. Considering the costs of coding an application, it is prudent to determine whether a problem is unique enough to warrant a custom solution. Taking all aspects of every feature that may be included in the Web site into account is integral to creating a successful site.

As the evaluation progresses, make every attempt to fully exhaust the analysis of the issues in the problem definition. Feature creep, or adding features after the project is well under way, is the most common cause of cost and schedule overruns in both software development projects and Web site projects. If there is an idea of adding a feature at a later stage, plan accordingly now. Even if the plan isn't fully fleshed out, get a sense of what the future features may be. Don't preclude the possibility of including a feature later by failing to acknowledge it now. Sites can get so far along without considering all the potential features that it becomes impossible to add new features without substantial rework. Imagine a corporate site organized a particular way with a nice full screen graphic. Adding a whole new department in this environment could ruin the design and navigation of the site. This would be like adding a spell-checking program to a word processor a few weeks before shipping. Even if such a feature could be integrated before the ship date, it probably would look as if it were simply tacked on, and may not work well.

Answering the Problem Definition: The Overall Purpose

The end result of the whirlpool experience is a revised and reduced problem definition statement that should accurately reflect the objectives for the Web site. After identifying the objectives, planning is complete. Leave the details to the Requirements Specification phase as discussed in Chapter 5. At this point in the process, only a very general idea of the required functionality is needed.

For example, imagine that the Human Resources department has established an objective of using the Web site for recruiting purposes. They wish to add and delete job listings online quickly and to retrieve resume submissions.

The job posting information may change quite often and the Human Resources department needs to control this area without coordinating with the technical staff. The general functions required to satisfy this objective can be drafted without providing the specifics necessary to actually solve this problem. With these basic requirements, using a database is probably in order.

Depending on the situation, static HTML documents may not be an appropriate solution to provide certain functions. A more complex solution may be necessary when the functionality requirements are spelled out. However, don't get ahead of the game in planning the actual features and functionality of the Web site. Though the decision to support commerce on the Web site may have been made, this is not the time to decide what shopping cart software to use. Concentrate on the purposes of the Web site and the *general functionality* that will be required to achieve those objectives. This phase is concerned with preplanning and may not be as precise as we would like.

In addition, the fundamental design of the site should be considered at this point as it will become important in determining budgeting issues. Many sites use a modular design where each section of the site (Human Resources, Technical Support, etc.) is the responsibility, both financially and content-wise, of that department. The example mentioned above is the one in which the Human Resources department is responsible for the job listings on the site. Another example may be the Marketing Communications department's responsibility for press releases, executive biographies, and general company information, which are usually included in the "About the Company" section. Additionally, Marketing Communications, working with product or service managers, may drive the Product or Services section of the Web site. From an intranet perspective, perhaps Marketing Communications establishes the general look-and-feel for the site while MIS coordinates the technology and then puts each department in charge of maintaining its section.

Software applications use modularity because it makes sense to separate functionally distinct areas from one another. This applies to Web sites as well. The needs of the Human Resources section are different from those of the Technical Support section. Be careful not to project solutions onto areas that do not require them. Consider each division of the site separately. Similar to a large monolithic software system with many functions, a site with many different goals probably should be divided into modules or subprojects that make up part of a larger whole. This reinforces the idea of a *microsite*—a very specific subsite that is a portion of a larger site, and may be built separately. Microsites have the advantage of allowing the focus, look, or technology of a segment of a site to change without having to change the site as a whole.

Establishing a Measurement of Success

In order to determine whether the site is successful, a measurement by which to judge the site must be developed. In most cases, the measurement will be closely related to the goal or purpose of the site. Imagine that a company builds a Web site with an information request form in order to collect leads that can be pursued by their sales forces. It seems logical that a measurement of success in this case would be the collection of a certain number of requests. However, in identifying the measurement, it is important to be specific. In the case of the sales leads, the goal may be 25 requests in the first two months after the Web site is launched. This may be an arbitrary number, but an objective must be set; otherwise, there will be little way to judge success.

Success measurements and objectives for Web sites vary depending on the site's purpose. Some Web sites judge success based on hard measurements, such as the number of orders received for a product, or the number of times that a certain file, such as an annual report, is requested. For another Web site, a measurement of success might be a decrease in technical support calls in relation to the availability of information on the Web site. In order to judge this, the number of technical support calls received prior to the launch of the Web site must be recorded. The success of a new intranet might be determined by the cost-savings realized as a result of the automation of previously time-consuming tasks.

However, the success of some sites may be based on a "soft" measurement where the success cannot be directly attributed to the Web site. Often, statistics provided by Web servers such as requests or visitor counts are incorrectly considered valid measurements. Contrary to what many people think, the number of requests or visitors is not necessarily related to the success of the site, as will be discussed further in Chapter 9. Measurements for some sites can be difficult to define when the results are indirect.

For example, consider the benefit of a promotional or advertising-oriented Web site for a movie. The Web site is part of the overall marketing plan for the movie, and ideally, will induce ticket sales. But how can the benefit of the site be measured? Is it possible that the site was very poorly received, but the movie did well? How about the scenario that the movie failed and the Web site was the only good thing associated with it? In either case, it is difficult to rate the effectiveness of the site. Maybe the number of visitors is the only metric that can be considered, in which case, the more hits the better. Figure 4-4 (page 105) describes some typical "hard" and "soft" metrics.

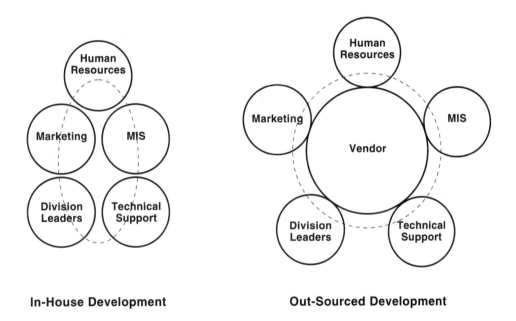

In-House Development　　　　**Out-Sourced Development**

The Players in a Web Site Development Project
Dashed lines indicate resources involved in project

Figure 4–5. Outsourcing versus In-house Development.

Aside from the satisfaction of realizing whether or not the site has achieved its goal, eventually the issue of the cost will arise. Management will initially allocate a "novelty budget" for the Web site, sort of a "let's try this and see what happens" approach. In order to get management to budget more money for the Web site, the site's success must be established. In order to show that it is successful, there must be a concrete measurement of success. Even with a novelty budget in place, a person's job may be at risk if there is no clear way to determine the value of having a site. While many sites may have to resort to a very indirect measurement of success, this is better than nothing. The advertising industry has long faced issues of soft measurements, but has used heuristics like "Spend 10 percent of sales on advertising" as a way to create a baseline for expenditures. While such statements may just be guesses, at least they can be used as a starting point for discussion. Waiting until after the site is launched to see the results will not help determine if the site is successful. Because all objectives will have been retroactively applied, judgment will be skewed, and there will be no way to defend against claims that the site wasn't successful.

Some measurements should focus on benefits in terms of cost savings rather than revenue generation. If a site is able to provide information to users to lower the number of support calls or if an intranet can provide previously print-based information to employees, then money saved is a very worthwhile measurement. This is particularly true for intranets where the automation of work flow and increase in efficiency can translate into significant savings.

Logistics

Upon making the basic decisions as to what the site will do, it must be determined who is going to implement it and how it will be paid for.

In-house versus Out-source

As far as the implementation issue goes, the choices are to do it all in-house, to out-source the entire project, or to do some combination thereof. Obviously, the ability to do any of it in-house is dependent on the skill sets of the company's staff. Remember, as discussed earlier, developing a Web site is not easy. Initially, it may seem financially imprudent to pay an outside firm to do tasks that company staff members have the intelligence to do. However, consider the time spent and the distraction from the person's core job responsibility. Doing the Web site in-house does not mean that it is free. In addition to the possibility that the primary work of those people working on the Web site may suffer, the quality of the Web site may be inadequate. It seems obvious that a group of people who make Web sites for a living could do a far better and more efficient job of building a Web site than those who are trying to learn as they go along while still fulfilling their primary job responsibilities. While some firms may be able to afford a dedicated in-house Web team that is equal to any outside vendor, many organizations will have neither the time, talent or budget for such a team. This argument is no different from the considerations facing managers trying to staff a software development project. However, having an outside vendor does not eliminate the need for a dedicated Web person in-house. It is at least a part-time job to communicate with the outside vendor and keep the Web site up to date and functioning. Regardless of the decision to develop a Web site in-house or to out-source some or part of it, the same principles apply.

Who Will Pay for It?/Company Dynamics

Having decided who is going to do the work, it now must be determined who is going to pay for it. As discussed previously, modular designs can be helpful in breaking down the cost. If the Technical Support section is technically complicated and involves a significant amount of programming and database integration, why should the Marketing department pay the bill for it? Initially, Marketing pays for most sites in their entirety. However, as sites get more complex, sharing the financial impact will become a reality. This applies to intranets as well. In some instances, though the look-and-feel of the intranet is directed by the Marketing department, each department may be responsible for developing its own section. Other concerns to address at this point include defining the business model for the Web site. With the rush to get the Web site up, financial issues may be ignored. Though the developer of the site may not consider the return on investment or finances of the site to be his or her responsibility, this responsibility should not be overlooked. If the business model of the Web site doesn't coincide with the objectives for the site, it may be necessary to rethink the project. While these issues are more managerial and business-oriented, it often falls on the Web development team to provide a sanity check, or at least act as a liaison with management to get fundamental site issues ironed out early.

It is important at this point to be aware of company dynamics, regardless of whether the project is in-house or out-sourced. Marketing drives the look-and-feel of a company. This includes the Web site. The MIS department determines networking and computer resource issues. Do not make the mistake of keeping MIS out of the loop. Developing the Web site using a database that the primary MIS manager dislikes is a very bad idea, both politically and financially. On the other hand, maybe MIS already has all the required hardware and software. The logistics of developing the Web site should take a team-based approach. MIS and Marketing need to work together to blend technical functionality with the appropriate design.

Summary

Thoroughness in the initial phase of the Web site engineering process can limit the problems that typically plague the development of software and Web projects. Clearly identify the motivations for the site. Develop a complete, detailed problem definition that states the issues without proposing solutions. Without an idea of what needs to be accomplished, efforts could be made to solve the wrong problem. Thoroughly research all aspects of the problem definition. For each idea, brainstorm possible solutions, considering the practicality and feasibility of each. Use the whirlpool method to eliminate those that are extraneous and the real purpose for the site will settle out. Have a general idea of the functionality of the site but avoid getting into specifics. Develop a measurement to determine whether the site is successful. Though the benefit may be indirect, it is important to have a measurement for success. Decide if the project will be completed in–house or relegated to an outside vendor. Lastly, in determining who will pay for what, acknowledge the company dynamics and take a team-based approach.

References

1. Card, D. N., 1987. "A Software Technology Evaluation Program." Information and Software Technology 29, no 6 (July/August): 291–300.

2. Card, D. N., McGarry, F.E., and Page, G.T., 1987. "Evaluating Software Engineering Technologies." *IEEE Transactions on Software Engineering* SE-13, no. 7 (July): 845–51.

Recommended Reading

Buchanan, R. W., Lukaszewski, C., and Buchanan Jr., R.W., *Measuring the Impact of Your Web Site,* John Wiley and Sons, 1997.

McConnell, S. *Software Project Survival Guide*, Microsoft Press, 1997.

Siegel, D. S. *Secrets of Successful Web Sites: Project Management on the World Wide Web*, Hayden Books, 1997.

Chapter 5

Requirements Analysis and Specification

In the previous phase, the main objectives for the Web site and a *very general* idea of functionality were identified. In this phase, the requirements analysis and specification phase, these goals are translated into requirements. If the objective is "to recruit potential employees using the Web site," the requirements statement might read as follows: "The Web site will have a section that lists all of the available jobs at the Company. There will be a feature that allows people to submit their resumes via email or an electronic form." The first step in turning the objectives into requirements is to classify the site in terms of the environment (intranet, extranet, Internet) and the general approach (static or dynamic.) These factors will influence the types of requirements to be addressed. The requirements analysis phase involves exploring the content, functionality, and system requirements for the Web site. Depending on the site's environment, corporate, and marketing requirements may also play a role.

The requirements analysis process concludes with the development of the requirements specification document. The requirements specification states *what* the site will do and the scope of the project. It does not address *how* to implement the functionality or what the site will look like. An estimate of resource requirements can be made using the detailed specification, and competitive bids may even be requested. The main goal of the requirements specification phase is to set boundaries and limits for the project. Failure to adequately specify features and requirements can jeopardize the project's viability to the point of cancellation [(1) Vosburgh et al. 1984, (2) Lederer and Prasad 1992, (3) Jones 1991, (4) Jones 1994, (5) Standish Group 1994] .

Classifying the Site

The first step in determining requirements is to set boundaries for the project. One way to do this is to classify what type of site it will be in terms of the environment and the general approach.

Environment: Internet, intranet, extranet

As discussed in previous chapters, there are three main types of Web sites: Internet sites, intranets, and extranets. Internet sites are traditional Web sites that are intended for access by the general public. Intranet sites are intended only for internal (intra-organizational) use. Extranet sites are a combination of these. They are typically private and secured areas for the use of an organization and its designated partners. For example, a distribution company might set up an extranet site for its primary customers. The site could provide order status, shipping information, and account balances on a private section of the distributor's Web site. In this way, the site functions like a traditional Internet Web site from the customer's perspective, but as an intranet site from the distributor's point of view.

Each of these three environments has requirements that are specific to type of site. An intranet, for example, has different system requirements than does an Internet site. With an intranet site, it may be possible to design for a very specific browser and platform; an Internet site must be more generic since the type of user access cannot necessarily be predicted or controlled. Intranet sites must address corporate guidelines; Internet sites involve marketing requirements. Extranet sites may involve both. All these requirements will be discussed in detail in the requirements analysis section. At this point, however, it is important to identify the site's environment to ensure that the appropriate issues are considered.

Infrastructure: Static versus Dynamic

After determining into what general category the site fits, the issue of a static versus dynamic site must be addressed as this will also influence the requirements. "Static" implies that the Web site will be a flat-file system of HTML files while "dynamically generated" sites require that the content be stored in a database. Consequently, the requirements for a static site are mostly content related, while the dynamic site will have content requirements *and* functionality requirements. It is important to note that the static and dynamic options are not mutually exclusive. Parts of a site may be dynamic while others are static. Not all sites require complete database functionality. A corporate site with minimal interactivity might require a partial database, while a complex online commerce-based site might be entirely database driven. The specifics of the requirements will be discussed in the next section.

In order to determine whether a database-driven site is necessary and appropriate, it is important to understand the differences between a static Web site and a database-driven Web site. In a static Web site, all pages reside on the server and have fixed content that will be served "as is" to the user. Web pages consist of text with HTML markup that controls formatting, links, navigation and the inclusion of images. Making changes to a page requires retrieving that HTML page from the server or where it may be centrally stored, making the necessary changes, and then putting the changed page out to the site. If there is a correction that is site-wide, such as a change in a copyright date from 1997 to 1998, each page must be updated individually. In addition to the redundant effort in making these changes, the large number of files in a static site in a flat-file system can be unwieldy. With a static site, the dynamic generation of Web pages is impossible; content and presentation are merged.

In contrast, a dynamic database-driven site separates content from presentation. There are two main components to a database-driven site: the database—where the information resides—and the HTML templates that provide the structure for the document presentation. The relational database consists of tables and fields that organize the information. Common databases used to power Web sites range from simple file-based databases like Microsoft Access to client/server relational databases like Oracle, Sybase, and Microsoft SQL Server. They may even include object databases or object relational databases. Determining which option is most appropriate for a specific site depends on the scope and type of the information, as well as existing company platforms, resources, and facilities. Databases are discussed in further detail in Chapter 7.

The second component of the database-driven site is the HTML templates. A template is a prototype HTML page that contains the code for the look-and-feel of the page, including the navigation and the layout. For example, a single site might have many different templates: one for the product pages, another for press releases, another for job opportunities, etc. By using templates, updating is simplified and the look-and-feel of the pages is preserved throughout the site.

The objectives of the site determine whether a database is needed. As mentioned before, electing to use a database is not an all-or-nothing decision. If the objectives include personalizing pages for individual or groups of users, a database is probably in order. With a database-driven site, users can search for specific information and content can be tailored to each user. For example, if a site has an international audience, different language versions of the content could be kept in the database and the appropriate version displayed depending on the user's domain. Queries can be constructed based on keywords, user preferences, and parameters passed via forms. Using the HTML templates, a new page containing the relevant information is built "on the fly."

In addition to increased usability and sophistication, a database-driven site may be practical if significant site growth is anticipated. The implementation of a database promotes and expedites site growth, maintenance, and consistency. By storing data separate from the actual page presentation, an infrastructure is created that easily accommodates adding future sections. Furthermore, a database-driven site expedites graphical redesign because it eliminates the need to individually reposition all existing content, instead using templates to apply a change to many pages simultaneously. Separating the content from the presentation encourages structured data organization, which makes the content more versatile.

For large sites, a database is helpful for managing files. Attempting to manage large numbers of files in a flat-file system is both inefficient and overwhelming. Along these same lines, it is important to maintain consistency of layout in a Web site. The use of predesigned templates ensures uniformity in page appearance.

Simplification of site maintenance is one of the most important features that a database-driven site can offer. Basic forms that involve minimal, if any, HTML can be created to enable the company to make changes to the information in the database and automatically update the Web site. This is especially advantageous in situations where many different departments (Human Resources, Sales, etc.) make changes to the site. With database level access control, each department can update only their own area and only within the prescribed template styles. This control preserves a consistent look and feel across the site and eliminates the need to channel content through one dedicated Webmaster before posting. A database may also provide a method of version control so that a "rollback" to older pages is possible.

Although it is initially more expensive to create a database-driven site, there may ultimately be a cost savings. The database solution can include an update tool that eliminates the need for heavy outsourcing to update or modify the site. In the event that outsourcing is required, such as for graphic redesign or major site additions, the scope of the project is less extensive due to the existing infrastructure. In our experience, the time to implement decreases over time when databases are used to drive sites, as do the costs. Furthermore, database-driven systems provide the opportunity for tool-based update by personnel who will not have to be familiar with HTML or other Web technologies.

Many firms feel that the expense of a database is not warranted. Instead, they opt for a static file-based site. When lookup facilities or dynamically generated documents are later desired, the site must be thrown away completely, or expensive work-arounds must be implemented to provide limited interactivity.

There is also the possibility that the database information may be used as the main data repository for the company. Database solutions can be developed using standard Structured Query Language (SQL), which is portable to and compatible with most other standard database products. For example, a company could use an internal database standard such as Microsoft Access to connect to the site database and download information for internal use.

Another aspect of cost that should be considered is the success of the site. Often, database driven sites are much more useful and process-oriented than static sites. Imagine that one of the objectives of a site is to help users identify which of the company's products fits their needs. While putting information about the products on the site may be informative, it may not really assist the user directly. However, creating a dynamic product finder that acts as a "virtual salesperson" facilitates the process and increases the likelihood that the visit will culminate in a sale. In this case, paying more initially to create a site that will better serve customers and increase sales will ultimately translate into financial gain. An intranet that consists of static documents for reference may be somewhat useful. In our experience, however, an intranet that increases productivity by using a database to integrate workflow will result in cost savings. Database-driven sites typically have a larger return on investment due to their process-oriented nature.

In summary, the objectives for the Web site should determine whether a database is necessary. In order to dynamically generate pages, serve individually tailored content, or offer complex search capabilities on a Web site, a database solution is required. If there are a large number of files or the ease of maintenance is a priority, a database is highly recommended. It is important to note that choosing to use a database is not a black and white decision. Often, it makes sense to implement a database in certain parts of the site but not in others. For example, areas that change frequently, such as press releases or job opportunities, benefit from a database. Pages that don't change often, such as the home page, probably should not be dynamically generated each time a person comes to the page. Rather, they can be pushed out once a day at a specific time into a flat file. This gives the benefits of a database by making available the most recent content, yet avoids the delay associated with dynamically generated pages. In this way, the database acts as a document repository system.

Figure 5-1 summarizes the issues involved in making the "database decision."

What is involved in creating a database-driven site?

- ❐ Choosing a database
- ❐ Choosing middleware
- ❐ Developing database schema (tables, fields) by studying the problem and talking to users
- ❐ Creating HTML page layout templates
- ❐ Creating update forms

How does a database-driven site differ from a static site?

- ❐ Dynamic generation of pages
- ❐ Individually tailored content
- ❐ Search capabilities
- ❐ Ease of file management
- ❐ Simplification of maintenance

What are the cost benefits of a database-driven site?

- ❐ Eliminates heavy outsourcing
- ❐ Expedites updates and redesign
- ❐ Allows for multipurpose use of database (used for in-house access as well)
- ❐ Possibly increases revenue due to site-effectiveness

What are the drawbacks of a database-driven site?

- ❐ Dynamically generated pages not easily indexed by robots
- ❐ Transfer performance penalty for dynamically generated pages
- ❐ Initially more expensive
- ❐ Possible lack of simple, consistent URLs for bookmarking

Figure 5–1. Factors Involved in Developing a Database-Driven Web Site.

Requirements Analysis

After classifying the site's environment and infrastructure, specific requirements can be developed for it. As mentioned previously, the classification of the site will influence the requirements and their respective degrees of importance for the different types of sites.

Environmental Requirements

Though system requirements will differ depending on the type of site, all sites should address the end-user system requirements of browser, connection speed, and monitor size as well as the server-side requirements. For an intranet, obtaining the end-user information is simple. While for this example connection speed and monitor size are not major issues, specifying the browser type is imperative. Imagine that an intranet is being developed by several different people and that the system requirements for it have not been established. One developer uses ActiveX (supported only by Microsoft Internet Explorer) and JavaScript to implement the functionality of one section, while another developer uses Netscape-centered JavaScript and Java on their section. There may be problems between the two parts of the sites because of the different technologies—even in the JavaScript, which varies between Microsoft and Netscape. Due to a failure to specify the system requirements, the intranet will not be completely functional using either browser. By not establishing the system requirements, one of the benefits of designing an intranet site is lost.

Determining the target platform for an extranet or Internet site can be even more difficult. While some general assumptions about the target audience can be made, surveying a sample of the user population or analyzing the statistical reports for the existing site can be very useful. A consumer-oriented site is likely to be accessed via a modem connection. It is probable that many of the users will have access through America OnLine (AOL), WebTV, or a similar online service and have only 14-inch monitors. Conversely, a Web site for a large components company probably will be accessed primarily by well-equipped engineers with high-speed connections who are most likely using either Netscape or Internet Explorer. In this case, optimizing a business-to-business site for use with the Prodigy browser does not make any sense.

It is a good idea to identify the most likely least common denominator (LCD) platform. Taken to the extreme, this translates into a text-only Web site, because when it comes right down to it the only thing people have in common visually may be text. Remember that some people may use text terminals on the low end, while at the high end huge high resolution monitors are used.. Obviously, this is too limiting. Another option is to provide a separate site for each type of browser. It is possible to design a site that can sense for connection bandwidth, browser type, screen size and other such variables. However, the cost and difficulty of deploying such a site probably outweigh the benefits. The cost/benefit ratio of the engineering effort to support all possible platforms must be considered. The solution to this problem is to identify the most common platform and design around that. Common Web design conventions, such as designing for 640 x 480 resolution in order to prevent the need for horizontal scrolling and avoiding the use of proprietary tags can be useful. Still, with all the different versions of browsers available, and their slightly different interpretations, results can be unpredictable.

With software products, we expect to see a system requirement and we don't expect the product to work on other platforms. For Web-based applications, system requirements disclaimers such as "this site must be viewed at 800 x 600 resolution with Netscape 3.0" are frowned upon. This lack of control over the end-user's environment is what makes Web design so difficult. Establishing system requirements is mandatory in order to provide a framework in which to develop the site. In addition, there will inevitably be comments that the site doesn't work on some browser. Attempting to retrofit the site each time a concern is raised can run a project into the ground. Establish the systems requirements based on the intended audience and adhere to those requirements. Table 5-1 summarizes some general system requirements based on the target audience and site environment.

In addition to end-user system requirements, the server-side requirements for the site should be addressed. The server-side requirements will state what type of server the site will reside on as well as general hosting information. The server-side requirements will be determined by the functionality demands of the site, corporate standards, and performance requirements. The functionality of the Web site must be considered when determining what Web server to use. For a dynamic site, the database platforms and middleware must be compatible with the server. If special software will need to be installed, such as an electronic commerce package, compatibility with the server should also be explored. The server should be chosen with consideration for the number of transactions that will be occurring. For example, a Macintosh server is probably not robust enough to handle the traffic of a large commercial site. In addition, it is important to ensure that other required resources, such as adequate disk space for storage are available on the server.

Corporate standards will also influence decisions such as what database, hardware platform, and software should be used. Corporate policy may dictate that the Web site should be hosted on a certain platform to ensure compatibility with other company processes. This is true for intranets, extranets, and Internet sites. Some projects may even have very specific compliance requirements. Government projects typically require that operating systems be POSIX (Portable Operating System Interface for UNIX) compliant, and that development conform to other specific standards.

In addition to functionality and corporate standards, performance issues will affect the server-side requirements. This is especially true in terms of who should host the Web site. The amount of necessary throughput should be estimated to determine what level of hosting vendor or service is appropriate. While hosting on an in-house server may be suitable for some sites, others may have enough traffic to warrant mirrored sites in other countries. Bandwidth and hosting issues are discussed in Chapter 3. Ultimately, the server-side system requirements should establish the platform on which the site will be developed and hosted as well as where the site will be hosted.

Marketing and Corporate Requirements

While system requirements are common to every Web site, there are other requirements that depend on the type of site. Intranets have corporate requirements that may include document format issues, internal communications standards, and document management systems. If the Human Resources department must legally keep track of Equal Employment Opportunity reports and statistics, the intranet must address this need. In this sense, corporate regulations must be addressed in the functionality requirement.

While Internet sites do not need to focus on the internal corporate requirements, they do need to address marketing and branding requirements. Marketing requirements are necessary to make sure that the Web site conforms to the company's current look-and-feel. A Web site is yet another reflection of a company. As such, it should be consistent with the other marketing collateral of the company. A site that does not project a strong image may speak poorly of the company. For example, imagine a company that has several "daughter" companies. If each of these companies has a completely different look-and-feel to the Web site with no unifying factor, it appears that the parent company is not in control. Conversely, if the main holding company's Web site clearly reflects its brand, and that brand is subtly reiterated on the other sites, a sense of cohesion and unity is promoted. The same standards that a company applies to its print literature should be applied to the Web site. Just as a brochure with spelling errors would reflect poorly on the company, and thus would not be sent out, errors on the Web site should not be tolerated. While intranets involve primarily corporate requirements and Internet sites have marketing requirements, extranet sites involve both corporate *and* marketing requirements because they serve both the company and its customers.

Content Requirements

The content requirements should list what information will be included on the Web site, if it exists, and in what format. Figuring out the content to use ahead of time is of great importance. Unfortunately, more often than not the content is not well specified nor collected ahead of time. This often causes delays later on in the project. In our experience such content problems are the number one delay of Web site projects once they are started.

What to Include

Too often, the tendency of Web site builders is to gather everything they can find that is in digital format and put it up on the Web. Content that is not already digitized is simply scanned and then put online. When deciding on the content to include on the Web site, there are two main concerns: first, what to include and second, how much to include. Determining whether the content is relevant is the first step. In some cases, such as with product information, the answer may be obvious. But what about old press releases? How far back should they go? Should there be an archive, or should only the releases from the current year be posted? Budgetary constraints may determine which content makes it to the Web site. The real goal is to give the users what they want and need, which may not be what you currently have. The "less can be more" heuristic applies in assembling the content for a Web site. Putting up a lot of content just to make the site look like it has substance is not the correct approach.

■ Repurposing Existing Content

Even if the content does exist, the format may be an issue. If there are 100 pages of articles that exist in hard copy, somebody is going to have to scan or type them in. If a company's monthly newsletter is produced in Quark XPress™, creating a Acrobat™ PDF (Portable Document Format) of it each month may be more cost-effective than converting it to HTML. In addition to text, multimedia will need to be prepared for delivery over the Web. Images will have to be repurposed for the Web; there are resolution and color issues that cannot be ignored. Sound and video must be reduced in quality or frequency of sampling, or downsampled, and compressed for acceptable download time. Repurposing existing content can be very time-consuming. Chapter 7 covers issues with writing for the Web and with text presentation.

■ Creating New Content

Another important question, and one that is rarely given enough attention, is whether the content even exists. Lack of content is probably the number one cause of Web site schedule overruns. Do not underestimate the time, effort, and cost of creating content. Depending on the volume, it may be more expensive than the creation of the Web site itself. It is far better to plan and execute a small Web site for which all content exists than to design a large Web site that never goes anywhere because it has no substance. Putting up "under construction" signs all over a Web site is not acceptable. Returning to the analogy of Web sites as software, imagine trying to format a document in Microsoft Word and receiving an error box stating that "This feature is not available." If it's not ready, don't include it.

After determining what types of information to include and addressing issues of content creation and repurposing, decide how much to include. The determining factor in this decision is money. The bigger the site, the more it costs. However, issues of economies of scale do apply. This is especially true for database sites where the content and presentation are separate. The real cost in the creation of a database site is in the development of the infrastructure and templates, not in the formatting of individual HTML pages. The content requirements should address what content will be included, whether it exists, and in what format.

Functionality Requirements

When addressing the functionality requirements, there is the temptation to focus on issues of implementation. Remember, the functionality requirements state *what* the site will do, not *how* it will do it. The specifics of design and implementation are addressed in the next few chapters. Even if a site is almost entirely static, it will probably have some functionality requirements. Remember, sites can be purely static, completely database-driven, or a combination of the two.

The functionality requirements should be detailed, as they are the specifications that the designers and programmers will use to develop the site. For example, the functionality requirements for an interactive product finder on an Internet Web site might be as follows: The product finder will allow searching by part number, specification, and integrated circuit (IC) manufacturer. Users should have access to data sheets, application notes, and any other relevant product information, using as few mouse-clicks as possible. The pages should be conducive to printing. Online commerce capabilities will be added eventually; the system should be built to accommodate this feature. The product information must also be easily updateable. Notice that this description does not mention databases or other specifics about how the site will be engineered. The description simply states the needs and leaves the rest up to the designers and programmers.

For a very simple, mostly static site, the functionality requirement might be only that the site contains a form that allows users to enter requests for information. A simple, static site might also treat navigation as functionality. For example, the functionality requirement might specify that there should be immediate access to the request form from all pages. An intranet might have functionality requirements for a detailed time-tracking system as well as a feature that allows the easy upload of files. Among other features, an extranet will most likely be password-protected and should be dynamically generated from an up-to-date information source. No two sites will have the same functionality requirements. The important thing to understand is that the functionality specification should be comprehensive. Enumerate every functional feature that the site should have.

Specification

In the requirements analysis, the site's content and what the site will do were explored. In the specification, actual requirements are documented. A flowchart should be developed to gain a general idea of the overall structure and scope of the site. The architecture of specific sections, such as the product finder discussed previously, should not be developed. It is sufficient to show a box that indicates where the section goes in the overall structure of the site (see Figure 5-1). In addition to the flowchart, a detailed written report should be part of the specification. The report should list the system requirements, content requirements, functionality requirements, and, where applicable, marketing and corporate requirements. The specification is of utmost importance. In software engineering, different degrees of requirements specifications are used. For example, a project might have a specification that is intentionally very general. Rapid Application Development (RAD) approaches such as JAD (Joint Application Development), evolutionary prototyping, or staged releases might be used to shorten the requirements specification phase for a certain project. Software engineering has a long history in which these practices have been fine-tuned. Web site design is not yet mature enough to benefit from these techniques. Even if it were, first-time Web developers should probably not attempt rapid development. Furthermore, RAD doesn't always work in a client/server environment.

The specification should be detailed enough that a development team of average skills would be able to design and build the site using the specification as the guide. In addition, based on a detailed specification, competitive bids

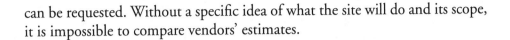

can be requested. Without a specific idea of what the site will do and its scope, it is impossible to compare vendors' estimates.

Estimation and Resource Requirements

With a detailed project specification completed, the process of estimation can begin. The previous phase (Chapter 4) should have addressed the question of outsourcing versus in-house development. The decision should be revisited at this time to determine if it is still valid. If the Web site development will be outsourced, the estimation process involves comparing bids and then allocating resources. If the project will be completed in-house, the resources required must be carefully evaluated, and time, resources, and money must be designated for the project.

Compared to software engineering, project estimation in the Web arena is very difficult. Because the Web is so new, there is no real history. Consequently, there is no real valuation for Web sites. There is a lack of familiarity with the Web and Web publishing. While software projects are assigned based on expertise, Web site projects often go to the lowest bidder. There appears to be a lack of awareness and common sense among the general public regarding Web site development. A person who would balk at a company that offered to design, create and print a four-color brochure for $100 may believe that there is no significant difference between a Web site that costs $300 and one that costs $10,000. This is changing slowly, as people become more familiar with the Web, and as the return on investment from certain sites becomes evident.

In addition to this Gold Rush mentality, there are other implications of the Web's newness. Because software engineering has a relatively long history, there is much to be learned from the experience of others. Sections of programs may be reusable; the likelihood that something similar has been done before is high. On the contrary, Web sites depend on innovation. Though there are code libraries and tutorials available, the Web is still young. Consequently, there is not a lot of information available for comparative estimation.

Defining the scope of Web sites can also be troublesome. Software engineering uses "lines of code" as a measurement. However, in Web site design, the concept of a "page" is hard to define. It could be a typed page—single or double-spaced—it could be a screen-full, but using what size monitor? Furthermore, not only does the size of the page differ; the complexity of pages can range dramatically. The time required to code a complex table-based HTML page is far different than that required to make a page with a heading and a few lines of text. Because the Web is so new and bug-ridden, the issue of complexity becomes even more subjective. Visual editors and other RAD-like tools mislead people into thinking that Web development is easy. Consequently, no consideration is given to testing or real design. This haphazard approach, combined with the idiosyncratic behavior of different browsers, can lead to trouble.

Design complexity is also a factor in the estimation process. Developing a site for a company that has no corporate look-and-feel is very difficult. In a sense, the project involves creating not only the Web site, but also the corporate identity. On the other hand, simply assembling scanned images for online viewing is not very complex.

Software engineering has developed estimation models, such as COCOMO, that can be used to determine the resources and schedule for a project. Though some software engineers maintain that these types of models are not accurate, the Web is not disciplined enough to even have such models.

However, one estimation factor is common to both software engineering and Web development. The project time is directly proportional to the size of the project. For both software and Web sites, this assumes an ideal environment. If a small project is mismanaged and the requirements are not adequately specified, it could take far longer to complete than a well-run project of twice the size. Software engineering has documented that adding more people to a project won't necessarily expedite the delivery. In his book *The Mythical Man Month*, Frederick Brooks concludes that adding manpower to a late software project may not help; it may even make it later. This is true for Web site development as well; sites with twenty-person committees often get delayed by internal politics and inefficient decision making.

Though estimation is difficult, it is necessary. Typically, a consideration of the design, scope, and technology will give a good idea of the cost and/or resource requirements of the Web site. Just as the functional requirements enumerate what the site will do, the resource requirements detail what will be needed to complete the project and how long it will take. If the site will be outsourced, the core estimation process will be done by the vendor. The hiring company's estimation process will consist of comparing vendors, selecting one, and then deciding where the budget comes from.

Typically, vendors are compared by the appearance of their previous work and by price. Unfortunately, these factors do not guarantee Web development expertise. Sites that look good may not be designed for cross-browser support. Firms that charge exorbitant fees do not necessarily produce the best work. When choosing a vendor, visuals and price are important but they are not the only consideration. The vendor should understand the specific needs of the company and develop a custom site rather than imposing a cookie-cutter solution. The vendor should be technically knowledgeable. Even if a database is not required at this point, it is helpful if the vendor is knowledgeable and designs the site with room to grow as necessary. The vendor should be receptive to the needs of the hiring company. There are many Web site development companies. Not every client is right for every company. Some Web firms may work better with consumer-oriented sites while others focus on business-to-business solutions. Web development is more of a service than a product. Consequently, a vendor should be selected based on their capabilities, a confidence in their ability, and a synergetic working relationship.

Once the project is assigned to the vendor, the vendor will typically set the development schedule. Remember that outsourcing does not absolve the hiring company of all work. An internal person will need to be designated to work with the vendor. Though the vendor is adept at Web publishing, they do not know the contracting company's business. For an outsourced project, the resource requirements for the hiring company might be one full-time, dedicated Web person and the cost in dollars of the Web site. The vendor has a different set of resource requirements for completing the site.

For a site that will be completed in-house, the effort and resources required will need to be explored and then documented. A schedule should be developed that explicitly states what the status of the project should be at given intervals. The project should have a project manager that oversees the development of the Web site by facilitating communication and coordinating resources. Thus, the resources requirement for a site developed in-house consists of the schedule, an account of the number of people and hours required as well as a consideration of any equipment or software needed.

Conclusion

The goal of the requirements analysis phase is to take the objectives for the Web site and translate them into requirements that can be used by the designers and programmers to develop the site. Depending on the type of Web site, different requirements will need to be addressed. All sites must have content and system requirements. Sites, particularly dynamic or interactive sites, will also have functionality requirements, though the degree may vary. Intranets must observe corporate requirements while Internet sites must address marketing requirements. Extranets must deal with both. The culmination of the requirements analysis is a specification that is detailed enough to enable an outside company to prepare a bid. Though the specification does not address how things will work, it reflects the overall structure of the site. The process of Web site estimation can be difficult due to the newness of the Web and its short history. Nevertheless, the development of resources requirements that address cost, schedule, and people resources is imperative. With a firm set of requirements, the design of the Web site can begin.

References

1. Vosburgh, J.B., et al., "Productivity Factors and Programming Environments." Proceedings of the 7th International Conference on Software Engineering, Los Alamitos, Calif.: IEEE Computer Society 1984: 143–152.

2. Lederer, A. L., and Jayesh, P., 'Nine Management Guidelines for Better Cost Estimating." *Communications of the ACM*, 51–59; February 1992.

3. Jones, C., *Applied Software Measurement: Assuring Productivity and Quality*, McGraw-Hill, 1991.

4. Jones, C., *Assessment and Control of Software Risks*, Yourdon Press, 1994.

5. The Standish Group, *Charting the Seas of Information Technology*, The Standish Group, 1994.

Recommended Reading

Frenza, J.P., and Szabo, M.. *Web and New Media Pricing Guide*, Hayden Books, 1996.

Gascoyne, R. J., and Ozcubuckcu, K., *Corporate Internet Planning Guide*, Van Norstrand Reinhold, 1997.

Chapter 6

Designing the Web Site and System

During the Requirements Analysis and Specification phase, the objective is to document what the Web site should do and establish an abstract structure and requirements for the functionality of the Web site. In the Design phase, it is important to determine what the site will look like, both structurally and graphically, and how it will work are developed. Though the different aspects of design are intricately related and overlap each other, we will present them as distinct processes in the most logical manner. First, *information design* involves the construction of a detailed flowchart of the structure of the Web site using the principles of hypertext theory. Closely related is *program design*, which deals with constructing a prototype of the site's functionality using software design principles and methods. Concepts of *navigation design* combined with the *graphic design* of the site are eventually used to construct the interface. *Network and server design* should also be addressed during the Design phase.

What Does Web Design Include?

Defining Web design is very difficult. To some, design focuses on the visual look-and-feel of a Web site. For others, Web design is about the structuring of information and the navigation through a document space. Others might even consider Web design to be mostly about the technology used to build interactive Web applications. In reality, Web design includes all these things and maybe more. The question is, in what mixture? Different types of sites will focus on different aspects of design. A very complex intranet may focus more on program design and functionality than graphic design. Conversely, for a static, marketing-driven Internet site, the graphic design will be the core of this phase. As Web sites move away from the "page" paradigm and towards a "program" paradigm, the emphasis of design will certainly change. Whatever the design phase's primary focus, the result should be the same—the development of the components necessary to implementing the preliminary Web site. These components generally include the development and refinement of a site flowchart and design document, the development of any prototypes necessary to show site functionality, and the creation of a graphical composite that suggests the final look-and-feel of the Web site.

Information Design

Previously, the Requirements Analysis phase documented a general idea of the scope and architecture of the Web site. Using this as a basis, a very specific architectural plan for the site should be developed. Remember that most people visit Web sites to retrieve a particular piece of information or to accomplish some task. Though sites with attractive graphic design may entice visitors initially, it is the information and functionality that guarantees the longevity of the site. Consequently, the information should be organized in a manner that facilitates its access. The site's functionality should be designed in a way that enhances its usability. *Information design* describes the organization of information which provides clarity, meaning, and context for the information [(1) Mok 96]. Information design involves taking data like text, pictures, multimedia elements, and programming elements—the raw goods of a Web site—and organizing them in a way that is meaningful and hopefully useful. Information design can be a subtle subject, but its usefulness should not be underestimated. Given the torrent of information on the Web, techniques to help communicate a message to a viewer and bring order to a site or document are mandatory. Unfortunately, in Web site projects the Web team often has little input to the design of raw information to include in the site. While content may not make sense at the page or paragraph level, it is often difficult to restructure it without careful consideration of the political fallout. Remember that the marketing department and others that contribute content may not be receptive to the idea of rewriting copy or changing it into a form more appropriate for the Web. A Web site manager should attempt to educate content contributors about well-designed information. In the best case, Web site managers may actually have control or input over the form of the content provided. Many times, however, site developers may have to resort to simply trying to structure and organize the information given them the best way possible. At this level of granularity, it is important to understand hypertext theory and different hypertext models in order to effectively structure a Web site.

Hypertext theory

Hypertext is not a new idea. As discussed in Chapter 1, the idea has been around for nearly 50 years. In some ways, the Web has been the first exposure many people have had to hypertext systems. Despite its recent popularity, there is actually quite a bit known about hypertext, which leads to three basic "rules" [(2) Shneiderman 89] of hypertext:

1. A large body of information is organized into numerous fragments, or, in the case of the Web, into pages
2. The pages relate to each other
3. The user needs only a small fraction of the information at any given moment

These rules should seem obvious to anyone who has ever been to a Web site, but it is interesting to note how often they are broken. Think about sites that put huge documents into a single page. Does that not break rule number one? Many sites attempt to do too much by providing links back and forth from pages that are hardly related. This would certainly seem to break rule two. Sites that provide links to every page in the site right away or attempt to provide a huge amount of information at once seem to ignore rule three, which simply states users can't handle everything all at once.

Because hypertext and hypermedia are the basis of the Web, a thorough understanding of their theory and conventions is essential to the design of a usable Web site. Just breaking the information into small chunks is not enough. Without a logical structure to the information, users may not know where they are or how they got there. They may literally feel "lost in cyberspace." Consequently, depending on the type of content and the user's mode of consumption, different hypertext models should be used so users don't get lost and can navigate the information presented quickly and logically.

Content Organization Models

There are four main hypertext organizational schemas in use on the Web: linear forms, hierarchies, grids, and pure Web. Slight variations on some of the basic schemas are also common. Choosing the correct site form is important in making a site accessible. For example, a sales presentation generally requires a linear form: slide two follows slide one. While the presentation could be presented in a tree or hierarchy form, it would encourage viewers to access slides out of order— possibly reducing the impact of the sales pitch. However, some information collections might benefit from hypertext links allowing viewers to find more information about the topic or about closely related subjects. Hypertext organization often closely mirrors the nonlinear way that people access and process information. When a Web site is organized around the most appropriate hypertext form, it can make the complex clear.

Linear

A linear form is the most familiar of all document collection styles because traditional print media tends to follow this style of organization. Books are generally written so that one page follows another in a linear order. Certain books such as dictionaries, "choose your own adventure," as well as many reference books may present a different structure than pure linear. Presenting information in a linear fashion is often very useful when discussing a step-by-step procedure, but there are times when supplementary information may be required. Linear forms can be modified slightly to provide more flexibility but will eventually degenerate into a grid, hierarchical, or pure web form when overextended.

Pure Linear

A *pure linear* organization facilitates an orderly progression through a body of information. On the Web, a "slide show" style tour could be used to give new visitors an overview of the company and its products. By using a controlled sequential organization, the designer can ensure that the user receives the information in the intended order. Likewise, if the information is intended for online consumption, presenting small chunks in a linear fashion can increase the likelihood that the user will read it. The linear style of organization provides a great deal of predictability in that the designer knows exactly where the user will go next. Because of this knowledge it may be possible to *preload* or *precache* the next bit of information to improve the perceived performance of the site. For example, while the user is reading the information on one screen, the images for the next screen can be loaded into the browser's cache. When the user advances to the next screen, the page is loaded from the cache, giving the user the illusion that the page downloads very quickly. Preloading is not a viable solution unless the user's next path can be anticipated, as is the case with a linear organization. Note that on the Web pure forward linear style is not quite possible because of a browser's backtrack facility. Figure 6-1 presents a diagram showing a linear structure.

Pure Linear

Figure 6–1. Linear Structure.

Linear-with-Alternatives

While a linear organization is useful to present information in a predetermined order, it may provide little room for the user to interact with the information. A *linear-with-alternatives* organization simulates interactivity. Imagine a quiz Web site that prompts the user for a "yes" or "no" answer to a question on each page, and advances the user to the next page based on the answer. Though it might appear to the user that there is some back-end technology at work, in reality, the two tracks are already established and the user is just presented with an illusion of interactivity. A health care site might use a General Health Quiz to attract people's interest. The quiz might begin with a question such as "Do you smoke?" Users who answer "yes" advance to a page that describes the hazards of smoking while users who answer "no" see a message congratulating them on their to decision to abstain from cigarettes. Regardless of their answers to the first question, both users advance to question two. Though the pages are static and there is no dynamic generation of pages, to the user it appears that there is some interactivity. Despite the appearance of choice, the linear-with-alternatives structure preserves the gen-

Linear with Alternatives

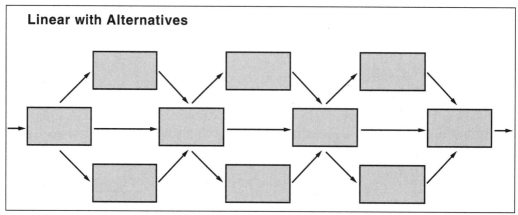

Figure 6–2. Linear-with-Alternatives Structure.

eral linear path through a document collection. An example block-diagram of a linear-with-alternatives structure is shown in Figure 6-2.

Linear-with-Options

A *linear-with-options* structure, as shown in Figure 6-3, is appropriate when a general path must be preserved but slight variations must also be accommodated. This type of hypertext organization might be useful for an online survey where some users might skip certain inapplicable questions. Given that linear-with-options generally provides a way to skip ahead in a linear structure, this organization is often called linear with skip-aheads. An example of this structure in action might be a survey given by a Web hosting company to determine the needs of potential customers. The first question might be "Are you interested in co-locating a machine at our facility?" Users who answer "yes" skip the questions that refer to the amount of disk space required and other questions specific to shared hosting. Again, this organization simulates an intelligent system even though it is nothing more than static files in a well-thought-out hypertext structure.

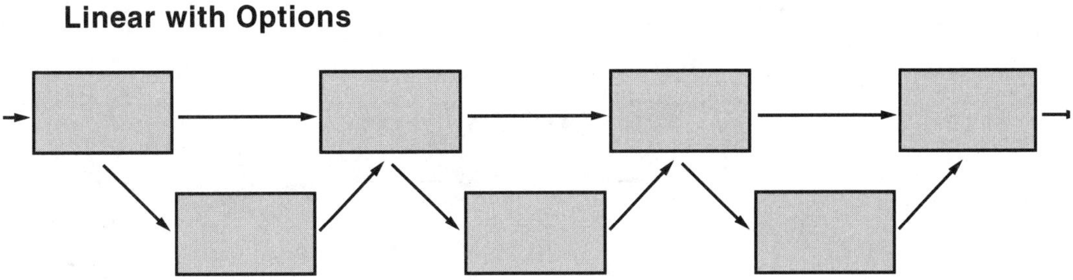

Linear with Options

Figure 6–3. Linear with Options.

Linear with Side Trips

A *linear with side trips* organization allows controlled diversions. Although the user might take a short side trip, the design forces the user back to the main path, preserving the original flow. Perhaps a technical article is presented in a linear fashion. A hyperlink on a particular word on the main page leads to a tangential page with the definition of the word and then links back to the main page. Rather than distracting the user from the main path, this bit of information enhances the experience. Making the side note part of the main linear progression would dilute the continuity of the primary message. However, when many side trips are added into the linear progression the structure may look like a hierarchical form to the user. An example of a linear-with-side-trips organization is shown in Figure 6-4.

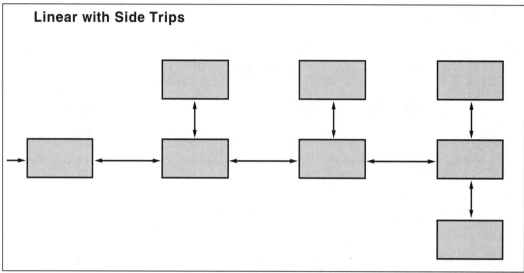

Figure 6–4. Linear-with-Side-Trips.

Grid

A *grid* is a dual linear structure that presents both a horizontal and vertical relationship between items. Because a grid has a spatial organization, it is good for collections of related items; so far, a pure grid structure remains uncommon on the Web. When designed properly, a grid provides horizontal and vertical orientation so the user may never feel lost. For example, items in a virtual software catalog might be linked horizontally based on a common quality such as operating system compatibility. Items might also be linked vertically based on the type of application such as graphics, word processing, or a spreadsheet program. While a grid structure is highly regular and may be easy for a user to navigate, not many types of information are uniform enough to lend themselves well to this organization. An example of a grid structure is shown in Figure 6-5.

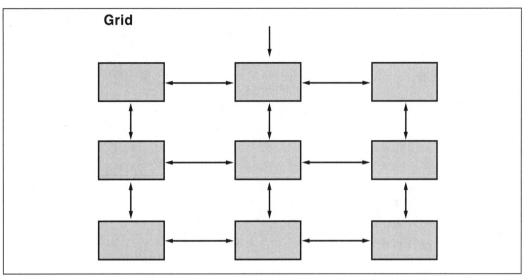

Figure 6–5. Grid Structure.

Hierarchy

The most common hypertext structure on the Web is the tree or hierarchy form. While a hierarchy may not provide the spatial structure of a grid or the predictability and control of a linear structure, the hierarchy is very important because it can be modified to hide or expose as much information is as necessary. Designers might be tempted to expose all information at once, but remember the hypertext rule that states that users don't need to see all information at once. However, providing fewer choices and hiding the information deep within the hierarchy may frustrate the user looking for a particular item. This is the balance between the narrow and wide hierarchy.

Narrow Hierarchy

A narrow hierarchy presents only a few choices but may require many mouse clicks to get to the final destination; this organization emphasizes depth over breadth. Though there is some spatial orientation, the user is required to drill down to get to the detailed information. For some sites, this is a very effective way of quickly funneling users into the correct category. For example, a Web site for an employment service generally has two main audiences: job seekers and employers looking to hire. Making this distinction obvious on the home page and requiring the user to choose a category facilitates quick and easy access to relevant sections of the site. Expanding the top-level choices to include the specific options for job seekers and for employers would be distracting. Using a narrow hierarchy as a means of progressive disclosure can help keep the user focused. However, it may increase the number of clicks required for the user to get to the ultimate destination. It is important to balance these two factors and to avoid putting up unnecessary "doors" between the user and the information. One way to understand if a site hierarchy is too narrow is when there are many pages that are purely navigational beyond the home page. Remember that users want "payoff." Endlessly clicking through pages provides little more than frustration. An example of the depth-oriented narrow hierarchy is shown in Figure 6-6.

Narrow Hierarchy

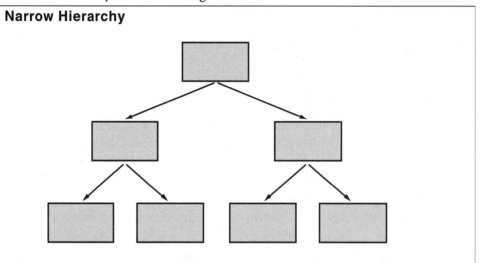

Figure 6–6. Narrow Hierarchy Structure.

Wide Hierarchy

A *wide hierarchy* **as shown in Figure 6-7** is based on a breadth of choices. Its main disadvantage is that it may present too many options. While the user only has to click once or twice to reach the content, the time spent hunting through all the initial choices may be counterproductive. Many people think that everything important must go on the home page. However, if everything gets a link from the home page, then the hierarchy is not preserved and information may lose its effectiveness, in some sense becoming lost in a crowd. With many choices, users may focus on extremes when making choices. The phone book serves as a good example of trying to stand out from many competing choices. For example, in alphabetical listings of nonpreferential choices, the letters A, M, and Z sections tend to be selected the most. Notice how in the plumbing section of the phone book how many firms have names like AAA Plumbing or A-1 Automotive. Also notice the use of bold text, display advertisements, and color to stand out from the crowd. Similarly, Web designers try to remedy this by calling even more attention to certain areas with larger font sizes, brighter color, animation or blinking—the digital equivalent of shouting. While at first these persuasion techniques may work, they may also cancel each other out or leave the user feeling overstimulated and annoyed. In fact, over time a user will become accustomed to any extra stimulation, and the attention-grabbing techniques lose their power. This is a known phenomenon from cognitive science called *sensory adaptation* [(3) Coe 96]. Ideally there should be just enough choices for users to give each choice equal weight when deciding what to do. Experience suggests that between six and ten main choices on a home page is ideal. At deeper levels in a site, more extensive numbers of choices may be appropriate. Note there are may exceptions to this rule, such as news sites or directories where the point may be to provide as many items at once.

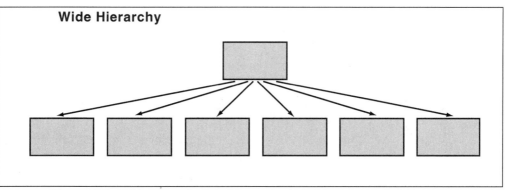

Figure 6–7. Wide Hierarchy Structure.

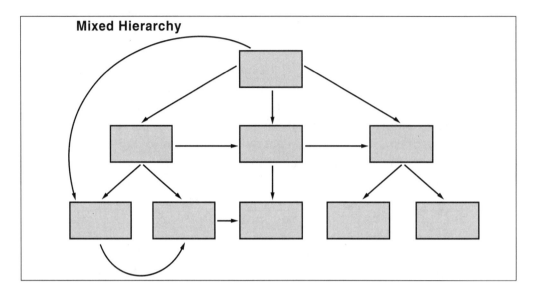

Figure 6–8. Mixed Hierarchy Structures.

Mixed Hierarchy

While a wide hierarchy may present too much, too narrow a hierarchy will hide too much information. In some cases there will be a need to augment the hierarchy to allow choices to bubble up to the top. This structure is called a *mixed hierarchy* and is probably the most common form of site organization used on the Web. A hybrid of narrow and wide hierarchy, a Web site using a mixed hierarchy may present main choices, such as About, Products, Technology, and Contact, while simultaneously providing the ability to skip ahead to deeper parts in the site. A prime example of a skip ahead is the "Download Product Now!" button found on the home page of many sites. This link takes the user directly to the download section, providing a quicker route than the traditional path through the Products section. Though spatial organization is not as pronounced as in other hierarchical structures, a hierarchy is still generally evident.

■ Pure Web

When too many cross links, skip-aheads, and other augmentations are made to a structured documentation collection, the form will become unclear to the user. When a collection of documents appears to have no discernible structure, it is called a *pure web*. A pure web structure can be difficult to use because it lacks a clear spatial orientation as shown in Figure 6-9. Though information can be accessed quickly if the correct choice is made, it may be difficult to orient oneself in a Web site with an unclear structure. If a site's structure is unclear or unfamiliar, the user may resort to a home-page-based navigation, always returning to a top level when beginning a new task. The benefit of a less structured form is that it provides a great deal of expressiveness. A technical paper might provide links to related diagrams, supporting statements and papers, and even excerpts from outside resources. The organization of the site may not easily fit any one of the more structured forms. While some might argue that the confusing pure Web structure may cause the user to lose focus and make it difficult for a participant to form a mental map of the site, this may actually not be a problem when information or task is properly designed.

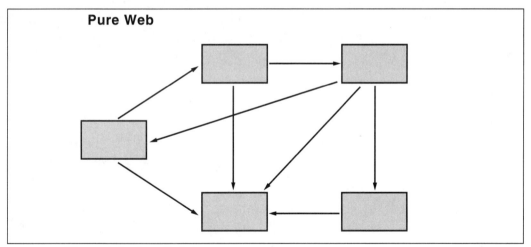

Figure 6–9. Pure Web Structure.

Picking the Correct Structure

Picking the correct structure for information is not an easy task. The idea of picking the correct structure for a document collection or breaking up information into a collection of pages is called information mapping [(1) Mok 96]. The first step of the information mapping process is to understand the data that will be included on the site. This may include the type of the data—such as text, graphic, video, sound, and so on—as well as the amount of information and its eventual purpose. Often it is very useful to understand if information is to be consumed onscreen or in printed form. This can be very important because it may influence chunking the data dramatically. Because of the difficulty of reading online, small chunks work well; however, collecting small chunks to print a document can be difficult, so a larger document might be warranted. The overall purpose of the site, including the amount of control that the user should have versus the designer, is also important in determining structure. Each document collection form has its own pros and cons. Figure 6-10 shows the relationship between the expressiveness and predictability of the different organizational structures. While linear is very predictable, it provides a limited relational view. While Web is very expressive, it can be confusing. The grid and hierarchy share the middle ground.

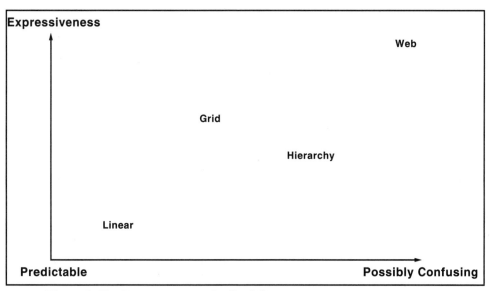

Figure 6–10. Expressive versus Predictability.

Proper information design is key to the development of a successful Web site. If a site has great content and a great interface but poor information architecture, it may be relatively useless. If the user cannot easily find the information, the site loses its effectiveness. Most sites now use a mixed hierarchy approach that is familiar to many Web users. Depending on the goals of the site, however, the use of several types of structures might be combined. For example, while the overall structure of a site might be a hierarchy, a pure linear structure could be used to provide an introduction to the company, and a narrow hierarchy could be used in the technical support section. Ultimately, the issue is that the designer, not the user, should be in control of the *presentation* of the information. It is the designer's responsibility to structure the information in a way that will make it most useful to the user. The user should not be hampered by the information design of the site. However, he should not be overwhelmed by it either. Allowing too many choices, or failing to provide linearity where it is needed, can be an equal disservice. In some cases, innovative information structuring can be used to simulate interactivity. It is important to anticipate what the user will want to do and how he will use each section of the site. The structure should be planned accordingly and documented in flowchart form, as shown in Figure 6-11.

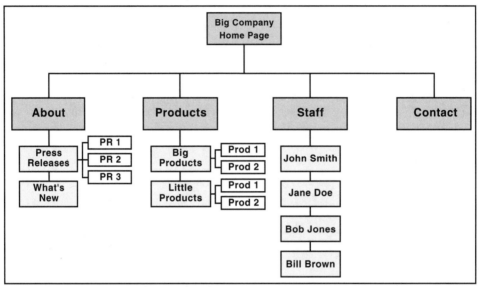

Figure 6–11. Sample Site Flowchart.

The flowchart is the simplest site design diagram. While there may be many conventions about what shapes, icons, or lines to use in the flow chart, the main point is to create a diagram that is easily described and understood so it can be implemented properly.

While the flowchart serves to document a site's structure for implementation, any scheme used should be clear enough so individuals who are unfamiliar with the information or the site's architecture will understand the organizational scheme. This doesn't mean that the users will memorize the layout of the information or visualize a flowchart in their head as they move around. In some sense, information structure may not matter if the user's focus can be retained. Whether something is back, next, or up from a current page in the site should not be the user's focus. The main point is what the user is doing, or what content they are consuming. If users are content and accomplishing their goals, they really aren't lost. Even so, don't throw out logical information structuring like linear, grids, and hierarchies in favor of a pure Web structure. Remember that people are spatially oriented and prefer to navigate in terms of location. Web sites are locations. People generally talk about "visiting" sites, not about reading them.

When organizing information, always attempt to retain the perspective of the user visiting the site. Many, if not most, of the visitors will be relatively unfamiliar with the site and its structure. Don't assume that the organization will be clear to them. Remember that organization may not have to be clear if the site is providing a service to the user.

Web Site: Application versus Information

Organizing the information on a Web site is only half of the picture. Remember that Web sites are now starting to *do* something. In this sense, the Web site becomes an application or software tool, and not just organized information. This mixing of application and information is what makes Web design difficult. From a user's perspective, they may be simply moving around pages looking for information and trying to fulfill some goal such as buying airline tickets. However, from the developer's perspective, the way this information is generated is by a software application. Like information design, the functional aspects of the site must also be designed particularly when visitors will use the site like a tool. Functional and program design is pure software engineering with slight Web twists that acknowledge the speed of Web development and the content focus of the medium.

Program Design

Concurrent with the idea of structuring the information into a flowchart is the idea of structuring the programmed elements of the site. Web design does not necessarily have unique system design schools yet, but some of the programming methodologies of software engineering, such as modularity, can be applied to the Web site development process. In general, most sites take a structured approach, though complex systems may require object-oriented ideas. Structured design may not be as glamorous as object-oriented design or as familiar as the "printed page structure" style design often used today for Web sites. However, it serves as a good way to bring order to a Web site; it even applies to simple Web sites. Remember that many Web sites may still be more about presentation and information than function. This will probably continue to be the case for some time. Even those sites that do have interactive elements may limit their use or restrict them to very distinct areas of a site. Because of the relative lack of programmed features in most Web sites, adopting an overly complex design methodology or one that requires excessive formality might actually hinder the development of a Web site. Remember that there isn't one correct way to build a Web site.

Design Principles

Certain principles are common to nearly every approach to program design. These principles are so fundamental to well-designed systems that they should be discussed outside a particular methodology, lest they are overlooked based upon a particular preference for one methodology or another.

Modularity

Structured design and object-oriented design both rely on the concept of modularity. Modularity describes the idea of breaking a system up into independent parts, called modules, which combine to make up the system. The flowchart produced in the requirements phase should provide an overview of the structure of a site and present some kind of a modular view of the site itself. This concept of breaking a system down into modular subsystems is known as decomposition. A high-level module within a Web site that has its own purpose and design can be deemed a microsite, subsite, or subsystem. For example, a company might build a small Web site that is separate from their main corporate Web site expressly to promote a new product. Within this subsystem, there might be a module that allows users to request information about the product as well as enter comments. Within the information request module, there might be one module for processing contact information and another module that handles the comments. The decomposition process should continue until it is easier to implement the subsystem than to further decompose it.

Cohesion and Coupling

It is good practice to design modules with high *cohesion*. Cohesion describes how strong the relationship is between the routines or code that make up a module. Imagine that there are two main modules to a Web site: the product finder and the job listings section. The module that controls the product finder should work only on issues involving the product finder. It should not be involved in the functionality of the job listings section. Likewise, for the job listings module to exhibit high cohesion, all of its routines should be dedicated only to implementing the job listings. The idea of cohesion can be taken to a more granular level as well. For instance, a page in a Web site should be designed with cohesion. All HTML, links and content on the page should be related to the purpose of that page. This presents the concept of maintaining a sense of *relevance* on pages. Code that is not necessary for the implementation of the page should not be included. Unnecessary graphics and content, or navigation that is better found elsewhere in the site, should also not be included. In page development, there is a tendency to code pages based on the HTML from other pages. This can result in the unnecessary inclusion of irrelevant pieces of HTML or client-side script code, resulting in low cohesion.

Sequential cohesion describes the orderly execution of functions and data transformations within a module. This linear progression relates to the idea of maintaining state between pages (to be discussed later). It may be appropriate for modules within Web sites to exhibit sequential cohesion. However, the idea of hypertext browsing can present problems with this concept. Consider the idea of an online ticket ordering system. A user must go through a logical series of steps on a number of pages to obtain a final result. With poorly constructed navigation or unintended user actions such as bookmarking, it may be possible to enter in the middle of the intended process and circumvent necessary first steps. This would throw a user out of context. Modules that depend on sequential cohesion should be designed to ensure that users follow the intended path. This may be possible by using techniques that control navigation such as built-in ActiveX controls or Java applets within pages, by using pages that are dynamically generated from a server, or even simply by embedding the environment within an HTML frame. Highly cohesive modules tend to be more robust than modules with low cohesion.

Cohesion refers to the *intra*-relationships *within* a module. *Coupling* refers to the *inter*-relationships *between* modules. Modules with high cohesion are typically loosely coupled to other modules, while modules that lack cohesion tend to be tightly coupled to other modules. As such, a system of modules that can be loosely coupled indicates good modular design practices.

Information Hiding

Another concept common in software engineering that can be applied to Web site engineering is the concept of *information hiding*. This is the idea that modules should contain two types of information: private and public. Private information concerns the internal details that make up the actual functionality of the module, including HTML code, scripting, binary objects and links. It might also involve other processing such as external calls to server-side programs. The private information of a module provides the "inner workings" of a page or site and is not accessible to the public.

The public part of the module provides the information that enables modules to interact with each other. The functionality, such as a displayed page made up of HTML code or the back-end program that processes a form submission, is called by a known public interface available to other modules or developers. In the case of a Web site, the public information might simply be a URL (Uniform Resource Locator). The URL links to a section of a site that performs a particular function, such as calling a program to calculate the tax for an online purchase. If another module needs to access this function, only the public address information to link to this module is needed. The module requesting the information does not need access to the private information of the module providing the information. The public address can be used to reference a particular module and its functions even if the content changes. It is interesting to note how careless Web developers are when moving information, subsites, or modules as they do not truly understand the ramifications of such a move. In traditional programming, changing an interface to a particular module without updating calling modules would be considered very poor practice. As discussed in Chapter 9, the cost of making changes during future maintenance phases can be reduced when modules are used. The current ad hoc nature of moving links is probably due to the more document-centered nature of Web site design rather than the functional view of a Web site as a software system. If the address of a module changes, a server-side redirect should be used to reach the module.

One of the main benefits of information hiding is that it makes programs easier to modify. This is because the private information is specific to the module. When details must be changed, the effects are limited to the module containing the private information. Information hiding also reduces the complexity of systems by relegating details to the private information of the module. Because modules designed in this manner tend to have high cohesion and be loosely coupled to other modules, in a sense information hiding ensures good modular design.

■ The Benefits of a Modular Approach

Modular design offers many benefits that make it an appropriate approach for Web site design. Modules can be explained and described easily, and developed one at a time with clear relationships between modules. With proper specifications, modules can be developed independently, by different team members. Because time is often a factor in the launch of Web sites, and because most Web sites have multiple functions, this can be particularly important. Modules are also comparatively easier to maintain since changes are limited to a single component. Modular approaches are also easier to document than are design approaches that do not break a system down into parts. A modular approach also facilitates testing, where each module can be tested independently, tested in conjunction with other modules, and then be integrated into the entire site. Testing is discussed in depth in Chapter 8. A modular approach can be applied to high-level site design, as well as to the actual programming that is involved in individual subsystems. Lastly, segmenting a Web site project into modules facilities managing the development project. Because individual modules or subsections of a site can be considered in turn, it is easier to remove sections or save development for later if there is a budget change or delay in development.

Structured Design

The software design philosophy that applies most closely to Web sites is structured or *top-down* design. The structured approach to dealing with a complex system is a straightforward "divide-and-conquer" method that attempts to decompose a complex system into manageable pieces or modules that have clearly defined functions and relationships with other modules.

The entire Web site design process can be viewed as a structured approach. First, abstract ideas are formulated and then represented in a flowchart. From there, each section of the flowchart is further decomposed into manageable elements like pages or programmed objects. For example, in a large programmed Web site, the section of the Web site that contains the online catalog system might be considered a module. Within the catalog module, a sub-module might control order entry. The order entry submodule contains a JavaScript routine that deals with data checking and HTML elements that make up the page. In this sense, the entire system is broken down into modules at different levels as shown in Figure 6-12.

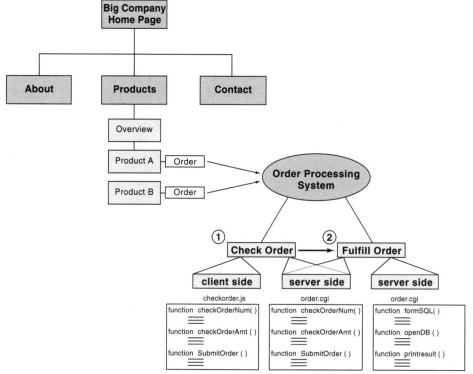

Figure 6–12. Site Design Breakdown.

A structured approach can also be used with HTML markup. Far too often, HTML structure is ignored at the document level, and the Web page is treated as a large binary object. In reality, it is possible to decompose a page into its components. A page may consist of a heading, three paragraphs, two images, a horizontal rule, and an address as shown in Figure 6-13. While this structure says nothing about how the document looks, it does provide a level of modular organization that facilitates the manipulation of the components or objects. This idea lies behind the document object model, or DOM (www.w3.org/DOM/), which describes an HTML document as a collection of objects that can be manipulated by a scripting language.

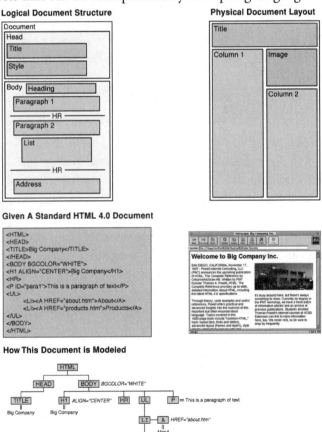

Figure 6–13. Document Structuring.

A structured approach to document design facilitates updating. If the page is coded so that individual components such as paragraphs or pictures are independent of each other, the design is more flexible and allows sections of pages to be swapped in and out. For example, imagine that a Web page contains a marketing paragraph, a picture, a feature list, and a detailed specifications for a product. If the structure of the page is well defined at the HTML level, it may be possible to reuse the page for a similar product. Coding structured pages is especially important when building dynamically generated sites. Imagine a database dynamically filling the paragraphs of a document. With careful document structuring, manipulation such as document population from a database and manipulation from a scripting language are possible. When documents are very well structured it is even possible to automate the retrieval or aggregation of information (www.webmethods.com). However, automation and manipulation of document content may be difficult unless the rules of HTML are well enforced or new technologies like XML are adopted [(4) Powell 98].

There are many advantages to the structured design approach. Most are similar to the benefits of modularity discussed earlier. First, structured design is relatively easy because it tends to follow the structure of the problem and the way people think about problems. Because structured design moves from the abstract to the specific, implementation details can be deferred. This is especially advantageous in the development of Web sites because it preserves options until the design and implementation phases. Probably the biggest advantage of structured design is that it is relatively easy to grasp. Remember, that many site developers are only now moving from a page to program paradigm and requiring them to use a complex distributed object-oriented philosophy may be too much to handle or even unnecessary for the bulk of sites built.

Object-Oriented Design

Object-oriented design arose out of information complexity and the need for a new paradigm to address that complexity. It involves modeling a system into a collection of objects with certain characteristics or *properties*. Objects also have actions, called *methods*, that they either perform or that act upon them. Object-oriented design is useful for taking real-world systems and describing them in terms of objects with certain behaviors and relationships to other objects. This approach is probably too sophisticated for most document centered Web sites. Each page could be considered an object, but, in general, the only real methods are "load" and "unload." However, some complicated systems deployed on the Web may require this approach, particularly those transaction-based systems that need to scale for large numbers of simultaneous users. An example of an organization having such requirements is Dell Computer Corporation, which sells PCs from their Web site (www.dell.com) using a complex system composed of ordering, manufacturing, and tracking components that have been modeled with object-oriented design.

While most small-scale systems don't quite yet require object-oriented facilities, many of the ideas of object orientation are useful immediately. In fact, many of the technologies used to build sites are object-oriented by nature. Technologies such as JavaScript, Java, ActiveX, and server-side components accessed by servers for functions such as database access or messaging take an object-oriented approach. JavaScript is more objectlike, while Java is truly object-oriented, but the point should be not to ignore the ideas of object-orientation when building systems. Even HTML elements are being based on a Document Object Model (DOM), so being familiar with object-oriented concepts will aid in the use of these different technologies. However, a mad rush to a modern programming methodology like object-oriented design may not be warranted. Web sites have yet to consistently demonstrate simple structured practices. With the document-centered nature of most sites, object-oriented decomposition may add needless complexity to a project.

To augment a structured or object-oriented design, a data-centered approach can be used, which involves developing detailed "dataflow" charts showing graphical depictions of the data flow in a system. These charts show data inputs and outputs to various parts of a system, along with how the data is transformed. Many programmed Web sites can be modeled in terms of data flow through a system. For example, a job recruiting system on a Web site may be depicted by a number of steps with input and output data. First, there is a job description that is input by human resources and results in output of posted job listings. In response to job listings, job seekers would submit a resume as input to a system that is then output as applicant data to human resources. This idea can also be viewed as a "workflow" where the activity through a Web site is defined in terms of the work users accomplish, as opposed to data transformations.

Choosing a Design Approach

When thinking about design methodologies, consider the variety of sites that range from print-oriented design to structured design to object-oriented design. On the most basic end of the spectrum, "brochureware" Web sites can be developed using printlike methods. Pages are developed separate from each other and may or may not relate. Each document in the Web site might be crafted by a single individual according to unique requirements, and little planning may be required. As sites, even print-oriented ones, get larger or more important, the number of pages may increase dramatically. On large sites, many people may have to work on the site to keep it up to date. Keeping things consistent in such an environment may become very difficult. Adopting structured design principles in such a situation might facilitate the distribution of the work load for the project. The site could be broken up into sections and then into pages. Pages might be grouped and templates developed. If the templates are made in regular fashion, it may be possible to automate their production and population, even allowing a database to dynamically generate pages. As a database is added, other programmed elements may be included. The site may then require structured techniques to build the functionality. The gadget order entry section of the site would be developed with the widget order entry section in mind so that the two could share code and functionality. However, a structured design thinking from the site down would be the only easy way to achieve such a design. As the site gets increasingly complicated, and programming and function play a larger role, it then may be beneficial to use object-oriented principles.

While this continuum of sites and methodologies uses different approaches for different site scales and forms, it is not an all-or-nothing approach. A simple site may need little formality except in the development of its order entry system, which might need structured design or object-oriented principles. Object-oriented design will not make sense in many cases because it will add useless complexity to sites that are often too document-centered. While, as we discussed earlier, a document or page can be modeled as objects as shown by the Document Object Model (DOM) central to HTML, not everybody needs to know this. In many cases the granularity does not need to extend beyond a document. Further consider that, in many organizations, nontechnical users ranging from human resources to sales may be involved in creating pages or at least the content for them. Adding a major dose of OOP philosophy to a discussion will cause eyes to glaze over.

After considering the design approach, a design document will have to be produced. In some cases, such as for large projects, especially those that are more like software than simple interactive brochures, a design document for the programming aspects of a site will be necessary. For "brochureware" sites, however, a flowchart is usually sufficient. In software engineering, a design document describes the actual modules used in code and how they are structured to address the requirements. This is used as a roadmap or blueprint for developers involved in the project. A formal breakdown and description of each module is specified, including an explanation of each module's behavior, inputs and outputs.

Once the design document has been developed, it is time to make sure that things will work. At this point, a demo or prototype of the site's functional aspects should be developed. This model serves only as a "proof of concept" so that the feasibility of the implementation is ensured. The prototype does not need to encompass all aspects of the site's functionality, but rather, provides a general idea of how it will work. In the development of a Product Finder Expert system that is capable of locating products in a huge catalog by idea, the prototype might consist of a mini-Product Finder for only one category of products. While this prototype won't necessarily uncover all the potential problems that may arise during the implementation phase discussed in the next chapter, it can provide some indication that the project is on the right track as well as be used to rally support for management. Remember that this is only a demo; it should lack polish, and is meant only to reflect the general interface and functionality of the finished programmed aspects of a Web site. Avoid the desire to turn the prototype into the site in one quick and easy step. The prototype is meant to be thrown away. Furthermore, always present a demo as just a validation of design. Otherwise, a misinformed manager may quickly decide to push the project ahead and release the prototype as the finished product.

Navigation Design

Information design deals with the structure of the site as a whole. Program design covers the methodologies used to develop the function of the site. Navigation design deals with how the user interacts with the interface and is related to the feel of the Web site, namely how it feels to use the site. The look is concerned with how the site appears and, while navigation does intersect with visual design, they should be considered separately, particularly considering the importance of navigation. Simply stated, if the user cannot move through the site quickly and easily, the function, graphic design, and content are irrelevant. There are several schools of Web interface design and different navigation models, each with advantages and disadvantages. The appropriate interface design and navigation depend on the purpose and audience of the site. There are Web conventions and usability concerns that should also be observed.

Web Interface Design Schools

In a general sense, Web interfaces can be classified as text-based, GUI or metaphor-based. Through the generations of Web design, interfaces have evolved due to increased layout capabilities and image support. The school of design adopted for a particular site will depend on the goals for the site. If one of the objectives is to project an innovative and creative sense of style, a metaphor-based design is probably in order. Conversely, if simplicity and quick loading pages are the aim, a text-based interface may be the proper choice. Unfortunately, selection of appropriate site navigation can be difficult because it begins to intersect with matters of personal taste.

▉ Text-Based Navigation Design

A text-based interface relies solely on text links to provide navigation. While text-based navigation is the lowest common denominator, this style of Web site navigation is often just too plain for most public Internet applications. People think of the Web as a visual medium, so images can be very helpful in conveying a message. However, unless an image is required to illustrate an idea, Web pages don't really need fancy images. Think about an intranet: while speed may no longer be an issue, there may be no point for sophisticated graphics because the site is mainly functional. While text-based navigation seems very easy, it is not simply a matter of linking generic words or phrases like "click here" to sections of a site. With such a design, choosing the appropriate linking words or organizing the links may be the difference between an easy-to-use or confusing site—regardless of download speed, as shown in Figure 6-14.

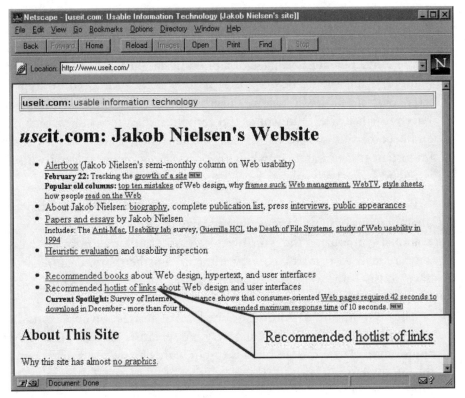

Figure 6–14. Text-Based Navigation.

Even if a more graphical navigation style is adopted, it still may be appropriate to use text links to augment the graphical navigation and make the page more accessible to those people who wish not to use images.

GUI-Based Navigation Design

The most popular navigation approach for software applications today is the graphical user interface, or GUI, style, which consists of elements like menus and buttons. As Web sites become more like software applications, it is no wonder that GUI designs are extremely popular for Web navigation. GUI style designs may be either icon or text-button oriented. An icon GUI style often implies the use of real-world metaphors to convey functionality or direction. For example, in a software application, an icon of a disk symbolizes the "Save" feature. For a Web site, an icon of a telephone or postcard might indicate "Contact" while an image of a building might indicate "Company Information." Icons should be designed carefully as they can become cryptic. If an icon is too simplistic, it becomes overly abstract, like a hieroglyphic character. Given its small size, if an icon is too complicated, it looks like a blob of colors and becomes indistinguishable. Even if the right level of detail is chosen, it is important to be aware that when an icon is sized down, it looks worse. What is a good style at a regular size begins to look like a mistake.

Because icons are the basis of the user interface, it is important to have unambiguous designs. Some concepts may be difficult to express as icons. For example, symbolizing the Northwestern Customer Support unit of a company with a small icon might be very difficult. Furthermore, creating icons that have consistently well-understood meaning can be challenging, particularly for an international audience. In Figure 6-15, the icon could be a megaphone or a bear's footprint, depending on the level of abstraction applied to the interpretation. Aside from developing very conservative, unambiguous icons, one approach to clarify this problem is to put words below the icon to remove any misinterpretation. User testing is another way to ensure that the icons are intuitive enough that users won't have to guess.

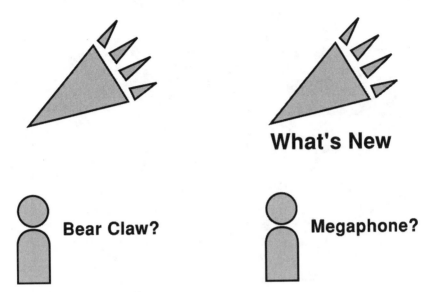

Figure 6–15. Icon Ambiguity.

Text buttons are another feature of GUI design. Though text buttons are good because they tend to look inherently clickable and use words instead of cryptic pictures, other issues can be troublesome. Buttons lend themselves well to relatively short section names. For example, in Figure 6-16, the section name "About" fits well on the button. An expanded section name like "About Acme Corporation" does not. Because there is a limited amount of screen space, button size and names become an issue of clarity versus implementation. Though it is more explanatory to include the long section name, it may not be feasible from a screen area perspective.

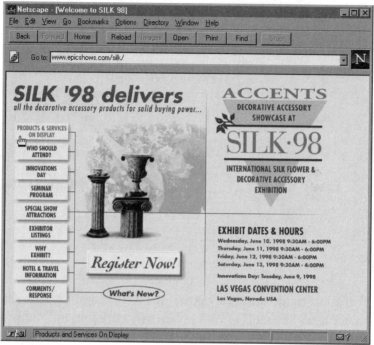

Figure 6–16. Length of Section Names on Buttons.

The benefit of using GUI design on the Web is that people are familiar with it. The drawbacks are that it is often uninspiring. Remember that many sites will be significantly market-driven; it will be difficult for a visual designer to establish an identity by the curve of a button or the use of drop shadows. It may be possible to use a theme or color to improve a GUI-driven design, but this can be limiting. While GUI interfaces are well understood in traditional software development, the Web doesn't afford the same degree of layout control. As discussed in Chapter 3, Web designers must deal with a range of system capabilities including screen size, bandwidth, and color support. As a result of this diversity, the pixel level control of traditional GUI design is almost impossible, making it extremely difficult to create perfect GUI "cross-platform" designs as shown in Figure 6-17. Note that any visual design approach, be it GUI or Metaphor as discussed in the next section, will encounter this limitation as well.

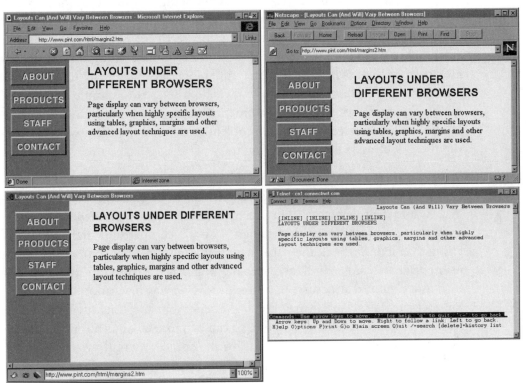

Figure 6–17. Different Browser Views of the Same Web Site.

The final issue that makes Web GUI design difficult is that users often don't spend enough time on any particular Web site to become very familiar with it. Users expect there to be a learning curve with software applications. With Web sites, users don't want to, and shouldn't have to, spend time learning the site's navigation. One way to ensure this is by adhering to Web conventions, which will be discussed later. Though traditional GUI design is by no means easy, Web GUI design involves factors that make it even more challenging.

Metaphor

Though GUI style design is familiar to many people and popular on the Web, it is often not terribly inspiring visually and may be too limiting for effective branding and market building. Metaphor-based design is similar to icon-based GUI design in that it relies on the mapping of real-world ideas. While GUI design uses icons and buttons, metaphor-based design is typically more integrated into the site. For example, a job recruitment firm might have a "cork board" interface as the home page. Many online communities use the idea of metaphor when they create different areas that map to real-world places to signify what types of content reside where. For example, Hollywood might signify movie and entertainment related items while Silicon Valley implies technology content. The problem with such metaphors is that they run the risk of users just not "getting it."

With metaphor-based design, use and navigation are intuitive and familiar. However, sites that use metaphor design tend to be more gamelike or informal. While it probably wouldn't be appropriate for a high-technology company to use a strong metaphor design, a subtle comparison might be useful. Using a design on the home page that clearly indicates the content of the site is important. A biotechnology company might use a common industry idea, such as a chemical structure, in an innovative way as navigation. To the average user such a metaphor may not make sense, but to a chemist it may seem familiar or inviting. The metaphor also can be more obvious but not necessarily as functional, as in the case of Southwest Airlines (www.iflyswa.com). Their home page is a clickable image map of a reservations desk with links to reservations, news and company information. In this case, the metaphor appears only on the home page. It is not really integrated into the design of the site. It is used more for design than for navigation purposes.

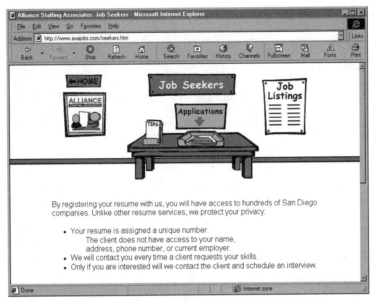

Figure 6–18. Example of Metaphor Design

Metaphor designs do have some drawbacks. They can be graphically inten-sive, causing long download time. In addition, they may seem forced or cli-chéd, causing negative reactions in the user. This is especially true in the case of the "power user," who may be uninterested in the creative aspects of a site after the first visit. Remember, as with icons, if users don't understand the metaphor, it fails.

It is impossible to engineer the choice of a site design school. The target audience of a site and the objectives for the site will help determine what school of design to use, as well as the preferences of the site's builders. Don't confuse site design ideas with navigation or even graphic design. It is possible to create a GUI driven site that uses illustrated points that look cartoonlike and playful, as well as a GUI design that uses large, professionally-shot photos as buttons.

Navigation Models

The navigation will only be determined by the design school (text, GUI, metaphor) to the extent that GUI designs will involve icons or buttons while metaphor-based design will involve more of a map approach. Beyond that, there are choices involving the placement and orientation of the navigation methods.

Left-Oriented

Left-oriented navigation as abstractly illustrated by Figure 6-19 is very common on the Web. In this model, buttons, icon,s or text links are lined up vertically along the left side of the page. Unless frames are used, the navigation tools may scroll off the screen. Right-oriented navigation is not common on the Web because browser and screen widths vary, and the results would be unpredictable visually. Lastly, given current practices, looking to the right for important content or navigation just isn't common for users. A right-oriented site runs the risk of being confusing for the sake of being different.

Figure 6–19. Left-oriented Navigation.

Top-Oriented

In a top-oriented design, the controls are in a banner at the top of the page as shown in Figure 6-20. Like left-oriented navigation, it is likely that the navigation tools will scroll off the page unless a frame is used. In addition, because top-oriented navigation items must share space with the page headings, this design can frequently look cluttered.

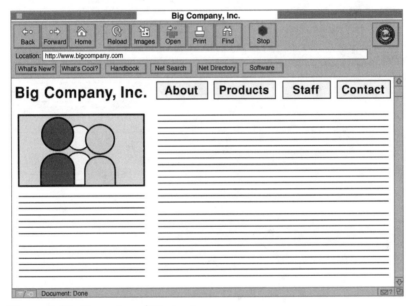

Figure 6–20. Top-oriented Navigation.

Bottom-Oriented

With bottom-oriented design shown in Figure 6-21, the user nearly always has to scroll to reach the navigation items unless frames are used. In many cases, users don't scroll and remain unaware of these additional choices.

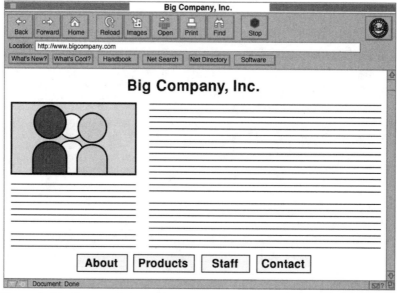

Figure 6–21. Bottom-Oriented Navigation.

Map or Center-Oriented

Map or center-oriented design is typically graphics heavy, but is useful for metaphor-based designs. Figure 6-22 shows how a map or center-oriented design dominates the screen. However, because content will occupy the majority of the space on subpages, a modified approach will need to be developed. The look-and-feel of the home page can be used to create an alternative navigation scheme for the subpages.

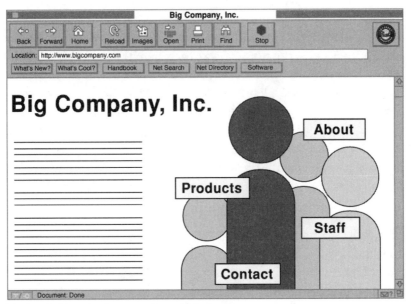

Figure 6–22. Map/center-oriented Navigation

It turns out that most sites use a combination of navigation approaches. For example, a site might use a maplike design on the home page and a simpler, top-oriented navigation for the subpages. Given that an entire Web site may be considered a collection of microsites, navigation should be chosen relative to the particular task and audience of the section developed.

The Nuances of Navigation Designs

Designing useful site navigation is very difficult. A well-designed site should provide flexible navigation that enables the user to move freely through the site. Web sites do not tend to exhibit the same degree of control over user navigation as traditional software, which makes their design difficult because different user paths must be anticipated and accommodated. For example, a user may end up at a page (via a bookmark or search engine) in a way the designer never intended. In some sense, there are parallel navigation forms on the Web—those provided by a browser and those provided by a site. Neither provides everything a user needs. Sites must accommodate situations like a user coming into a process midway and not being able to use a browser back button to reach previous steps. Providing site-specific navigation on all pages and attempting to give the user context for where they are in a site can help alleviate such situations. Don't try to control the user's navigation too much. Inventing navigation elements or providing local forms of scroll bars, windows, link colors, and back buttons can confuse a user. Don't be tempted to use unique navigation as a way to brand the site and give it identity; this plan tends to backfire and results in people leaving a site. Consider that your Web site is part of an overall software system called the World Wide Web.

■ Navigation Conventions

As mentioned previously, there are Web design and implementation conventions that should be respected. While doing something different to establish a brand identity is good in marketing, on the Web it undermines the established usability principles that users have come to expect. For some sites, such as purely artistic ones, a non-traditional approach may be appropriate. However, most sites should strive to conform to established Web principles, and avoid novelty for the sake of novelty. Users do not view Web sites as individual entities that have their own unique navigation schemas. They expect to apply the same principles from site to site.

Anyone who has browsed a few Web sites is probably familiar with common Web navigation aids and principles. For example, those items which are graphical links tend to look clickable. Beveling the edges of a button and using drop shadows can make buttons look more pressable. User feedback mechanisms such as graying out the currently selected button or animating buttons when a mouse passes over them can also help indicate which functions are available. Just as it is important to make clickable items obvious, nonclickable items should not be confused with links. Text should not be underlined for emphasis since underlining typically represents a link on the Web. Rather, use bold or italics. Similarly, colored text has significance on the Web. Typically, links are blue when they are unvisited and red or purple when they have been visited. It is important to adhere to these types of conventions. Some visually oriented designers set all links (visited and unvisited) to the same color, which makes it impossible for the user to see where they have been. Other sites reverse the established text link colors, which is bound to cause confusion.

The most important rule for Web navigation is that any conventions applied must be used consistently. The navigation should remain the same from page to page except for minor variations that indicate state. The placement of the navigation should not jump from page to page. Sections should not be removed; they should change color or be altered to otherwise indicate the state. Consistency in navigation should be augmented by headings used to show the user what section he or she is in. Even when all conventions are applied there may be requirements for navigation ideas or Web features which are inherently difficult for users.

Navigation Aids

Even when all conventions are followed and sites are structured well, users may still not be able to find what they want. Web sites should provide navigational aids like site maps, keyword indexes, and search engines to help users find what they are looking for. Web sites should also attempt to provide help systems including context sensitive help or pop-up windows or tool-tips that explain what things do. Imagine shipping a software application without documentation and a help system. Now think about Web sites and ask how many actually have adequate help systems. Remember too that the Web is bringing more and more people online and assumptions should not be made about familiarity with software navigation. For example, on a recent project it appeared that intranet users with no Web background would not scroll pages automatically while users familiar with the Web do. Frames serve as a prime example of careful consideration of the use of navigation devices.

As mentioned earlier, one way to ensure that the navigation choices do not scroll off the screen is by using frames. Despite this one advantage, there are many drawbacks to using frames. Users may be confused by the location to where they are taken when pressing the browser's back button. Printing is problematic; only one frame at a time can be printed, which may not be useful if related information is split between frames. In addition, pages with frames cannot be accurately bookmarked. Lastly, using frames wastes valuable screen real estate as the scroll bars take up space. The major benefit of using frames is to maintain navigation on the page at all times. Another benefit of using frames is that they allow multiple subwindows at once, which may make it easier to display complex data. Frames may serve a purpose for a given site, but they should not be used just for the sake of using them. Showing a sophisticated site implementation is meaningless if the user is unable to navigate the site properly. Yet despite all their problems, frames may make sense in certain applications like a site table of contents or on a site such as an engineering intranet that is mainly for sophisticated users with large monitors.

Navigation aids will depend not only on audience but on purpose. In a site with a large product catalog, a site map and search engine will provide little benefit for the user trying to find a particular product they can't describe well. Conceptual search tools such as automated product finders may help in such situations. Don't get hung up on the process of navigating to a particular piece of information. The user doesn't appreciate order if it takes twenty clicks to get to the information they want.

The culmination of the navigation design phase is a thorough understanding of the different navigation models and design schools, and an idea of what type of navigation the Web site should have. Navigation design is the crux of the site's usability. Navigational devices let the user move through the site as well as provide an indicator of the current location. While graphic design is often a matter of personal taste, navigation conventions should be respected.

Graphic Design

After considering the design school, navigation design, and graphic design, the site's interface can be built. However, the graphic design aspect of building the site's interface is not in the realm of engineering. The technical professionals on sites are often quick to attack the visual elements as wasteful, or to abdicate any responsibility for visuals with the claim that it is an artistic discipline. However, is it not true that the main point of graphic design is to communicate, not decorate? If so, engineers may have something meaningful to say, particularly in the case of Web sites where the engineering and content must intersect with art. Remember the relevance issue; graphic design must add to the site in a meaningful way. On the other hand, don't forget that some sites are only about art, and that the point may be to decorate. The best approach is not be dogmatic about a graphic design philosophy but apply visuals for navigation and content based on the situation.

While it is difficult to provide hard and fast rules for visual Web design, certainly the site's visual design will be determined by the company's current marketing collateral, issues of personal taste and the limitations of the medium. Corporate Web sites must promote and reflect the company's brand identity. If the Web site looks one way and the print literature looks entirely different, the company is promoting an inconsistent image. In addition, the graphic design should help communicate the message, not just decorate it. While market branding of the company drives the design of an Internet site, an extranet site may involve the brand of another company as well. The design of an extranet site typically needs to convey a partnership between two or more companies. Consequently, the site may have a look-and-feel similar to the main company's Web site, but also include the logo and company colors of the partner. In this way, the design is driven both by marketing and by the user's desires. An intranet site is similar but may pay even less attention to corporate image. Users of an intranet typically are not interested in graphics, nor does the brand identity of the company need to be continually reiterated in a creative fashion. Rather, the user's desire for simple, fast-loading pages will drive the design.

From a base visual standpoint, sites typically fall into one of three categories: illustrative, photorealistic or typographic. Illustrative designs may be either icon- or metaphor-based. Benefits of illustrative design include small file size due to generally simple images and predictable reproduction with little or no image degradation even under systems with limited color support. However, illustrations may not be appropriate for certain types of sites. For sites that must reflect professionalism, illustrations can appear too cartoonlike. Photorealism can be used with either GUI designs or metaphor designs, and is often useful to create a professional or "real-world" look. However, using photos requires careful optimization, as the file sizes can be quite large. Furthermore, photos may not display well under all conditions, particularly on monitors that support a limited number of colors. While text-only design can be limiting, when implemented by experts, type-oriented design can be very interesting and fast loading. Technologies like style sheets can be used to create layouts that emulate print as they provide fine control. The spacing between lines can be controlled. However, type-based designs can also be potentially confusing since there may be too much regularity in the design thus making it difficult to discriminate important things such as links. The choice of a particular design style is not really an engineering issue, but there are implementation issues that should be considered before developing any design.

Web Design Issues and Limitations

Issues of the Web and the Internet as a medium are discussed in depth in Chapter 3. Implementation issues will be discussed in the next chapter but, just like building a technical prototype, before getting too far into a design, a visual prototype that considers some of the Web graphic issues below should be implemented.

File Size

Download time is probably the biggest complaint about Web sites. Complex designs generally equate to long download times unless careful attention is paid to byte savings techniques such as optimizing and image reuse. As mentioned, photos tend to be larger, byte-wise, than illustrations. Images that use print techniques such as gradients tend to have large file sizes because they do not compress well. Designers strive for small file sizes. However, without considering the network and server conditions as discussed in Chapter 3, even the most optimized graphics may appear to download slowly.

Color

There are technical limitations to using color on the Web. Depending on the end user's system, the designer may be limited to a mere 216 colors. The reason for this, as discussed in Chapter 3, is that browsers use a special safe color palette that is common across Macintosh, PC, and UNIX systems. If colors outside this palette are used and the user's video system does not support the specified color, the image may be degraded by attempting to approximate the color using a process called dithering. Even if images are designed only with these colors, there are other system variations that should be considered, such as gamma and contrast. Representing colors perfectly on screen is difficult because different systems exhibit different gamma values and not all monitors will display colors the same way. Because variables that control contrast are partially out of the designer's control, designs that have little contrast, such as dark text on dark backgrounds and light text on light backgrounds, should be avoided. Again, it is this lack of control over the end user's system, even with something seemingly as simple as color, which makes Web design challenging.

Fonts

Reading on screen is difficult. Font selection can either improve this situation or make it much worse. Traditional graphic design ideas hold that sans-serif fonts are used for headlines and serif fonts are used for body text. However, given screen readability issues, sans-serif fonts make more sense for small text such as body copy. In general, text needs to be larger, and there should be less of it for users to effectively consume it online.

Anti-aliasing

Anti-aliasing describes the smoothing of jagged images on screen. This is accomplished by gently blurring the image to the same color as the background. While anti-aliasing will smooth images, it may make them appear "fuzzier." It may also be necessary to increase the size of the image to keep things clear, particularly in the case of text. If the design must be small, designers should consider the use of aliased images or text, which can be very effective when used properly.

Layers and Margins

Print designers are accustomed to making complex layered designs. Layering images can be difficult on the Web, particularly when limited to traditional HTML. It is possible to create images that have transparent regions so that they can be layered on background, but the position of the image is often difficult to control because of variables such as browser margins. Because of a lack of control over the margins in the browser, print-oriented designs such as bleeds are not easily implemented on the Web. To achieve the look of a bleed requires the use of a background color or tile. Yet, even when objects can be positioned, if the images are anti-aliased there may be a residue or halo effect around the layered image. There are ways around these problems, but designers should think about how layered designs will be implemented when they create design mock-ups.

■ Resolution and Screen Region

Monitors do not have the resolution of print. While print is generally at a minimum of 300 dots per inch (dpi), monitors usually display 72 dpi. Therefore, images must be large in dimension if detail is to be preserved. This can be problematic, both because the file size will be large and because the image may take up the majority of the screen. The effective region available on the screen should also be taken into account. Consider the audience of users on 640 x 480 resolution systems running Netscape on a Windows95 machine. Under Netscape 3.0 with all the toolbars on, there is a mere 570 x 260 pixel (approximately) area in which to design a page that will not scroll (see Figure 6-23). Even if larger monitors are common, consider well that many users print pages; designs that don't fit the paper dimensions may be useless. While the size or at least the width of a piece of paper may not be the appropriate design size for a site, the available screen real estate should be determined before the design stage proceeds.

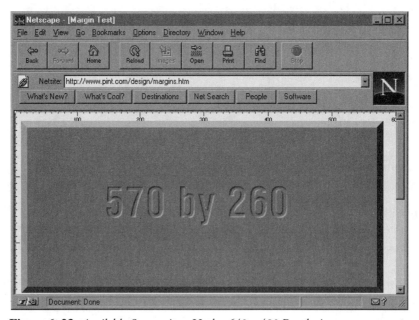

Figure 6–23. Available Screen Area Under 640 x 480 Resolution.

For examples of some of the technical aspects of visual design such as color use, transparency, margins, and font use see the design references at http://www.pint.com/design.

The Visual Design Process

After considering the issues that may affect the visual design, a visual prototype should be developed. Like the technical prototype, this may just be an exploration of what to do. It may not represent the actual implementation.

Sketches and Visual Prototypes

Design ideas should first be sketched out on paper, preferably in a mocked-up browser window as shown in Figure 6-24. Remember to consider the amount of screen real estate available and create sketches that reflect this. The designer will probably start work by looking at the existing content and collateral that the site draws from. The design should play off the print ideas and brands in a complementary fashion but may not necessarily mimic them. Simply translating print to the Web generally falls flat. Working the ideas out on paper provides more flexibility in the initial stages, and allows the designer to explore ideas without working up full designs.

Figure 6–24. Sketching a Site Design Ide.a

After some preliminary designs have been developed on paper, graphic tools like Adobe PhotoShop can be used to create a basic screen composite. Creating many designs on different visual layers is useful in providing flexibility for design experimentation. Eventually, the various candidates for the visual design should be saved as large GIF or JPEG images. These "comps" (compositions) can then be loaded into a browser window to give a sense of what the site will look like. Far too often, decision makers won't be able to envision what the design really looks like until it is actually in a browser. Remember, the browser does provide a framing effect that may influence the pages' appearance. Make sure to decide exactly which design to use. Just as the implementation of the technology aspects of a site won't proceed without a finalized prototype, so should the continuation of the project be dependent on the final visual mock-up. At this stage, there is no need for complex HTML markup or optimization of the image for download. Preparing the image for delivery over the Web and integration into an HTML page is discussed in the next chapter.

Network/Server Design

At this point, a firm development plan is in place and both technology and design prototypes have been finalized. But don't rush into the implementation phase quite yet. Double-check how the site will be delivered. The network and the server design should be considered. As discussed in Chapter 3, the end user's perception of the site will be heavily influenced by the speed of delivery. This stage cannot be skipped. Networks may need to be designed or modified to handle the performance and traffic demands of a Web site. Corporate LANs and WANs may already have existing traffic issues. The effect that the addition of intranet servers or public Internet Web servers will have on network traffic should be considered. Specific segments may need to be allocated for Web servers, as well as network upgrades to switched Ethernet, Fast-Ethernet, or FDDI topologies, as necessary. Internet access may need to be upgraded or a new connection established for dedication to a particular Web site. Network security issues, beyond the scope of this book, may also need to be addressed. Additionally, network design should account for scaling needs and potential bottlenecks. Servers need to be designed or built to fit the application. Sufficient performance is critical. This requires adequate hardware and

RAM. It may also require tuning of the operating system for performance at the network level as well as the Web server software itself. One potential bottleneck is hard disk I/O. Servers and networks may run fast enough to handle traffic, but if data cannot be pulled off the disk fast enough, this will have to be addressed. High-grade SCSI drives or RAID arrays or even dedicated disk-drive appliances may be necessary. Finally, the costs, resources, and labor required in terms of network and server administration can be enormous. Because of this, outsourcing these services to hosting facilities makes sense in many cases. This includes external hosting of intranet and extranet servers for private use within and between companies.

Summary

The point of the Design phase is to figure out exactly what should be done. Starting from the site specification, a design document should be built. Depending on the site, this might range from a simple flowchart to a complex programming plan. The structure of the site should be well considered, along with how the user will navigate the site. Designing the structure and technology of a site may benefit from considering the design methodologies used in software engineering, including structured design and object-oriented design. The choice of a particular design methodology will depend greatly on the scope and purpose of the site. There is no one right way to design things. The correctness of design is particularly difficult when considering site visuals. Visual design is certainly a major part of the design phase. While it may not be easy to formalize the creative aspects of site development, it should still be held to the same rigorous standards as the programming design. Prototypes of both the technical and visual aspects of the site should be built and agreed upon. Finally, how the site will be delivered should be revisited. Only after all these stages are complete should the site be implemented. Implementing too soon means that the resulting site is really just a prototype for the end user to play with, which may reflect poorly on the site designers.

References

1. Mok, C., *Designing Business*, Adobe Press, San Jose, CA, 1996.

2. Shneiderman, B., "Reflections on Authoring, Editing, and Managing Hypertext" in *The Society of Text*, Barrett, Edward editor, The MIT Press, Cambridge, MA, 1989.

3. Coe, M., *Human Factors for Technical Communicators*, John Wiley & Sons, New York, New York, 1996.

4. Powell, T., *HTML: The Complete Reference,* Osborne/McGraw-Hill, Berkeley, CA, 1998.

Recommended Reading

Barrett, E., ed., *The Society of Text*, The MIT Press, Cambridge, MA, 1989.

Black, R., with Elder, S., *Web Sites That Work*, Adobe Press, San Jose, CA, 1997.

Horton, W., *Designing and Writing Online Documentation*, John Wiley & Sons, New York, New York, 1994.

Horton, W., *The Icon Book*, John Wiley & Sons, New York, New York, 1994.

Nielsen, J., *Multimedia and Hypertext: The Internet and Beyond* AP Professional, Boson, MA, 1995.

Weinman, L., *Deconstructing Web Graphics—Designing Web Graphics 2*, New Riders Publishing, Indianapolis, IN, 1997.

Weinman, L., Heavin, B., and Karp, A., *Coloring Web Graphics 2*, New Riders Publishing, Indianapolis, IN, 1997.

Wurman, R.S., *Information Architects* Graphics, NY, NY, 1997.

Chapter 7

▶ # Implementation: Building a Web Site

The implementation phase involves producing a beta site using high-level specifications in the form of requirements, a structural representation of the site (a flowchart), prepared content, and a design document. The site's specifications must be defined as clearly as possible before implementation begins. If they are not well defined, and new or modified specifications are introduced during the implementation phase, valuable time may be lost, as work already done may have to be scrapped. The requirements specification phase concentrated on describing what the site should do, the design phase specified how these things will be done, while the implementation phase involves the construction and integration of the technology to realize the requirements.

The implementation phase of site design is the most concrete in the Web Site Engineering process. However, diving into site development by simply starting to code HTML pages will never yield the best results. The key to implementing a good site is choosing the most appropriate tools, technologies, and design methodologies for the job. In order to make accurate decisions, you must understand the capabilities and limitations of various client and server-side tools and technologies. The implementation process also requires knowledge of coding and programming conventions, and project management logistics. The overall implementation approach taken will depend greatly on whether the focus is on technology or design. The names of development products will certainly change over time, but the underlying ideas and technologies stay the same. This chapter provides a general and somewhat theoretical overview of the different elements involved in the implementation phase, as well as details on the practical use of each in the Web Site Engineering process.

Programming Technologies

Once you understand the site design philosophies and design documents (if necessary), it is time to consider how to build the site. The diagram in Figure 7-1 depicts the familiar holistic view of how a Web site works, including technology and programming issues. (The network components, while shown, will not be a focus here.) The medium that Web sites use is discussed in Chapter 3 along with the ramifications of networks and servers.

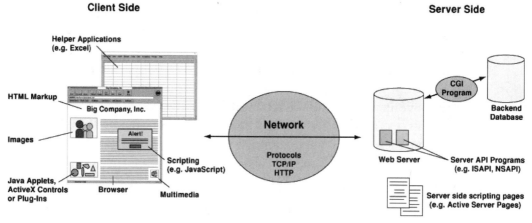

Figure 7–1. Overview of Web Technology Mix.

Not every site needs all the technologies shown in Figure 7-1. There is a great difference in complexity between a "brochureware" site and a full work-flow-driven database application written in Java. If a site is simply an electronic brochure, its focus is on the interface. The more the site "does," the more it is like a traditional software application with a focus on programming. Understanding the basic concept of adding programming to a site isn't hard, but there are various technologies to choose from when implementing a site. Web programming technologies can be grouped into two basic groups: client-side and server-side. Client-side technologies are those that are part of the Web client (the browser) or run on the Web client. Some client technologies, such as ActiveX controls, may run outside of the browser. Server-side technologies are those that run on the server. The chart in Figure 7-2 presents an overview of Web programming technologies. Each type will be discussed, as will how they fit within a Web project.

Client Side	Server Side
HTML	CGI
- CSS	- Java Servlets
Plug-ins / Helpers	ISAPI/NSAPI Programs
ActiveX Controls	Server-side Scripting
Java Applets	-Active Server Pages
Scripting Languages	-Server-Side JavaScript
-JavaScript	- Cold Fusion[a]
-VBScript	Database Middleware
-Dynamic HTML	

Figure 7–2. Client Side and Server-Side Web Technology.

Client-Side Technologies

As stated earlier, client-side technologies are those that depend on the client to run. Some client-side technologies are built into the Web browser, such as HTML, Cascading Style Sheets (CSS), Java, and JavaScript. Other technologies are added to the browser or supported through outside programs such as ActiveX controls, Netscape plug-ins, or helper applications.

HTML

HTML (HyperText Markup Language) is the most basic building block for site creation. Nearly all Web pages are defined by an HTML file that consists of tags, or, more accurately, of elements that describe the structure or presentation of the page. HTML elements have a relatively simple syntax and consist of a pair of angle bracketed tags, for example <B> and </B>. User agents, such as browsers, read HTML files, interpret the elements, and display text enclosed within the tags accordingly. A fragment like <B> is important. </B> might be rendered in bold by a browser reading the markup. HTML elements can be modified by attributes that provide more information for the tag or act as parameters. An example of attribute use would be setting the <IMG> element to include a particular image by setting the SRC attribute to <IMG SRC="companylogo.gif">. More complex HTML elements like <IMG> may have numerous attributes separated by spaces, such as <IMG SRC="companylogo.gif" HEIGHT="50" WIDTH="100" ALT="Big Company, Inc">.

At first glance, HTML appears to be a very trivial technology. Picking up the syntax of the tags is not difficult. Less than 50 tags will probably be used in any given document. There is, however, a general misunderstanding of HTML's purpose. HTML is a structured language defined as an application of SGML (Standard Generalized Markup Language). The syntax of HTML is very carefully defined by the World Wide Web Consortium (www.w3.org), which has issued three standards. These standards have been at least partially implemented by major browser vendors. The standards include HTML 2.0, 3.2, and 4.0.

HTML Design Philosophies

By design, HTML is not meant to be used for presentation. Unfortunately, support for presentation is exactly what people desire. Browser vendors such as Netscape and Microsoft initially responded to user demands by introducing proprietary extensions to the markup language. Designers have taken it upon themselves to create work-arounds to allow improved layout, including HTML tricks and embedded binary forms like images and Adobe Acrobat files [(1) Powell 98]. Until the advent of style sheets, HTML served double duty as a structural and presentation-oriented markup language, regardless of the original intentions of its designers. Given the focus on Web site appearance, such abuses were inevitable. A brief overview of the various approaches to HTML design philosophies is presented here.

Mixed Structure and Presentation

This school of thought holds that HTML can be used to define the structure of documents, as well as to control presentation such as formatting and layout. To provide presentation capabilities, some tricks must be used to make structural tags deliver presentation. Examples include relying on tables or unordered lists for layout, or using proprietary HTML elements like <SPACER> or <LAYER> to literally push objects around the browser screen. Figure 7-3 shows a simple HTML file using the structure and presentation design philosophy of HTML use. Note that this approach is still the most common way to mark up Web pages.

```
<HTML>
  <HEAD>
<TITLE>Typical HTML File</TITLE>
</HEAD>
<BODY BGCOLOR="white" LINK="blue" VLINK="red">
<TABLE WIDTH="560" BORDER="0">
<TR>
<TD WIDTH="50"> </TD>
<TD>
    <H1 ALIGN="CENTER">
    <FONT COLOR="green" FACE="Arial">
    Big Company, Inc.</FONT>
    </H1>
    <HR>
    <UL> <!-- Indent this -->
        <P>This is a paragraph of text. . . </P>
    </UL>
</TD>
</TR>
</TABLE>
</BODY>
</HTML>
```

Figure 7–3. Example HTML File Mixing Structure and Presentation.

There is a major problem with using HTML to force design: browser incompatibilities. Not all browsers support the same proprietary extensions, nor will they render even standardized tags in the same way. To deal with such inconsistencies in browser support, the page developer may be forced to keep multiple versions of his file. This can be seen on sites that have buttons that read "click here for the Netscape version of the site" and "click here for the Internet Explorer version." Besides the additional work required to maintain multiple versions of a page, future maintenance difficulties may arise. Mixing the structure of the document with the presentation may also cause complications when migrating the document to a new form of HTML.

HTML for Structure and CSS

A purist philosophy sees the original intent of HTML as providing structure for documents. Additional methods such as Cascading Style Sheets (CSS) can be used to control presentation of documents and provide features like absolute positioning. The benefit to this may not be altogether obvious. Imagine using an HTML element like <H1> to define a heading for a document and then associating a style rule to all occurrences of <H1> so that the heading is rendered in 36-point green Arial font. An example of the use of style sheets in a file is shown in Figure 7-4.

```
<HTML>
<HEAD>
<TITLE>HTML and CSS Example</TITLE>
<STYLE TYPE="text/css">
<!--
 BODY{background: white;
         font-size: 14pt;
         margin-left: 50px;}
 A:LINK {color: blue}
 A:VISITED {color: red}
 H1      {text-align: center;
          font-family: Arial;
          font-size: 36pt;
          color: green}


   P.indent { text-indent: 10px; }
   #screencanvas {position: absolute;left: 10; top: 10;
                 width: 560; }
 -- >
</STYLE>
```

(Continued)

191

```
</HEAD>
<BODY>
<DIV ID="screencanvas">
<H1>Big Company, Inc.</H1>
<HR>
<P CLASS="indent">This is a paragraph of text. . .</P>
</DIV>
</BODY>
</HTML>
```

Figure 7–4. HTML with Style Sheet Example.

Style sheets offer a major benefit. By separating the structure of the document in HTML from the presentation as specified with a style sheet, it may be possible to create a different style sheet for the same content, or at least easily modify the style of an existing document. Imagine a printing style sheet, a style sheet for a 640x480-resolution environment, a style sheet for a text-only browser, and so on. This approach makes sense[1]—but do designers necessarily approach documents this way? Does someone making a Web page think to use the <STRONG> element and associate a style with it, or do they think about using the <BOLD> element? WYSIWYG-based editing environments like modern-day word processors tend to discourage this way of thinking about documents. In fact, some designers may take a drastic approach to nice looking pages, such as embedding huge text-laden images into their pages.

HTML as Container

The third and most problematic approach to using HTML is to use it solely as a container language and let some other format deal with the issues of presentation. Imagine creating an entire Web page as an image, and then just including the image in the page. This approach is heavily used, particularly in

---

1. Note: While HTML and style sheets seem like the best approach, their support is still not consistent across browsers. Even with the 4.0 generation of Netscape and Internet Explorer, there are numerous style-sheet rules not implemented. There are compatibility issues between the two major browsers regardless of standards.

design-focused sites, to force layout or include fonts. Besides making large images with embedded texts, a few developers make heavy use of Adobe Acrobat files, Java applets, Microsoft's HTML Layout Control, or other binary formats to circumvent the design limitations of HTML. Given this approach, HTML files eventually just act as stub files for other technologies, as shown by the example file in Figure 7-5.

```
<HTML>
<HEAD>
<TITLE>HTML as Container</TITLE>
</HEAD>
<BODY BGCOLOR="white">
<CENTER>
<EMBED SRC="page1.pdf"
          HEIGHT="100%"
          WIDTH="100%">
</CENTER>
</BODY>
</HTML>
```

Figure 7–5. HTML as Container Example.

The binary approach to improved layout makes sense when it's not abused. HTML will never be suitable for some things, such as video. Why attempt to build a video tag for HTML when another technology like QuickTime can be used and referenced more generically? Given this, it seems that the best approach to HTML design would be one that leverages all three designs. Pages should be built primarily with structure in mind, since it will facilitate dynamic page generation. Style sheets can be applied to format the document. Programmed components like plug-ins, ActiveX controls, or Java applets can be included to handle new media forms and features. Finally, scripts can be written to tie everything together. For the moment, some structuring facilities, like tables, may have to be used for backward compatibility with the large number of older Web browsers still in use.

Helpers

One approach to client-side programming comes in the form of programmed solutions like helper applications or Netscape plug-ins. Initially, Web clients had limited functionality and support for media beyond HTML. If new media types or binary forms were encountered, they had to be passed to an external program called a "helper application." Helper applications generally run outside the browser window. An example of a helper application would be a compression or archive tool like WinZip, which would be launched automatically when a compressed file was downloaded from the Web. Helpers are often problematic because they are not well integrated with the browser, and lack methods to communicate back to the Web browser. Because the helper was not integrated within the Web browser, external media types and binaries could not be easily embedded within the Web page. Lastly, helper applications generally had to be downloaded and installed by the user, which kept many people from using them.

The idea of a helper application is rather simple: It is a program that the browser calls upon. Any program can be a helper application for a Web browser, assuming that a MIME type can be associated with the helper. When an object is delivered on the Web, HTTP header information is added to the object indicating its type. This information is in the form of a MIME type. For example, every Acrobat file should have a content-type of application/pdf associated with it. When a browser receives a file with such a MIME type, it will look in its preferences to determine how to handle the file. These may include saving the file to disk, deleting the file, or handing the file off to another program such as a helper or browser plug-in. With MIME types and helpers, a developer can put Microsoft Word files on their Web site; users may be able to download them and read them automatically, assuming they have the appropriate helper application. Figure 7-6 overviews the basic way helper applications operate.

1. Browser checks look-up table mapping MIME to action

2. If no action, browser prompts user.

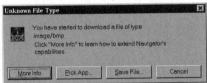

3. Pass to plug-in if plug-in is registered.

4. Pass to helper application if set up to do so.

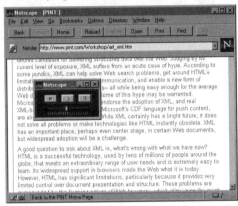

Figure 7–6. Overview of Helper and Plug-in Use.

Intranet environments often shun data in formats like Word or Excel, which require helpers or plug-ins, in favor of HTML, which is less capable and requires reformatting of the data. This is partly due to the ubiquity offered by HTML. It is also caused, in part, by ignorance of the use of helper applications and of the fact that Web servers can serve any form of data equally well (or poorly) that is to be handled by helpers. Another reason that helpers may be shunned is that content viewed under them may not be well integrated with the Web. Under Microsoft Windows, at least, helper applications that are written properly may actually run within the browser window, since the browser can be considered an OLE (Object Linking and Embedding) container. (See the section below on ActiveX for more discussion on

ActiveX and OLE technologies). Plug-ins, described below, also address some of the integration issues that make helpers troublesome.

Netscape Plug-ins

Plug-ins, first introduced by Netscape in Navigator 2.0, address the communication and integration issues that plagued helper applications. Plug-ins are like small helper programs (components) that run within the context of the browser itself. Plug-ins are well integrated into Web pages, and may be included using the HTML elements <EMBED> or <OBJECT>. However, as with helper applications, cross-platform compatibility, installation, and security can be a problem. Plug-ins are compiled for a particular platform, so they are fast, but not always available. More than 80 percent of all plug-ins run only on Windows 95. Less than 5 percent of available plug-ins run on UNIX. Plug-ins may be difficult to deal with since they must be found and downloaded. Initially with Netscape, the burden was on the user to find and install the plug-in. Though users can be pointed to a main repository or go to other directories to find plug-ins, they must still install them. Starting with Netscape 4.0, the installation of plug-ins has become far easier. They are still not as seamless as ActiveX controls, which may be downloaded and installed automatically. While this is a major improvement over the Netscape plug-in model, it also introduces potential security risks because it may facilitate the introduction of malicious programs or viruses.

ActiveX

ActiveX (www.microsoft.com/activex) is the new name of Microsoft's Object Linking and Embedding (OLE) technology, which embeds small components or controls within an application. ActiveX is intended to distribute these controls via the Internet to add new functionality to browsers like Internet Explorer. Microsoft maintains that ActiveX controls are more like generalized components than plug-ins: They can reside beyond the browser, within container programs like Microsoft Office. ActiveX controls are like plug-ins since they are persistent and machine-specific. While this makes resource use a problem, installation is not an issue—the components download and install automatically.

Security is a big concern for ActiveX controls. Because these small pieces of code may potentially have full access to a user's system, they could cause serious damage. This unlimited functionality of ActiveX controls, combined with automatic installation, creates a gaping security hole. End users will be quick to click a button to install new functionality, only to accidentally get their hard drive erased by an errant or malicious program. To address this problem, Microsoft provides authentication information to indicate who wrote a control, in the form of code signed by a certificate. In other words, safe Web browsing should be practiced by accepting controls only from reputable sources.

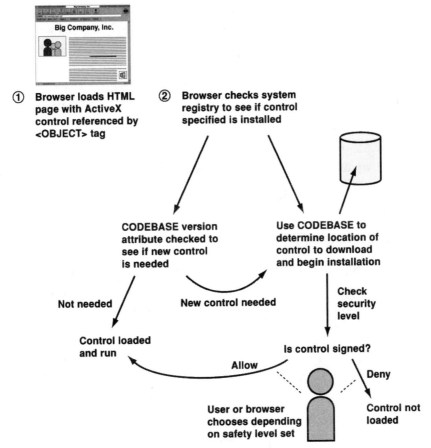

Figure 7–7. ActiveX Overview.

Figure 7-7 shows the process of an ActiveX control downloading and executing within a browser. This can be described in a series of steps. First, the browser loads an HTML page that references an ActiveX control with the <OBJECT> tag. The browser checks the system registry to see if the control specified is installed. If it is installed, it compares the CODEBASE version attribute stored in the registry against the CODEBASE version attribute in the HTML page. If a newer version is specified in the page, a newer control will be needed. Similarly, if the control is not installed, the CODEBASE must be used to determine the location of the control to download. Before the download begins, the browser checks to see if the code is signed. If the code is not signed, the user will be warned of this. If the code is signed, an authentic-code certificate will be presented to the user bearing the identity of the author of the control. Based on these criteria, the user can allow or deny the installation of the control on his or her system. If the user accepts the control, it is automatically downloaded, installed, and invoked in the page for its specific function. Finally, it is persistently stored on the client machine for further invocation.

ActiveX may be more suitable on a Windows-only intranet where security can be managed than on the potentially unsafe Internet. Development for controls is platform-specific, and currently only Windows-centered. ActiveX on other platforms such as Macintosh or UNIX will require new binaries to be compiled, and won't be compatible with Windows controls because of operating system differences.

Windows developers can access an abundance of available controls for various purposes. They can also write their own, though in some cases this may be like re-inventing the wheel. Controls can be created using a variety of languages such as Visual Basic, C++, and Java. It is also possible to convert existing programs to controls. Controls expose their interfaces through the Component Object Model; this can be accessed and controlled easily through scripting languages. Beyond security, the biggest complaint that can be made about ActiveX is that it is too platform-specific. Within a cross-platform environment like the Internet, Java attempts to address this issue, as well as security, but it has its own problems as discussed in the following section.

Java

Sun Microsystems' Java technology (www.javasoft.com) is an attractive, revolutionary approach to cross-platform, Internet-based development. It has been positioned as a platform-neutral development language that allows programs to be written once and deployed on any machine, browser, or operating system that supports the Java Virtual Machine that includes Macintosh, Windows, UNIX, OS/2, and a variety of other machines.

Java-enabled pages access small Java programs, called *applets*. Applets are downloaded and run directly within a browser to provide unique functionality. Applets are first written in the Java language and then compiled to a machine-independent byte-code in the form of a Java class file. Java applets are embedded into a Web page using the <APPLET> or <OBJECT> HTML element to reference the binary object. The intermediate binary is downloaded automatically to the Java capable browser and then run within the browser environment. Figure 7-8 presents an overview of how Java applets are used within a Web page.

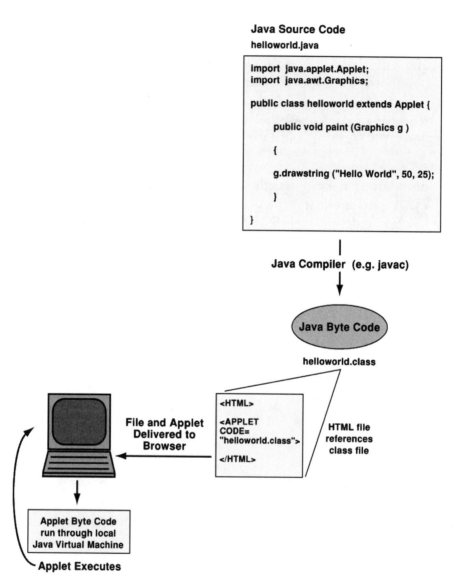

Figure 7–8. Overview of Java Use.

Java applets are intended to run safely in a browser, not accessing any system functions, so the browser automatically downloads the applet unless Java is disabled. The bytecode is interpreted by a Java Virtual Machine or may be run by a Just-In-Time (JIT) compiler. A JIT compiler takes bytecode and converts it into native system code on the fly when run on a client system. Normally, Java bytecode is interpreted by the Java virtual machine. When using a JIT compiler, this bytecode is turned into native machine code and executed directly instead of being interpreted, which should result in a substantial performance boost. Regardless of whether it is interpreted or quickly compiled, an applet undergoes a life-cycle where it is initiated, executed, and finally discarded when a different page is loaded. Accordingly, it is not persistently stored on the client machine.

Java has inherent performance issues; even with a fast processor, the end system runs the bytecode slowly compared to a natively compiled application because the bytecode must be interpreted by the Java Virtual Machine. Even with recent JIT compilers in newer browsers, Java doesn't always deliver ideal performance. It is possible that special hardware, including Java chips, may eliminate such problems, but for now this hardware is not widely available. Even if compile time was not an issue, Java applets may not be persistent; they must be redownloaded for future use. Java browsers act like thin-client applications—they only add code when they need it.

Security in Java has been a serious concern from the outset. Because programs are downloaded and run automatically, a malicious program could be downloaded and run without the user being able to stop it. However, Java applets actually have little access to resources outside the browser's environment. Within Web pages, applets can't write to local disks or perform other harmful functions. This framework has been referred to as the Java "sandbox." Developers wishing to provide Java functions outside of the sandbox must write Java applications, which run as separate applications from browsers. Other Internet programming technologies (plug-ins, ActiveX) provide even less safety from damaging programs. Oddly, Java developers often want to add just these types of insecure features, as well as powerful features like persistence and inter-object communication. Newer versions of Java are addressing these issues and some browsers will support these features with a capabilities-based security model determined by end-user settings or LAN administrators.

The broad functionality of Java can cost both time and money. Java programming assumes familiarity with C++ and object-oriented design. Like ActiveX, Web professionals lacking programming skills or budgets will find many free premade components available for reuse or sale. These Java components, called *JavaBeans*, are reusable, and can be customized by developers with visual tools to distribute as Web-ready applets. However, JavaBeans are not nearly as widely available as ActiveX controls, and lack the history of OLE behind them

Another issue with Java is that it is an evolving standard with different versions in the field and in development. There are versions 1.0, 1.01, 1.02, and 1.1, as well as different foundation class libraries from Microsoft, Sun, and Netscape. There also is the issue of "100 percent Pure Java" versus Java implementations that make specific operating system calls to achieve performance improvements or access certain platform-specific functions such as multimedia capabilities. While Java and ActiveX are often compared, the two appear to be moving closer to each other in philosophy and capability all the time. Both are moving toward a distributed component model with different functions placed on the client and server with inter-object communications between components.

Regardless of the component technology being used within a Web page (plug-ins, controls, or applets), eventually the issue of "glue" arises. How will the various elements that make up a Web page communicate with each other? How will the small programming tasks that do not require the overhead of Java or ActiveX be handled? The answer to these problems, as well as similar server-side issues, is by using a scripting language such as JavaScript or VBScript (Visual Basic Script).

JavaScript

JavaScript is a scripting language developed by Netscape. Microsoft also supports JavaScript in the form of JScript, a clone language used in Internet Explorer. The language was turned over to the international standards body ECMA (www.ecma.ch), which announced approval of ECMA-262 or ECMAScript as a cross-platform Internet standard for scripting. Browser vendors will comply with the specification, but will still use the commonly recognized JavaScript name.

As a scripting language, JavaScript is meant to be easy to use, noncompiled (interpreted), and useful in small chunks. This sets it apart from Java and other languages that might be used on the Internet, which tend to be compiled and relatively hard to master for the nonprogrammer. JavaScript has basic object-oriented capabilities, but is not a true object-oriented programming language and retains features like weak typing common to simple scripting languages. As a scripting language, it is useful for small jobs such as checking form data, adding small bits of HTML code to a page on the fly, and performing browser, time, and user-specific computation. JavaScript is also a powerful means of controlling events in browsers and accessing the Document Object Model for programming Dynamic HTML. An important potential function of JavaScript is to act as the glue between different technologies such as plug-ins, Java applets, and HTML pages. An example of JavaScript code that performs simple form validation and illustrates the relationship between HTML and JavaScript is shown in Figure 7-9.

```
<HTML>
<HEAD>
<TITLE>JavaScript Example</TITLE>
<SCRIPT TYPE="JavaScript">
<!--
function validate()
{
  if (regform.name.value == "")
  {
  alert("You must enter your name");
    return;
  }
  else regform.submit()
}
//-->
</SCRIPT>
</HEAD>
<BODY>
<H1 ALIGN="CENTER">Registration Form</H1>
<HR>
<FORM ACTION="mailto: info@bigcompany.com" METHOD="POST" NAME="reg-
  form">

Name: <INPUT NAME="name" TYPE="TEXT" SIZE="20" MAXLENGTH="40">
<BR><BR>
<INPUT TYPE="BUTTON" VALUE="Register" onClick="validate()">
</FORM>
</BODY>
</HTML>
```

Figure 7–9. JavaScript Example.

Historically, only Microsoft Internet Explorer 3.0 and Netscape browsers (version 2.0 and greater) have supported JavaScript. The JavaScript specification has changed rapidly. Cross-platform support has not been consistent. Developers should be very careful with the use of JavaScript with browsers. One technique is to "hide" JavaScript code from older browsers with comments.

There are a few major dialects of JavaScript including JavaScript 1.0 (Netscape 2.X), JavaScript 1.1 (Netscape 3.X) and JavaScript 1.2 (Netscape 4.X). JScript in Internet Explorer 3.0 is approximately equivalent to JavaScript 1.0 and does not support JavaScript 1.1 features such as dynamic image replacement. IE 4.0 appears to support JavaScript 1.1, but with a richer object model. Finally, there is the ECMAScript standard. Figure 7-10 shows a chart of JavaScript versions supported by different browsers:

Browser	JavaScript Support
Netscape Navigator 2.X	JavaScript 1.0
Netscape Navigator 3.X	JavaScript 1.1
Netscape Navigator 4.X	JavaScript 1.2
Internet Explorer 2.X	None
Internet Explorer 3.X	JScript (JavaScript 1.0)
Internet Explorer 4.X	JScript (JavaScript 1.1), ECMAScript compliant

Figure 7–10. JavaScript Support by Browser Release.

Programming of JavaScript requires an awareness of programming principles, including the concepts of variables, operators, statements, functions, objects, and events. To obtain specific functionality and control features in a browser, it also requires an understanding of certain objects and their properties such as the Document, Date, and Window objects. Bringing all of this together to produce useful and properly functioning JavaScript code also requires developers to learn the nuances of the particular language and to develop a good coding style for maintainability.

Problems with JavaScript include the scripts not behaving the same on different platforms, bugs in different implementations of the language, and the results of poor programming. Memory leaks and security holes, such as e-mail address collection, are still a possibility. Even simple bugs like infinite loops can force a user to shut down the browser to recover. Historically, many of JavaScript's problems have to do with incomplete and inconsistent implementation and a misunderstanding by developers about adding programming code to a Web page. Accordingly, a fair amount of cross-platform testing on different browser versions may be necessary to ensure consistent performance. Considering these issues, approach JavaScript use with caution. However, this is a general rule for all programs: Approach the coding of all programs in a defensive manner. Never assume anything. JavaScript has been widely used to perform a variety of embellishment functions such as animated buttons and form contents validation. Since users may turn off JavaScript, pages should still be able to work acceptably without these features and not rely on the support for the language. All scripts added to a Web site should be coded in a defensive manner. Never assume that a particular feature will be available in all forms of a language like JavaScript. Testing to see which browser is being used and which objects are supported in a particular JavaScript implementation can help avoid errors. However, errors still may occur, so make sure to use an "onerror" event handler to provide custom error messages and alert the user on how to report the bug. If JavaScript use is targeted for a specific browser and the functionality is tested and known, as could be the case in an intranet environment, then reliance on the functions the language provides is generally acceptable.

All of these issues must be considered, realizing that the language must be seen as an important part of the Web programming puzzle. Accordingly, developers should treat JavaScript as more of a programming language and apply generally accepted programming principles to achieve maximum benefits. There is an abundance of JavaScript code available on the Web that can be easily cut and pasted, but this practice should be used with caution. Code should be carefully examined and tested. In contrast, the idea of script reuse and libraries of stable and well-coded scripts for various purposes should be adopted as discussed later in this chapter.

VBScript

VBScript is somewhat more defined and stable than JavaScript because of its Visual Basic ancestry. The language should be familiar to the many Visual Basic programmers in the world. VBScript is less prevalent than JavaScript on the Internet, largely because it is fully supported only in Internet Explorer. The language can be used to provide the same functionality as JavaScript, and is just as capable of accessing the various objects that compose a Web page, termed a browser's Document Object Model. It should be avoided for use as a cross-platform scripting solution. Used with ActiveX controls in a more controllable environment, such as an intranet, VBScript might just be what the Microsoft-oriented developer needs. Figure 7-11 shows a sample of VBScript to give a flavor of its syntax. The example has the same functionality as the JavaScript example in Figure 7-9 and performs simple form validation. While syntactically the two languages are different, the way they interact with HTML is very similar.

```
<HTML>
<HEAD>
<TITLE>VBSscript Example</TITLE>
<SCRIPT LANGUAGE="VBScript">
<!--
Sub Reg_OnClick
Dim TheForm
Set TheForm = Document.regform

   If (TheForm.name.Value) = "" Then
       MsgBox "You must enter your name"
   Else
      TheForm.submit
   End If


End Sub
-->
```

(Continued)

```
</SCRIPT>
</HEAD>
<BODY>
<H1 ALIGN=CENTER>Registration Form</H1>
<HR>
<FORM ACTION="mailto:info@bigcompany.com" METHOD=POST NAME="reg-
  form">



Name: <INPUT NAME="name" TYPE="TEXT" SIZE="20" MAXLENGTH="40">
<BR><BR>


<INPUT TYPE="BUTTON" VALUE="Register" NAME="Reg">


</FORM>
</BODY>
</HTML>
```

Figure 7–11. VBScript Example.

Dynamic HTML

Dynamic HTML (DHTML) is not about new tags or attributes that can animate pages. Dynamic HTML actually extends the current set of HTML elements, and a few other things like style sheet properties, by allowing them to be accessed and modified by a scripting language like JavaScript or VBScript. Dynamic facilities can be added by exposing tags to a scripting language; this allows pages to come alive with movement and interactivity. The tags in a page are accessed through the Document Object Model, or DOM.

Every Web document is made up of a variety of tags like <B>, <IMG>, and <FORM>. Browsers read pages in a regular fashion because they understand the extent of the objects that are possible in a page. A page might be composed of three image elements, two paragraphs, an unordered list, and the text within these elements. The Document Object Model describes each document as a collection of individual objects like images, paragraphs, and forms, all the way down to the individual characters. Each particular object may have properties associated with it, typically in the form of HTML attributes. For example, the paragraph element has an alignment attribute that may be set to left, right, or center. In the object model, this attribute is called a *property* of the object. An object may have methods that are associated with it, and events that may occur and affect it. An image tag may have an "onmouseover" event that is triggered when a user places the cursor over the image. A form may have a submit method that can be used to trigger the submission of the form and its contents to a server-based CGI program. See Figure 7-12 for an illustration of these concepts.

① Given A Standard HTML 4.0 Document

```
<HTML>
<HEAD>
<TITLE>Big Company</TITLE>
</HEAD>
<BODY BGCOLOR="WHITE">
<H1 ALIGN="CENTER">Big Company</H1>
<HR>
<P ID="para1">This is a paragraph of text</P>
<UL>
        <LI><A HREF="about.htm">About</A>
        <LI><A HREF="products.htm">Products</A>
</UL>
</BODY>
</HTML>
```

② How This Document is Modeled

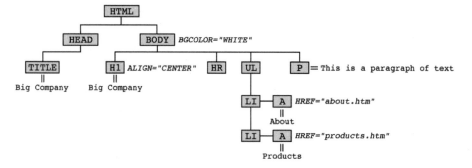

③ How Scripting Works Within the Document

Scripting has access to the elements either directly by binding script code,

```
<A HREF="products.htm" onMouseover="this.style.color=red"

onMouseout="this.style.color=blue">Products Section</A>
```

or

by referencing items by names or collections,

```
para1.style.color=green
```

Events like "onclick" or "onMouseover" are used to bind script code to user actions.

Figure 7–12. The Idea of DHTML.

The only major difference between the idea of DHTML and scripting languages like JavaScript and VBScript is the degree of integration. DHTML proposes to make Web pages fully modifiable on the client side, while previously scripting languages generally could only manipulate certain portions of pages such as form elements and, in any case, not after page load. Before the DOM and DHTML, scripting has mainly served in a support role for server-side technology, for example by validating the contents of a form before submission. However, full accessibility to the page may bring more power to the client side.

When to Use Client-Side Technologies

Client-side technologies can be used to control the presentation and structure of documents and to call on embedded elements such as plug-ins, ActiveX controls, and Java applets to provide enhanced content and functionality. Client-side scripting and DHTML can be used to control these elements and add logic to pages as well as access the Document Object Model to dynamically change content on pages. Different client-side technologies have unique development, installation, security, and cross-browser and cross-platform concerns.

While client-side technologies have their place in a Web site, focusing development strictly on the client has its limitations. The evolution of these client-side technologies has offloaded some of the processing that traditionally occurred on the server. For example, validating form field entries by using JavaScript on the client makes more sense than relegating this processing to the server. However, with a defensive programming approach, it may be necessary to account for lack of scripting support by providing a means of validating entries on the server with a CGI program. Server-side technologies have their appropriate place, although many designers have traditionally focused page design on the client. Web site engineering requires a holistic approach with an understanding of how to use client- and server-side technologies together. Server-side technologies typically require more programming and often require consideration of the server itself as well as integration with other systems such as databases.

Server-Side Technologies

As discussed earlier in the chapter, server-side technologies are those which run at the Web server. The benefit of using a server-side technology to add interactivity to a Web site is that there is a great deal of control over the execution environment; little is required on the browser's part. While server-side programming is relatively safe compared to client-side programming in that it should work regardless of user setup, it tends to put too much responsibility on the server. This is the big drawback of server-side technologies. Common server-side technologies include CGI (Common Gateway Interface) programs, custom server applications such as NSAPI and ISAPI programs, and parsed HTML solutions. Often, the whole point of these technologies is to access a database, so the technology may simply be a form of middleware. As sites scale and add database facilities, advanced designs such as tier systems with transaction processors or distributed object systems may become necessary. However, like client-side technologies, each technology has its place and will be discussed individually.

CGI

The first server-side technology was CGI or Common Gateway Interface. This protocol standard specifies how information can be passed from a Web page via a Web server to a program and back to the browser in the proper format. Many people often confuse what the application does with the idea behind CGI. In reality, Web server-based applications are just plain programs that are enabled to pass information back and forth across the Web using the CGI specification. The passing of data (the part CGI defines) is easy; the actual function of the program is the hard part. This is what people seem to be confused about when they think about CGI.

CGI can be used for anything, as it is just a specification. However, common uses tend to limit CGI to form interaction, database queries, and dynamic document generation. It is possible to create complex applications with CGI, but many tasks are often limited by the problem of maintaining state between HTTP requests from the client. The only magic of CGI is understanding how to read data in from name-value pair environment variables that are passed along with each HTTP request, and write data out to talk to a Web browser using a HTTP header such as "Content-type: text/html".

Because a CGI program is external to a Web server, it must be launched as a separate process. The overhead of launching and running a program can be significant in many operating systems. Some solutions attempt to keep the CGI loaded in memory. Some take advantage of operating system facilities such as Dynamic Linked Libraries (DLLs) to keep processing time to a minimum, but there is still a lag between a Web server receiving a request and an external program actually handling it. Another approach is to use an improvement to CGI such as FastCGI (www.fastcgi.com), which provides better memory and process management, with an open standard that is not tied to a particular server. Figure 7-13 presents an overview of how CGI programs are used.

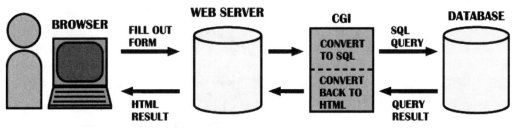

Figure 7–13. Illustration of CGI Use.

Another solution to CGI's performance problems lies in the choice of the programming language used to write CGI programs. Many CGI applications are written in Perl, which can have serious drawbacks for large-scale systems. Perl's interpreted nature and slow execution speed can be a problem, especially when coupled with the inherent performance penalties involved in launching CGI programs. An alternative is to write CGI programs in a compiled language such as C or C++. This would be particularly appropriate for sites that service a large number of CGI requests and must handle a large volume of processing. Smaller tasks on less busy sites can be accomplished with a language like Perl.

To facilitate the development process, there are libraries of functions for CGI processing and free code for a variety of applications available in most languages. Implementing canned solutions can save time and development costs, but developers should be wary of the quality of code and possible bugs.

Developers should also be aware of the lack of built-in state management with the CGI protocol. This must take place in CGI programs themselves, with techniques such as processing hidden form fields and dynamically generating new pages with these same fields. Such an approach would commonly use the HTTP POST method to pass name-value pairs from forms as environment variables. An illustration of this approach is shown in Figure 7-14.

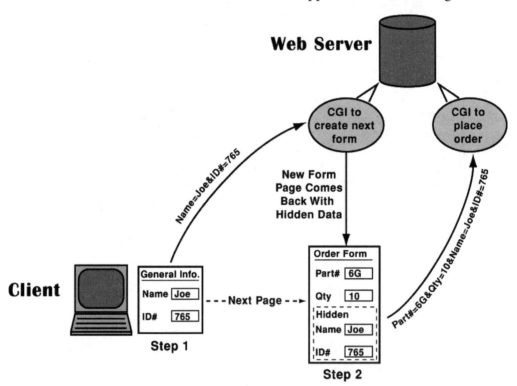

Figure 7–14. CGI State Problem Solution.

An alternative state maintenance technique could use CGI program to retrieve cookie information from a client to generate dynamic pages, as well as send back updated cookie information. Another approach for state management uses the HTTP GET request method to embed state information in a URL. This can allow for bookmarking of URLs with state information to revisit previous pages. An example of this can be seen in many search engines where the search results page uses the information submitted by the user to generate the result embedded into the URL as shown below:

```
http://www.hotbot.com/?SW=web&SM=MC&MT=San+Diego&DC=10&DE=2&RG=NA&_v
=2
```

While the GET form of data passing has limitations to the amount of data that can be passed, one advantage is that the resulting pages can be bookmarked or canned queries can be built for them.

Server APIs

If total avoidance of CGI performance and bottlenecks is warranted, writing programs that are tightly bound to the actual HTTP server via server APIs is possible. Netscape servers offer the cross-platform API (Applications Programming Interface) called NSAPI, and Microsoft appeals to Windows developers with its own API, called ISAPI. Server API solutions are analogous to plug-ins on browsers. These API programming solutions provide performance improvements over CGI by supporting tight integration with the actual Web server. Similar API approaches exist on most Web servers. The widely deployed and freely available Apache server (www.apache.org) lets developers add or create different server modules to add functionality. Because of the tie-in at the server level, applications written using server APIs can access core server functions such as authentication, access control, and various levels of HTTP request processing.

There are serious downsides to the server-side API approach. The complexity of server-side API programs makes development cycles long and expensive. Worse yet, buggy API programs can bring down an entire Web server, while a bad CGI would just take up processing time. Server API-oriented solutions are obviously faster and, if well developed, more robust, but the difficulty of developing such applications makes them unrealistic for many Web professionals. Furthermore, developing software for a particular server API will lock the application into that particular server platform. If a newer version of the server is released, new APIs will likely be available as well. Code may need to be rewritten to ensure compatibility.

Because of these issues with server-side APIs, other approaches for generalized applications may be more appropriate. However, when there is a need to write or use modules that perform specific functions at the server-level such as authentication or access control, the use of server API programs may be warranted.

Parsed HTML Middleware

If it is necessary to avoid the problems faced by CGI or the complexities of server-side APIs, it is possible to use server-side script engines or other forms of middleware installed as part of the server. The point of the middleware is to provide some way to add logic to a Web page without complex programming, typically in order to access a backend system such as a database. A simple precursor to this, supported by many servers, is the concept of Server-Side Includes (SSI). SSI commands are inserted into an HTML file and reference external files to be included. These external files contain HTML fragments in separate files that are added to pages by the server to display simple items such as copyright notices. This idea has been extended to a more a general and programmable approach with middleware that is installed as part of the server. The middleware typically interprets *parsed HTML,* which contains additional code with HTML to produce dynamically generated pages. The simplest solutions use specialized tags included in HTML that are parsed by a product such as CFML (Cold Fusion Markup Language) in Allaire's Cold Fusion (www.allaire.com). Other approaches embed a variety of standard scripting languages, such as JavaScript, VBScript, or Perl, in HTML code to be run by a server-side script interpreter. Importantly, middleware often provides a programmable interface to access to other system and server-side facilities including the key feature of database access using SQL (Structured Query Language) and ODBC (Open Database Connectivity) standards. Figure 7-15 depicts how middleware works to generate dynamic pages:

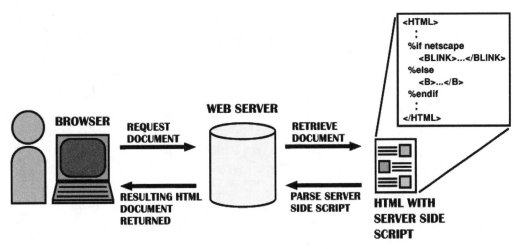

Figure 7–15. Parsed-HTML Middleware in Action.

There are various middleware solutions, many of which are dependent on the server and platform being used. In addition to parsing server-side script code or specialized tags, there are usually server-side components or objects that can be accessed through the middleware programming interface. Similar to CGI, there is typically an object that can access HTTP request information, including form data. There is usually a state management object that uses cookies to retain state information between pages. A database object will include the means of executing SQL commands on a database and retrieving the results in the form of record sets that can be manipulated by code to generate dynamic pages. Also common is an object to access the local file system. In addition to these standardized components, middleware will usually provide the means to access or develop other third-party server-side components for functions such as messaging or directory services.

Server-Side JavaScript

Though this is not commonly known, JavaScript can also be used on the server side.[2] Server-side JavaScript is available as part of the LiveWire® devel-

---

2. As a programming language Java can also be used on the server side to build CGI like programs.

opment tool from Netscape. Code is intermixed with HTML and applications are compiled into "byte code" that can be run on Netscape servers running on platforms such as NT or UNIX. LiveWire applications are installed as part of the server. Additionally, LiveWire provides server-side objects for functions such as database access and HTTP request information. The development environment features a database connectivity library with native support for major databases as well as ODBC support. However, LiveWire is a proprietary product specific to Netscape servers and must be run on this platform. The learning curves and development costs associated with this product go beyond simple knowledge of JavaScript. Finally, developing Web applications using LiveWire requires a commitment to the Netscape server platform.

Active Server Pages

Microsoft supplies a powerful Internet Information Server (IIS) extension known as Active Server Pages (ASP) for server-side program and script execution for dynamic content creation, database access, and other functions. ASP files are similar to parsed HTML or server-side includes and provides an easy way to add logic or "glue" code. ASP is scripting-language independent, meaning that scripts can be written using server-side VBScript, JavaScript[3], Perl, REXX and other languages, all which have full access to object models of server-side components. ASP was developed by Microsoft for Internet Information Server, although a third-party vendor has developed a product to provide ASP support on Netscape Web servers.

Active Server Pages allow programming of server-side script code directly in HTML pages. Code is interpreted, not compiled. The server must execute ASP script code in appropriate script engines. The result of code execution is HTML delivered to clients. Like other server-parsed HTML solutions, ASP files allow business logic to be hidden from the client. However, unlike other parsed HTML solutions, because ASP is part of the Active Server platform, it also provides access to object models of ActiveX Server Components for various functions such as database access, file access, and messaging. Premade

---

3. The server-side JavaScript used with ASP is not compatible with Netscape's server-side implementation.

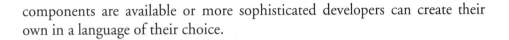

components are available or more sophisticated developers can create their own in a language of their choice.

Databases

A brief mention of databases is relevant, considering that they serve as a host for backend systems or a content store for many pages that are dynamically created. Database selection for a Web project depends on the scale of the application. The range of choices includes huge database systems on mainframes to small single-user desktop databases. The type of database will depend on development and scaling needs. Smaller file-oriented relational databases like Microsoft Access or FileMakerPro® are generally suitable for workgroup solutions. Medium- to large-size relational database solutions, such as SQLServer®, Oracle®, Sybase®, or Informix®, might be suitable for most Web site back-ends. However, as the site scales or complexity increase, a different architecture or even object technology might be in order.[4]

As mentioned, Internet database connectivity is usually through some type of middleware that communicates via native support or ODBC drivers for a particular database. SQL commands are used for common database functions such as queries, inserts, and updates as well as for accessing stored procedures. These create a quasi-two-tiered architecture. What is interesting is that on the Web there is generally a middle tier, often implemented as a CGI program, between the Web server and the database. As discussed previously, this could be migrated to a NSAPI/ISAPI program, or the Web server and the database can even be integrated. An illustration of this migration is shown in Figure 7-16.

---

4. Since databases are often the heart of a Web site, they should be considered carefully as part of the design phase. Plans should also take into account the performance and maintenance requirements of the database.

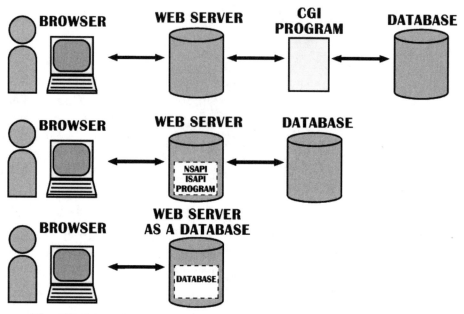

Figure 7–16. Web and Database Relationship.

While some performance issues can be resolved by merging the Web server and the database, scalability can become a factor. With traditional client/server models, the two-tier architecture can fall apart under high loads. We need to look to multitier architecture, potentially with many databases, and a transaction processor or other load-balancing mechanism.

Transaction Servers

Database solutions that must scale or require distributed load balancing between multiple database servers may require a transaction server. A transaction processor (TP) or transaction server can coordinate database transactions, which may be a series of actions on a database that collectively make up a single "atomic transaction." The traditional example given for this is the transfer of money between two bank accounts. This requires one account to be debited and another to be credited. The collective action is a transaction. If anything goes wrong in the process, the transaction is considered incomplete. The complexity of such activity may require several steps to perform, as well as a mechanism to "rollback" to previous database states before a transaction was processed. There is a trend to integrate a transaction server with the Web server as part of a larger model of Web client/server computing. An illustration of a traditional TP model for client/server database access and its migration of the TP into the Web is shown in Figure 7-17.

Web Server & Transaction Processor are one

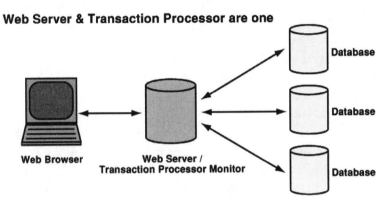

Seperating Web Server & Transaction Processor

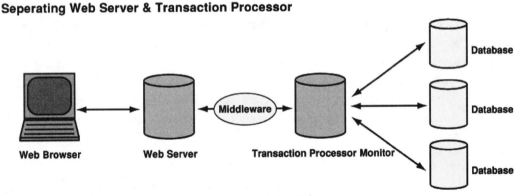

Figure 7–17. Transaction Processing and the Web.

■ Distributed Web Computing

A paradigm of distributed computing based on Web technologies is evolving. Behind all of this are component architectures for developing multi-tiered Web applications. Browsers function as clients that may also run controls or Java applets. Web servers receive requests for pages that can contain server-side scripts that call Java servelets or ActiveX server components for database access. These processes may be controlled by a transaction monitor that provides improved performance, load balancing, and reliability for transactions. Finally, the results of server transactions may be returned as HTML or via protocols, such as IIOP (Inter-ORB Protocol), RMI (Remote Method Invocation), or DCOM (Distributed Component Object Model), directly to the client that is running an ActiveX control or Java applet. This model relies on different architectures, such as the Component Object Model (COM) or JavaBeans®, and the distributed network component model of COM or CORBA (Common Object Request Broker Architecture). The benefit to the distributed object model is that the objects can be distributed around the network or served from different points, depending on network conditions. Also, the object protocols may offer better performance than traditional Web protocols like HTTP. However, note that distributed object technologies are not widely available on the Web nor are they simple. Typically, only very complicated applications such as airline ticketing, involving multiple servers running across enterprises, would require such an implementation. Smaller Web sites or applications do not need to be complicated by these emerging technologies. Again, the choice of technology should be based upon the problem to be solved.

When to Use Server-Side Technologies

Selection of server-side technologies involves carefully looking at the requirements of the application or task at hand, along with performance and scaling needs. Server-side technology also is often influenced by the need to integrate with other systems such as databases. Performance can be an issue with server-side technology; however, small tasks may be adequately accomplished using traditional CGI programs or server-side scripting middleware. High-performance applications may require custom-server modules written in a language like C++. Adding support for databases may complicate the picture, particularly when considering the performance of databases. A multi-tier architecture, even one using distributed objects, may be required by large-scale applications; this will result in a major increase in project complexity. Regardless of the server-side approach taken, careful consideration must be given to the quality of the hardware and software used. Otherwise, the server may turn into a bottleneck in the Web application. Projects will probably use a mixture of client-side and server-side processing. Client-side programming may be able to offload some processing from the server and make the system more responsive from the user's point of view.

Content Technologies

When assembling Web sites, consider the content-driven nature of the Web. Sites rely heavily on the quality of the images, sounds, videos, text, and other media forms—content—that make up a page. Given the importance of content to Web sites, mistakes in choosing the appropriate media form can ruin even the best Web sites.

Images on the Web

The most important media form to consider, beyond text, is images. When images have not been saved in the appropriate fashion, the quality of the image can suffer greatly, and file size may be less-than-ideal for Web delivery. Image compression and quality depend on the image file format. There are a variety of image formats in the computer world, including vector image formats like Encapsulated Postscript (EPS) and bitmap formats like GIF (Graphic Interchange Format) and JPEG (Joint Photographic Experts Group). A vector format describes an image mathematically as a collection of curves, while a bitmapped format describes an image as collection of colored dots. The HTML standard says nothing about what image formats can be used on the Web, but the browser vendors tend to support the same image types. On the Web, the primary image formats are GIF and JPEG. A new format called PNG (Portable Network Graphics), which should also eventually become a Web image standard, is being heavily endorsed by the W3C (World

Wide Web Consortium). Given the historical association between UNIX and the Internet, the X-image formats, X-Bitmaps (.xbm), and X-Pixelmaps (.xpm) are often supported natively by browsers. The table in Figure 7-18 summarizes a few of the basic Web image types.[5]

File Format	Description
GIF (Graphics Interchange Format)	• Lossless compression • 8-bit (256) colors only • Good for illustrations and line art • Supports one degree of transparency • Interlacing possible • Animation in GIF89a form
JPEG (Joint Photographic Experts Group)	• Higher loss rate (Lossy) during compression • 24-bit color possible • Good for photographs • Supports progressive rendering • No animation or transparency
PNG (Portable Network Graphics)	• Lossless compression • More than 256 colors possible • Multiple degrees of transparency • Progressive rendering • Not common to all browsers

Figure 7–18. Web Image Formats.

■ GIF Images

GIF images are used extensively on the Web. They are probably the most widely supported image format in browsers that handle graphics. GIF images come in two basic flavors: GIF87 and GIF89a. Both forms of GIF support 8-bit color (256 colors) and use the LZW (Lempel-Ziv-Welch)[6] lossless compression scheme, meaning that quality of the image is completely preserved.

---

5. Internet Explorer also supports the Bitmap format (.bmp) popular with Windows users. This format has yet to be adopted widely on the Web.

GIF 89a also supports transparency and animation, both of which will be discussed shortly.

The run length encoding compression scheme used by GIF works well with large areas of continuous color, so GIF is very efficient in compression of flat style illustration.

As mentioned earlier, GIF images support 8-bit color for a maximum of 256 colors in the image.[7] Consequently, some degree of loss is inevitable when representing true color images such as photographs. Typically, when an image is remapped from a large number of colors to a smaller color palette, *dithering* occurs. Dithering attempts to imitate colors by placing similar colors near each other. Dithering also produces a speckling or banding effect that may cause images to appear rough or fuzzy. Web authors should be careful to use GIF images appropriately. Netscape and Microsoft currently use a so-called "browser-safe" color palette of 216 colors that are common across systems like the Macintosh or Windows. If a GIF image using a color outside this color palette is displayed on an 8-bit system, dithering will occur and the result may look grainy or distorted on the user's screen.. Authors looking to avoid image problems should remap colors to the safe palette. Information on this technique can be found in numerous books on Web image design.

GIF images also support a concept called transparency. One bit of transparency is allowed, which means that one color can be set to be transparent. Transparency allows the background behind an image to show through, making a variety of complex effects possible. GIF transparency is far from ideal, as it can result in a halo effect in certain situations. For example, in order to smooth images, a technique called *anti-aliasing* is used. Anti-aliased images appear smooth because the image is progressively made lighter to fade into the background. However, because only one color of transparency can be set in an

---

6. There is some concern about the use of GIF images because of the patent on the LZW algorithm held by Unisys that would require payment for use of the proprietary scheme. This concern is somewhat unsubstantiated. Nevertheless, the PNG format described in this chapter has been positioned as a substitute for the GIF format.

7. According to the GIF specification, the idea of layering makes it possible to create a GIF image that supports more than 256 colors. However, not all browsers support this little known feature. Layering also allows for an interesting form of color interlacing which can bring in one set of colors before another.

image, the anti-aliasing colors may show up as a halo or residue around the image.

GIF images also support a feature called *interlacing*. Interlacing allows an image to load in a venetian blind style fashion rather than from top to bottom one line at a time. The interlacing effect allows a user to get an idea of what an image looks like before the entire image has downloaded. The pre-visualization benefit of interlacing is very useful on the Web, where download speed is often an issue. While interlacing a GIF image is generally a good idea, occasionally it comes with a downside. First, interlaced images may be slightly larger than noninterlaced images. Second, an interlaced image may not always provide its intended previsualization benefit. For example, if the GIF image is of graphic text, the text will probably not be readable until the image is fully loaded.

Using GIF89a format, simple animation is possible in a Web page. The GIF89a format supports a series of GIF images that act as the individual frames of animation. The animation can be set up so one image is displayed after another, similar to a little flipbook. The animation extension also allows for timing and looping information to be added to the image. Animated GIFs are one of the most popular ways to add simple animation to a Web page because nearly every browser supports them. Browsers that do not support the animated GIF format generally display the first frame of the animation in its place. Even though plug-ins or other browser facilities are not required, authors should not rush out to use animation on their pages. Excessive animation can be distracting as well as inefficient to download, particularly when frames are not used efficiently. One approach to combating file bloat is to replace only the moving parts of an individual animation frame.

In summary, because of their compression scheme and support for 8-bit color, GIF images tend to be best suited for illustrations. GIF images do support interlacing, which may provide previsualization for Web-based imagery. Because of the nature of their image compression, GIF images may not be suitable for photographic style imagery, which is probably better left to the JPEG format discussed in the next section. In their favor, GIF images are the most widely supported image format, and do have advanced features such as transparency and animation.

JPEG Images

The other common Web image format is JPEG, which usually is indicated by a file name ending with .jpg or .jpeg. JPEG, which stands for the Joint Photographic Experts Group—the name of the committee that wrote the standard—is a *lossy* image format designed for compressing photographic images which may contain thousands, or even millions, of colors or shades of gray. A lossy image format does not exactly preserve an image, but allows for a tradeoff by allowing the designer to give up image accuracy in favor of file size. For complex images like photographs, the loss in image quality may hardly be perceptible to the untrained eye. The JPEG format stores high quality 24-bit color images in a significantly smaller amount of space than GIF, thus saving precious disk space or download time on the Web.

While the JPEG format may compress photographic images well, it is not well suited to line drawings or text. When such images are saved in JPEG format, there may be significant residue or artifacts. Because JPEG is so well suited to photographs and GIF to illustrations, it is no wonder that both are used on the Web. JPEG images do not support animation, nor do they support any form of transparency. Web designers needing such effects must turn to another image format, such as GIF. JPEG images do support a form of interlacing in a format called progressive JPEG. Progressive JPEGs fade in from a low resolution to a high resolution, going from fuzzy to clear. Like interlaced GIFs, progressive JPEG images are slightly larger than their non-progressive counterparts. One problem with progressive JPEGs is that older browsers, particularly those before Netscape 2.0, do not support them.

PNG Images

The PNG (Portable Network Graphics) format has all of the features of GIF89a in addition to several others. Notable features include greater color depth support, color, and gamma correction and 8-bit transparency. In addition, the compression algorithm for PNG is nonproprietary, making PNG a likely successor of GIF. Though Internet Explorer 4.0 supports inline PNG images, Netscape Communicator requires a plug-in. PNG is currently not a viable image format for general Web use, but may be in the near future.

■ Other Image Formats

There are many image formats beyond GIF, JPEG, and PNG that may be used on the Web. These include vector formats like Illustrator and Flash (.swf), compressed Freehand files, AutoCAD files (often used for architecture sites), and images that require heavy compression such as fractal or wavelet. Most of the less common image formats may require a helper application or plug-in to the browser to allow the image to be displayed. Unless there is a specific need, special image types requiring browser add-ons should probably be avoided; users may become frustrated by the work involved in obtaining the extra software.

Web Audio

Audio may also be a very important content form in a Web site. However, the representation of audio in its most basic form can create huge data files. Digital sound is measured by the frequency of sampling, or how many times the sound is digitized during a given time period. Sampling frequencies are specified in kilohertz (kHz), which indicate the sound sampling rate per second. CD quality sound is approximately 44kHz, or 44,100 samples every second. For stereo, two channels are required, each at 8 bits. At 16 bits per sample, that yields 705,600 bits of data for each second of CD quality sound. In theory, the bits of data on a CD could be delivered over the Internet, creating high-quality music at the end-user's demand. In reality, transmitting this amount of data would take nearly half a T1 line's bandwidth. Obviously, this type of bandwidth is not available to the average Web user.

One approach is to lower the sampling rate when creating digital sound for Web delivery. A sampling rate of 8kHz in mono might produce acceptable playback results for simple applications such as speech, particularly considering that playback hardware often consists of a simple soundcard and a small speaker combination. Low-quality audio requires a mere 64,000 bits of data per second, but the end user still has to wait to download the sound. For modem users, even in the best of conditions, each second of low-quality sound takes a few seconds to be delivered, making continuous sound unrealistic.

Like graphics files, audio files can be compressed to reduce the amount of data being sent. The software on the serving side compresses the data, which is decompressed and played back on the receiving end. The compression/decompression software is known together as a *codec*. Just like image formats, audio compression methods are either lossy or lossless. Lossy data compression doesn't perfectly represent what was compressed, but it's close enough, given the size savings. Since lossless compression techniques guarantee that what goes in one end comes out on the other, most cannot compress files to any significant degree. Compression always involves a trade-off between sound quality and file size; larger file sizes mean longer download times. When dealing with sound, the compression and quality is determined by the file format. There are many standard audio forms as shown in Figure 7-19.

File Format	Description
WAV	Waveform or simply "wave" files are the most common format of sound on Windows platforms. It is also possible to play back WAVs on Macs and other systems with player software.
AU	Sparc-audio or *u-law* format is one of the oldest Internet sound formats. There is a player for nearly every platform available.
AIFF	The Audio Interchange Format is very common on Macs. Widely used in multimedia applications, it is not very common on the Web
MIDI	The Musical Instrument Digital Interface format is not a digitized audio format. It represents notes and other information so that music can be synthesized. MIDI is well supported and files are very small, but it is useful for only certain applications due to its sound quality when reproduced on PC hardware.
MPEG	MPEG format is a "standard" format that has significant compression capabilities. It is not as standardized as many people might think; it lacks widespread playing and encoding acceptance, despite its quality.

Figure 7–19. Common Web Audio Formats.

Early approaches to delivering sound via the Internet followed the "download and play" model. In this scenario, users must download sounds completely before they can play them, taking up valuable harddrive space even if they only want to hear the first few seconds of a file. Sounds must be degraded significantly in this situation, which may not be acceptable for content that requires flawless playback. Even at very low sampling rates, these sounds must be fairly short in order to spare impatient users the agony of prolonged download times, though on an intranet this may not be such an issue. Download time can be reduced by creating smaller audio files, which only accentuates the drawbacks of the download and play method.

Using HTML, the simplest way to support the download and play approach is by linking to a sound file and letting another application like a helper or plug-in deal with it. If no application is configured, the user will be prompted to deal with the sound. Generally the download and play approach to audio is appropriate for small bits of sound and, since most browsers such as Netscape Navigator and Internet Explorer include players for common audio forms, this approach does not require users to install special software just to hear the sound.

There are many proprietary audio formats that can be used. Of these, RealAudio® is by far the most popular. Why use RealAudio if audio is built into the browser? Proprietary audio formats offer one thing that many "standard" digital audio formats lack—the possibility of streaming data. If it is possible to represent one second of audio in the amount of bytes that can be transmitted in one second, the data could be effectively streamed to the user continuously. So if a user could receive 2K per second—the average for a 28.8Kbps modem user—and the sound could be compressed so that one second of sound equaled 2K, then the sound could be delivered in real time, assuming the necessary bandwidth was there.

There are a few potential drawbacks to streaming audio. First, to compress audio enough for streaming, there may have to be a serious reduction in sound quality. Second, as discussed in Chapter 3, the Internet protocols themselves do not readily support the requirements of streaming, so this may not always work. If this unpredictability is acceptable, using a streaming technology like RealAudio (www.realaudio.com) would be called for.

Web Video

Like audio files, video files can be compressed to reduce the amount of data being sent. Because of the degree of compression required by video, most video codecs use a lossy approach that involves a trade-off between picture/sound quality and file size, with larger file sizes obviously resulting in longer download times.

There are three standardized video file formats used on the Web: AVI, QuickTime, and MPEG (summarized in Figure 7-20). The file format usually determines which compression technique will be used. Some file formats, such as QuickTime, allow different codecs to be selected. In some ways, this makes QuickTime the most flexible video format.

Video Format	Description
AVI	Stands for Audio Video Interleaved. This file format for digital video and audio is very common and easy to save to. A growing number of video files in AVI format are being used on the Internet, but file size of AVI is significant. Both Netscape and Internet Explorer are capable of dealing with AVIs easily.
MOV (QuickTime)	MOV is the file extension that indicates the use of Apple QuickTime format. Probably the most common digital video format on CD-ROM, it continues its popularity on the Internet. QuickTime has a strong following in the multimedia development community. Various *codecs* and technology enhancements make QuickTime a strong digital video solution that may work in conjunction with MPEG.
MPEG	The Motion Picture Experts Group video format is the supposed standard format for digital video. While compression and image quality of MPEG files is impressive, it can be expensive and difficult to work with this format.

Figure 7–20. Common Web Video Forms

For download-and-play delivery, AVI and QuickTime are the safest formats for short video clips. Regardless of length, MPEG is typically the only choice for high-quality playback. AVI and QuickTime files are commonly supported via helper applications. They're even supported natively by Netscape (via LiveVideo) and Microsoft (by ActiveMovie) in a download and play style.

As with audio, many online video delivery systems follow the "download and play" model where users must download video clips completely before they can play them. Some Web video solutions allow the user to see the video as it comes down despite the slow speed; this allows users to cancel the download before it ends. Shortening video clips and reducing frame rates helps keep users from giving up during download time, but this may not be acceptable for content that requires flawless playback. Even at very low frame rates with no audio, video clips more than a few seconds long tend to exceed the patience of the average user. With download and play video, you should stick to common formats like AVI, QuickTime, or MPEG, unless the proprietary format has a wide degree of industry acceptance or provides a really motivating feature such as compression high enough to allow streaming.

Proprietary video formats offer one thing that many "standard" digital video formats lack—the possibility of streaming data. As mentioned during the audio discussion, if it is possible to represent one second of content in the amount of bytes that can be transmitted in one second, the data could be effectively streamed to the user continuously. Just like streaming audio, there are a few potential drawbacks to streaming video. First, to compress video enough for streaming, you have to sacrifice a certain degree of quality. Video files will be far larger than audio files, so the sacrifice may be much greater. Second, the Internet protocols themselves, as discussed in Chapter 3, do not readily support the requirements of data streaming.

Other Binary Formats

Besides audio and video, there are many other media forms that may be used in a Web site. The most common binary object inserted into a Web page (besides images, sounds, and video) are Adobe Acrobat files and Macromedia Shockwave files. (Adobe Acrobat files are cross-platform documents. Macromedia Shockwave files are complex multimedia files.)

■ Shockwave

One of the most popular plug-ins on the Internet is Macromedia's Shockwave for Director plug-in (www.macromedia.com). This program also comes in an ActiveX control version for use with Microsoft's Internet Explorer. Because of compatibility issues, the <EMBED> syntax should be used. Macromedia's Director authoring tool has a long history in the development of multimedia applications, including games and educational reference CD-ROMs. The program may be somewhat difficult to learn, but it is powerful enough to create any time-based animation that can be imagined.

The biggest problem with Director-built animations is that they tend to be very large. Most are built to be delivered by CD-ROM. A technology called Shockwave compresses Director files (as well as other media types like Authorware and FreeHand) for speedy delivery over the Internet. Shockwave also adds features to support interaction and playback over the Internet. To assemble a Director-based animation, a designer must create animation cells in a graphics program, put them together with Director, and compress the result with a tool called Afterburner[a] or by saving the file appropriately. The final step is to place it in a Web page with the <EMBED> element. End users with the Shockwave plug-in installed can then download and view the Director file.

The real advantage to using Director files for animation is the complexity of what can be done. As its name suggests, the program directs the flow of a program or animation. With Director, sound effects can be synchronized with animation, buttons can be activated, and games and interactive comic strips can be created.

■ Acrobat

Adobe's Acrobat technology (www.adobe.com/acrobat) is one approach to the distribution of electronic documentation. Originally proposed to help implement the mythical idea of the "paperless office," Acrobat has now matured into a product with uses both on and off the Web. Adobe Acrobat provides the capability to deliver an electronic document to an end user without requiring the reader to have the authoring environment to open the file. Visually, it preserves the exact look and feel of the document, both on-screen and in print. For design-oriented Web publishers, Acrobat provides a highly motivating alternative to HTML that easily surpasses HTML's relatively simplistic and imprecise layout features.

Acrobat files are created using a combination of traditional text authoring tools (word processors and desktop publishing software) and special Acrobat authoring software (Adobe Exchange® or Distiller®). They are then saved in a file format aptly named "portable document format," or PDF. PDF files are small, self-contained documents that can be transported in a variety of ways—by diskette, CD-ROM, or across a network. The files are read by the end user using special Adobe Acrobat Reader software. Thus, by its very nature, Acrobat Reader technology must be cross-platform. Acrobat Reader software is currently available for most major platforms. For certain content forms such as technical drawings, Acrobat is far more suitable than HTML or GIF images.

Choosing the correct technology to program a site is only half the battle. The content must also be represented appropriately. Choosing the wrong image, video, or audio format can result in huge files that the user must patiently wait to download. Some things such as complex drawings and specifications won't even work well in HTML form. While HTML and common image forms like GIF and JPEG are the most common media forms on the Web, depending on the requirements of the application other content forms must be considered.

Development Tools

After determining the technologies and content to use in implementing a site, the different tools available to implement the site should be considered. When considering tools, it is important to understand how the tool will be used. Will the tool be employed to accomplish some task like building an HTML page, or to aid in the process of building the site? If task-oriented tools are to be used, can they be integrated in a framework or must they be used alone? Lastly, if the project is to be conducted by a team, do the tools facilitate multiple users working on the same site at once?[8]

HTML Page Development Tools

HTML in first generation sites was produced mostly by hand using text editors. This process, still prevalent today, provides the most control and allows the use of the very latest tags. However, this method can be quite slow, and human coders are prone to making errors. One must know HTML well or use references to produce pages this way.

Tools have been created to aid in the HTML creation process. Tag editors were the first to appear. These were developed to enable the insertion of tags with appropriate syntax, and to enable editing of attributes and links. Some perform rigorous validation of HTML for correctness, which may be too stringent. This method can be faster than by hand, but may still require knowledge of HTML. With both tag editors and manual editing, it is difficult to actually pre-visualize a page.

HTML WYSWYG (What You See Is What You Get) tools that enable visual design of pages are one of the most misunderstood tools in the Web developer's arsenal. While these tools do not necessarily require knowledge of HTML, they provide the least amount of control over the code that is generated. The code generated is not always correct, many contain odd nuances, and can be difficult to edit by hand. Another difficulty with some of these tools is the built-in display mode for pages that do not match pages as actually rendered by browsers. In reality, the concept of WYSIWYG for the Web is not possible unless rendering environments become more regular and the final page rendering engines are incorporated directly in the editing tool. This would make the page viewing environment the same as the editing environment.

Another class of tools enables document translation from existing formats such as word processing documents in Microsoft Word® or pages laid out with Quark Xpress. Most recent versions of many document and graphics creation programs have the ability to translate or output directly to HTML. However, not all of the formatting may be maintained. It may not be translated in the

---

8. At the time of this writing, Web tools, even HTML editors, are still in their infancy. Most of the tools available are task oriented, not terribly well integrated, and are often totally unsuitable for team-based task management.

way intended, and may require manual editing of the HTML. Figure 21 provides a summary of the different types of HTML development tools.

HTML Markup Method	Pros	Cons
By Hand	Strict control Able to use latest tags	Error prone Slow Must know HTML well
Translators	Able to convert existing documents quickly	May still require hand or editor cleanup
Tag Editors	Tight control Faster than by hand	Still need to know HTML Difficult to pre-visualize the page Syntax checkers might feel constrictive
WYSIWYG Editors	Easy to use Knowledge of HTML not necessary other than to potentially fix improperly output HTML	Often behind in tag support Generated files may be hard to hand edit Not really WYSIWYG

Figure 7–21. Summary of HTML Page Generation Tools

Web CASE-Like Tools

Many Web tools approach the site from a single page at a time. This is counterintuitive, as most Web sites can be viewed as entire projects with additional requirements as well. There are tools that take this approach to development of an entire site. Some tools allow for the high-level construction and visualization of different site modules and their relationship with others. These will also visually show hyperlink relationships between modules. Some tools support team development and mechanisms for controlling different versions of sites. It may also be worthwhile to use scheduling or project management software in tandem with the development process.

Tools also need to support documents and technologies other than HTML and their integration into sites. Some tools function like visual application builders and allow drag-and-drop of components, including HTML, scripts, and ActiveX controls or JavaBeans. There may also be support for server-side scripting and programming technologies and database integration as well.

Tools that take this comprehensive approach to development are akin to rapid application development tools. Already there is too much implementation focus on the front end of Web sites. RAD tools only tempt page developers with the idea that the back end is a few clicks of a wizard away. In reality, the more mature database tools come from the traditional client/server environment and will probably require some custom development to hook into Web sites.

Tools for Managing and Preparing Media for the Web

In addition to development tools, there are a variety of tools that are used to fit media content to the Web and provide media management facilities. These include graphics tools that provide a variety of functions such as producing image maps; converting files into standard Web formats such as GIF, JPEG, and PNG; reducing the number of colors used; or providing color matching. Web project team members focused on interface and graphic design tend to use tools like Adobe PhotoShop and Illustrator®, Macromedia FreeHand®, and others that come from the traditional desktop publishing environment in conjunction with special plug-ins or utilities to help prepare files for the Web. Now that Web visual design is more commonplace, many of these tools support Web output natively, allowing visual designers to work in an environment they are comfortable with. Beyond illustration and photo manipulation tools, multimedia tools, as well as specialized audio and video encoding tools might also be used in some Web projects.

Assembling the Beta Site

It is helpful to think of sites in terms of "beta" and final versions. A beta site is a candidate site that is tested and changed before being approved as the final or release version of a site. A beta site provides a checkpoint from which to test the correctness and acceptability of the site. Just developing a site and considering it in final form is not the right approach. Before building the site, it is helpful to establish coding conventions and address project management issues. Media must be prepared for the Web before it can be integrated into a site with HTML. After the HTML skeleton is in place, programming modules and content must be added to the site. Testing is required from both developer and working system perspectives.

Once the assembly stage is finally reached, people are often eager to get started. However, before launching into coding and page markup, it is important to establish conventions such as naming and addressing issues of version control. A little forethought at this stage in the process can prevent problems later. Guidelines and standards for coding practices and file naming are imperative when multiple people are working on a project. A set of conventions should be published and made available to developers.

Naming Conventions

Naming conventions must be established at the beginning of a project. On a directory level, determine how the structure will be established. Logical directory structures for sites should be created with meaningful names that describe the high-level module that contains related files. Directory names such as "About," "Products," and "Services" are far more explanatory than names like "Dir1," and "Dir2." Appropriate subdirectories underneath should be created. The "Products" directory may contain subdirectories with names for specific products such as "Gadgets" or "Widgets."

In addition to proper directory naming, a scheme for file naming should be established. Decide on whether the file extension for HTML documents will be .html or .htm. The only reason to choose one over the other might be the legacy problem with file extensions with more than three letters. Otherwise, the choice of three- or four-letter file extensions is more dependent on operating system conventions and personal preference. Set guidelines for the use of upper- and lowercase letters in file names. Like directories, file names can be case sensitive. Determine what the name of the default file in each directory should be. Depending on the server, it may be *index.htm*, *default.htm* or some variation of these.

HTML Markup Conventions

Within each HTML document, it is also good practice to maintain consistency in style. Within an organization where many people may work on the same file, a uniform method of coding can be very helpful. HTML style issues cover syntax and good practices, as well as the overall appearance of the document. It is a common software engineering practice to include a *comments* header in the file that contains relevant information such as what the file is, what it contains, and who authored it. This information can be included between comment tags. Revision notes can be included in code with brief descriptions of what revision was made, who made it and the date. Names of those who made revisions can provide a reference for the appropriate people to contact concerning changes. A list of external files required or used in the HTML document can be helpful. A sample heading template is shown in Figure 7-22.

```
<!--
   Document Name: IRORI Home Page [index.htm]
   Author: PINT
   Coder: D. Whitworth
   Creation Date: April 9, 1997


  Document Requires:
  Images
---------

          tile2.gif [body background image]
          homelogo.gif
          hometext.gif
          HNabout.gif
          HNproducts.gif
          HNsitemap.gif
          HNcontact.gif
          HNYabout.gif
          HNYproducts.gif
```

(Continued)

```
            HNYforcust.gif

            HNYindref

            HNYsitemap.gif

            HNYcontact.gif

            space.gif


Modification History:

4/9/97 Created page DW

5/20/97 META info modified TAP

6/26/97 New intro paragraph image set DW

10/1/97 JavaScript modified for IE 4.0 compatibility  JTAM


-->
```

Figure 7–22. Sample HTML Comment Heading.

The actual style of HTML coding will play a role in the maintainability—and potentially in the correctness— of the page. HTML is not case sensitive, so this leaves room for a variance of styles. However, consistency in case provides readability. Uppercase is recommended over lower case because it makes the markup tags more obvious in contrast to the content they are identifying. Using tools to generate HTML may result in code that does not follow conventions. Some tools produce outright strange results. Attribute values should be in quotes and listed in alphabetical order to facilitate the adding, changing or modifying of attributes. Though browsers are very lenient in their interpretation of tags, it is good practice not to cross tags. For example, instead of <B><I>Test</B></I> where the tags are crossed, nest the tags like so: <B><I>Test</I></B>. Crossing tags could become a serious problem in the future as DHTML may not allow manipulation of nonconforming document objects.

Within code, there are links to other files and addresses. External addresses on other servers must be absolute links, as they are not relative to the current page displayed on the same server. Absolute links should be avoided for addresses on the same site. Relative links and file paths should be used. This makes the site more portable and maintainable than it would be with absolute links.

In addition to the specific syntax conventions such as casing, an overall structure style can make the file easier to understand. Indentation levels can be used to indicate where certain elements begin and end. Also, some HTML elements do not require end tags and it is possible to simplify structure in certain cases. The code examples in Figure 7-23 show how formatting affects the readability and ease of comprehension of code.

Poor Formatting	Structured Formatting
<TABLE><TR><TD>Row 1- Cell 1</TD><TD>Row 1- Cell 2</TD></TR> <TR><TD>Row 2 - Cell 1</TD> <TD>Row 2 - Cell 2</TD> </TR> </TABLE>	<TABLE> <TR> <TD>Row 1 - Cell 1 <TD>Row 1 - Cell 2 <TR> <TD>Row 2 - Cell 1 <TD>Row 2 - Cell 2 </TABLE>

Figure 7–23. HTML Formatting Example.

Indentation is not the only way to create readable code. Leaving white space and adding comments can also be helpful.

While the previous examples all refer to controlling the formatting and appearance of the HTML source document, style guides can also be used to ensure that specific information is included in each file. For example, it is usually beneficial to include metainformation in Web pages. This provides information about the Web pages themselves: the author, date of creation, subject covered, keywords, and so on. Metainformation can be used to provide a framework for content management and is essential to searching, as discussed in Chapter 9. The style guide can specify this. Likewise, copyright information should be included on all pages. To avoid repeated coding of these standard elements, templates can be developed that reflect the style guide. Templates should contain the basic information that is standard to every file. However, they should be generic enough so that information that is not applicable is not included. Be careful when copying and pasting code from one file to the next. It is easy to forget to change details such as the document title and descriptive information. Templates are key to dynamically generated pages as they can be built and pieced together into unique documents.

Scripting Style and Approaches

The guidelines that should be followed with scripting concern consistent naming conventions and coding styles, especially when teams are involved in development. Some form of naming conventions for functions and variable names using meaningful labels, as well as a style based on a notation such as the *under_score* style (e.g., _mysalesform) or *caseMix* style (e.g., mySalesForm), can be helpful. Coding styles should maintain some sense of structure and organization. Comments should be used to increase readability. There are also decisions about whether to place braces ({}) around code blocks or to use semicolons (;) at the end of lines, which is optional in some scripting languages like JavaScript. Other languages like VBScript do not require semicolons. Many of these issues, like the HTML style discussion, are simply matters of style, but some sort of standards should be set to facilitate readability and maintainability.

JavaScript's case-sensitivity should be noted. This can be troublesome for Web developers who often use mixed case tags in HTML. JavaScript, on the other hand, will distinguish between alert("hello"), and Alert(hello). The capitalized example should result in an error using Netscape. JavaScript is also very sensitive to carriage returns, since they signify the end of a block of code. If a line is very long, code may need to extend beyond the point at which it wraps. Unintentional line breaks within code will cause errors. Spaces are usually acceptable in JavaScript, so tabs and spaces should be used to space out scripts.

JavaScript is not backward-compatible with earlier versions. Some browsers won't even support it at all. In order to provide compatibility with browsers that support older versions of the language, scripts written using features from newer versions must use the LANGUAGE attribute in the <SCRIPT> tag to specify which version is being used. Potentially incompatible code should be hidden within comments to allow older browsers to ignore scripts with language versions they do not support. Multiple <SCRIPT LANGUAGE="">

tags with different codes that use the same function names for different versions can be included. This way, functions can be referenced by the same name to call the appropriate version. Different scripting language versions should be listed in the order of oldest to newest as browsers will use the code for the latest version listed. Another approach is to use code to check which version of a browser a person is using and then execute a particular piece of code depending on the result. A few scripting approaches useful in creating cross platform scripts are shown in Figure 7-24.

Comment out JavaScript to avoid old browser interpretation.	<pre><SCRIPT LANGUAGE="JavaScript">
	<!--
	 Script code here
	// -- >
	</SCRIPT></pre>

Use the LANGUAGE attribute and fall through concept with the same names version of code.	<pre><SCRIPT LANGUAGE="JavaScript">
	function DoSomething()
	 {
	 // Simple version
	 }
	</SCRIPT>
	<SCRIPT LANGUAGE="JavaScript1.2">
	function DoSomething()
	 {
	 // Complex version
	 }
	</SCRIPT></pre>

Determine browser version and use conditional statements.
 	
Note: The example shows a simplified version of this that does not account for the browser type, only the version.
	<pre><SCRIPT LANGUAGE="JavaScript">
	if (navigator.appVersion.charAt(0) ==
	'4')
	 {
	 // Do 4.0 stuff
	 }
	else
	 if (navigator.appVersion.charAt(0) ==
	'3')
	 {
	 // Do 3.0 stuff
	 }
	else
	 {
	 // Do 2.0 stuff
	 }
	</SCRIPT></pre>

Figure 7–24. Browser-Compatible Scripting Approaches.

Image Conventions

Like HTML files, graphics should be named appropriately. Graphics can be classified by type. There are background images ("tiles"), buttons, and navigation bars, as well as other elements. Saving all graphics to the default directory for images makes it easy to specify the path to the file. Using a naming scheme that reflects what type of graphic it is helps identify images as well as expedites the development process. Since the person who creates the graphics is rarely the person who is coding the HTML, a naming scheme can be very useful to the programmer.

The following paragraph illustrates one possible naming scheme for elements in a site. A single letter inserted can distinguish a slight variation between similar graphics. For example, ICONnew.gif is the name of the image that is the icon for the New section. When that is the current section, the icon should be disabled, or *grayed out,* to indicate that. Simply putting a G (for *gray*) in front of the image name indicates this difference. Similarly, the heading for the New section has an H (for *heading*) as a prefix. This type of consistent naming scheme keeps images well-organized within a directory. When listed alphabetically, similar images are adjacent to each other. Figure 7-25 shows a brief sampling of media files named in a logical fashion.

Icons at top of page	Icons that are "gray" to indicate that is the current section	Headings
ICONnew.gif	GICONnew.gif	Hnew.gif
ICONproducts.gif	GICONproducts.gif	Hproducts.gif
ICONjobs.gif	GICONjobs.gif	Hjobs.gif

Figure 7–25. Graphics Naming Example.

It may be helpful to have a list of all graphics used in the site. This list should include each graphic's dimensions to facilitate specifying height and width information for the images as well as any other information that the HTML coder might need. If the site is dynamic, providing different views based on user conditions and graphics may even be saved in varying resolutions and bit depths. A logical naming structure will make it far easier to create programs to insert the files automatically. There may be other media files,

245

such as sound and video, used within a site. These files should also follow a logical naming scheme.

The Implementation Process

Once conventions have been determined, it is time to start putting the beta site together. Integration of all the elements that make up a Web page (text content, HTML, programmed elements, and images) can occur in a variety of orders, but preparing images first, then HTML, then integrating programming facilities, and lastly incorporating content and adding polish seems to be the best way of going about building the candidate site.

Prepping the Images

The result of the prototyping stage of the Web Engineering process, as discussed in Chapter 5, was an approved design for the site. Typically, when developing the basic site design composite, single large graphic files such as PhotoShop documents are used to convey a general look-and-feel. In order to build the beta site, any visual design must be reformatted for the Web. Graphical mock-ups in formats such as PhotoShop Documents (PSDs) will have to be cut up into individual image elements as they would appear on a page. Additionally, graphics must be optimized for the Web. This involves reducing the number of colors in an image to lower bit levels, from 8-bit to 6-bit or 5-bit, which will reduce file sizes significantly. Optimizing the images for Web delivery also involves making sure that browser-safe colors are used. Netscape has a 216 color-safe palette. It is important to use hexadecimal color values (e.g., #FF0000) as opposed to color names (e.g., red) for background, font, and table cell colors. Browsers may arbitrarily render names such as "Deep Dark Purple" as opposed to producing a standardized color determined by an RGB value. Just as images are prepared for the bandwidth-sensitive Web, sound and video generally must be downsampled to achieve an acceptable download time and then converted to a supported Web format.

Coding the HTML

The next step in assembling the beta site is the actual coding of the HTML and integrating the prepared media. As mentioned earlier, different people subscribe to different HTML design philosophies. HTML is not a real programming language; it is a markup language. It does have a syntax that need not be strictly followed. Different browsers interpret HTML in varying ways. However, HTML can benefit from the same good coding practices that apply to conventional programming languages. A style guide should be developed so that the HTML is consistent for a project regardless of the number of people contributing, and so tools can be used to facilitate coding.

One general approach that is useful for building a site is to build a page template with the navigation and headings for the page. This template may be populated with mock text, images, and other media forms in order to provide a sense of what the page will look like. The template should then be carefully expanded to account for browser differences. Once the template provides the desired rendering, it can be used to create the site. Using a template-driven approach to HTML page design keeps pages consistent, allows for tool-based page population, and facilitates migration to a database-driven Web site.

Integrating Programmed Modules

It is typical to first develop a skeletal HTML structure for a site with placeholders for the parts that require programming. Programmed modules can be developed separately from the rest of the site and later integrated. A sensible approach is to develop the programmed modules to correctly work with stubs before moving them to their real context in the site. This way the focus is on developing proper functionality before integrating it into its final form. In a team approach, designers may build the visual interface that goes on top of the separately-developed program module.

Incorporating the Content

Because of the amount of effort that goes into the technical implementation of the site, it is sometimes easy to overlook the content: the text, images, and other informational aspects of a Web site. While the structure of the site is being built, mock text should be used as a placeholder in Web pages. Avoid incorporating actual text until the site is close to completion. Keeping content and presentation separate will make it easier to make changes to each if needed. Creating a directory structure for the text that mirrors the sections of the Web site can be helpful. Make sure to proofread the text before flowing it into the HTML documents. Furthermore, all pages should be spell-checked using automated tools, if available. Far too many sites are ruined by major typographical errors directly on the home page.

The effort required to collect content for Web sites is often underestimated. If content does not exist, creating it can be very time-consuming. Even if the content does exist, it may need to be rewritten for the Web just as images have to be saved in a different format. The problem with print-based content is that it is often not well suited for reading online. Newspapers employ the inverted pyramid writing style. This also works well for the Web. Instead of starting with the basics and gradually building to the conclusion, the inverted pyramid presents the conclusion first and follows it with supporting information. This is especially important on the Web, because it has been determined that users read 25 percent more slowly on screen than on paper and, as a result, tend not to read on screen. Consequently, content that is intended for online consumption must be concise and direct. Research suggests that writing documents that will be read online to be scanned rather than read can improve usability and understanding dramatically [(2) Morkes and Nielsen 98]. Font choice, which is discussed below, also may play a role in screen readability.

It is important to anticipate whether users will likely consume the content online or off-line. If the document is long and will be read online, separating the copy into multiple linked pages that don't scroll may facilitate reading. Information that will be read offline should be provided as one, long scrolling page that lends itself to printing.

Text formatting is an important part of implementation and should be considered part of the user interface. The way words are presented affects their ease of perception. For example, it is difficult to read bodies of text that are in all caps because there is no variety and the paragraph tends to turn into a visual blob. Likewise, text that is centered or right-aligned is problematic because lines of different lengths force the readers' eyes to jump around in order to find the beginning of the next line. While columns are usually intended to make reading easier, columns that are too thin present problems because they create too many pauses and hyphenated words. Fonts can also make a huge difference in the readability of text. Serif fonts, such as Times and Courier, typically are used for printed body copy but don't necessarily render well on screen at small size. Documents made for screen reading may be more readable in a sans-serif font such as Helvetica or Arial. In addition, issues of contrast between text and background should be well considered; things should generally be made bigger if they are to be read on screen. Once content has been added to the site and polished for proper use, it is time to begin the testing process.

Developer Test

The result of the implementation phase should be a beta version of a site. If a modular development approach is used, each module may be tested independently of the whole system in a unit test. The developer should perform general testing for proper functionality and look and feel according to requirements and design document specifications. At this point, a "code walk-through" may be appropriate to determine the correctness of the HTML code and of the programming techniques. The developer may go over both aspects of the site in detail, in some cases even line by line. Developers may use tools such as HTML validators that check the syntax of tags, link checking tools, and programming syntax checkers. Lists of errors from the developer's perspective should be compiled and corrected before undergoing a more rigorous system test or presenting the site to end users.

Summary

Web site engineering requires a thorough understanding of how to implement a site. One should first examine the requirements for building a site and understand site design philosophies. It is also important to evaluate different technologies on both the client- and server-side to determine which technologies are required and which tools can facilitate the site construction process. Technology evaluation may be difficult if the site is to integrate with backend systems or scale to high-volume use. Before assembling the beta site, management issues should be carefully considered. To support the team development process, standards should be adopted and a configuration management system used. Where programming is required, principles such as naming, comments, and code structuring should be utilized to aid in development and maintainability. Text issues should be a final consideration with the focus that writing for the Internet should be concise and direct and enable readers to easily comprehend intended information. Once assembled and tested by the developer, the beta candidate site can be passed on for more thorough testing and evaluation before release.

References

1. Powell, T., *HTML: The Complete Reference*, Osborne, Berkeley, CA, 1998.

2. Morkes, J., and Nielsen, J., *Applying Writing Guidelines to Web Pages*, http://www.useit.com/papers/webwriting/rewriting.html, 1998.

Recommended Reading

Gundavaram, S., *CGI Programming on the World Wide Web*, O'Reilly & Associates, Inc., Sebastopol, CA, 1996.

Flanagan, D., *JavaScript: The Definitive Guide*, O'Reilly & Associates, Inc., Sebastopol, CA, 1997.

Isaacs, S., *Inside Dynamic HTML*, Microsoft Press, Redmond, WA, 1997.

Linthicum, D., *David Linthicum's Guide to Client/Server and Intranet Development*, John Wiley & Sons, New York, New York, 1997.

Naughton, P., and Shildt, H., *Java: The Complete Reference*, Osborne, Berkeley, CA, 1997.

Nielsen, J., useit.com Web site, http://www.useit.com.

Orfali, R., Harkey, D., and Edwards, J., *The Essential Client/Server Survival, 2nd Edition*, John Wiley & Sons, 1996.

Seaman, P., and Cline, J., *Website Sound*, New Riders Publishing, Indianapolis, Indiana, 1996.

Chapter 8

Web Testing

This phase of Web Site Engineering involves testing sites as a whole for complete and proper functionality and content, as defined by specifications. This includes testing sites on target browser platforms and anticipating unexpected results on end-user systems and in the medium of the Web. The correctness of a Web site includes what it was designed to do and how it appears on the Web compared to other sites. The unpredictability of the Web medium can make testing Web sites a difficult practice. This area of Web development needs to be addressed more seriously, especially as Web sites begin to exhibit characteristics similar to software. Site development should embrace the use of test plans, procedures, and methodology. Avoid the mindset that deems a site tested if it loads correctly and looks superficially correct in common browsers. Remember that the ultimate testing and acceptance of a site is from the user's perspective, which points to the role of usability testing in site development.

Issues with Testing

Testing a Web site involves many issues. The most important hurdle to overcome is the Web testing attitude. Many Web developers regard testing as a low priority endeavor where things are assumed to be correct unless shown otherwise. A simple statement like "test on as many browsers as you can" is as formal as most ad hoc Web testing approaches get. To be effectively conducted, testing must take the approach that there are problems with a particular site, and that it is paramount to locate, identify, and correct any such problems.

Assumption of Correctness

Web testing often takes the incorrect approach of assuming everything is (or seems to be) correct—if it looks and loads right, it must be right. This lack of testing rigor is not surprising given that most past Web sites were simply a collection of documents linked together. In such sites, if the pages load relatively fast and look correct under most browsers, the links aren't broken, and the content is correct in spelling and presentation, the site is for all practical purposes correct. With the introduction of programmed sites, the rise of new technologies, and the proliferation of browser bugs, such simple testing is no longer acceptable. When sites do something, it is not just a matter of just seeing if the site loads—functionality must be tested. Imagine a benefits package calculation Web site. What testing issues might come up? What if the user enters bad data such as negative values or values beyond some allowed salary deduction? Shouldn't the page catch these errors? What if the user has turned off programming or scripting support? How should the site act then? Even basic static sites have major issues when you begin to consider performance of the site or esoteric browser configurations. The bottom line is that testing is getting a whole lot more complicated.

The Difficult Job of Testing

The second problem with Web testing is that many people, including developers and those in specific testing roles, regard the testing process as a tedious task to be avoided. Testing can often be a thankless job, particularly when one bug found by a manager seems to erase acknowledgment of the efforts made to catch hundreds of others before release. The rigor of proper testing is not often understood or appreciated. What should be considered paramount are the potential results of lack of testing.

While a broken link or spelling error on a Web site can leave a bad impression with a customer, a buggy site that includes programmed elements may cause browsers or systems to crash. Even worse, as sites begin to perform critical applications, the ramifications of bugs may become significant. Imagine an electronic commerce site that overcharges client shipping fees due to a software glitch. Not only is the site cheating customers, it may even invite litigation. Technical support, investor relations, employment systems, electronic commerce, and many other potential Web applications may have legal or reputation risks associated with them that bugs can bring to life.

Because of the serious ramifications of Web site bugs, Web teams need to think of testing as a priority task and apply some process or methodology to ensure adequate quality assurance. It may also be worthwhile to consider the concept of a specific Web team staff with a role of testing or quality assurance, as is the case in software engineering. Even with a testing process in hand, testing by its very nature cannot account for all possibilities and scenarios. Costs, labor, resources, and technical issues all limit the extent of testing. The costs and requirements for testing can be significant. As explained later in this chapter, the sheer number of browsers that render pages and perform slightly differently is enormous. It does not make sense to test for any and all browsers for every site. Consider the costs just to have the necessary hardware to test all the different platforms with the various versions of the two most common browsers. Then add the costs of the staff, time, and resources needed to test thoroughly. Like Web development itself, Web testing includes a compromise between what can be done and what should be done.

The Compatibility Issue

Many of the same issues, such as compatibility across platforms and multiple configuration testing, are not unique to the Web. Think about testing a new PC software application. It would seem that one would only have to test it on a few different types of platforms, such as Pentium 2, Pentium Pro, Pentium, and 486. However, clone chips exist, and different PCs don't always act the same. It is not commonly admitted, but even major applications may not load or run on all hardware configurations. A Compaq won't run all the same applications that a Dell will, and the Dell won't necessarily run all the applications a Gateway can. Conflicts abound at all levels including chip level, board level, BIOS level, and operating system level. The applications that seem to exhibit the most problems in the PC software arena are those that push the limits, most notably games. Trick code to improve speed or graphics and the use of the latest system features makes game compatibility testing a challenge. Now think of the analogous situation in the Web site world. Those sites that employ every plug-in, use the latest JavaScript or Java, and use HTML tricks to force layout are also pushing the limits. Compatibility across all platforms when using fancy tricks is impossible and rigorous testing of complex sites will certainly be difficult.

The software industry has attempted to address compatibility and testing issues with several approaches, such as standards, test labs, and platform simulators. In the Web arena, test labs will certainly be a growing business in the next few years. Some platform simulators, such as the WebTV simulator, are available, but so far Web platform simulators are difficult to come by. Under ideal circumstances, platform issues should be addressed by the adoption of standards for HTML, CSS, and other technologies by the browser vendors. So far this has not really panned out. Regardless of HTML or style-sheet specifications, the browsers simply don't work similarly enough to assume that standards conformance equals site correctness. Remember, a user isn't going to blame a browser vendor when they don't conform precisely to a particular standard. Even if standards do work themselves, and browsers begin to work consistently, the need to test for and support previous versions, rather than just the newest and best-working browser version, will be around for quite some time.

Realistic Testing

It is impossible to test every possible hardware, software, browser, and network configuration. Even when testing on a few platforms for a predetermined baseline, testing all possible user entries is impossible. A realistic approach to testing is needed. Extreme cases, such as bad or nonsensical data, can be tested for— but only in the general sense. Testing for a negative number of parts being ordered is easy. But there is always the rare chance that a particular negative number causes problems. It is impossible to test for all possible numbers.

It is impossible to enter all possible key sequences or resize a window all possible ways in a realistic amount of time. Automated Web site testing tools, combined with test plans that go after likely problem areas, can help catch most bugs, but there is no guarantee of catching everything. Web site testing should be done with a given plan in mind, in a given time-frame, within given resources, limitations, and costs, to accomplish the goal of finding problems and eliminating them. Web sites are evolving projects; changes can and always will be made. Testing should avoid potential problems, but remember that the speed of release is often important. A balance must be reached between what can be tested for by developers and testers and what can be released for outside users.

Test Plans and Procedures

The key to efficient Web site testing is a test plan. Formulation of test plans must be approached with specific goals in mind. The formality, specifics, and depth of test plans will vary depending on what is being tested. There are a variety of different tests that can be conducted to account for the various elements that comprise a Web site. *Functionality testing* ensures that the site functions properly and meets specification. Functional testing may include unit testing, integration testing, browser and configuration testing, and delivery testing. *Content testing* insures that the content of the Web site is correctly implemented; this includes visual reproduction issues, spelling, grammar, and other important details such as copyright information. *User testing* insures that the site meets user's needs and is usable. Many of the issues dealt with by testing should have been addressed in the specification, design, and development phases, and by tests performed at various stages to steer a project on the right course. One more possible form of testing for Web sites is *security testing*. While this might be considered part of functionality testing for sites that include online commerce, security can go far beyond the Web site and extend to server security, network security, physical site security, and other topics beyond the scope of this book. Leaving all forms of testing and quality assurance for the end of a project is not a good approach. Imagine determining that a database-driven site has problems with loads of more than five users at a time. If this is not discovered until the testing phase, the entire technological architecture of the site may have to be changed to rectify the performance problems. Another problem may have to do with user acceptance. Imagine implementing a whole site and finding that users do not respond well to the graphics. It is always important to test and receive feedback throughout the life-cycle of the Web project development.

A holistic approach to testing must be taken to account for the different elements in play in the underlying site. These elements should be spelled out in the test plan. This approach requires knowledge of the overall makeup of a site at different levels. It may require that documentation or information from different Web team members in various capacities (technical, design, content) be provided detailing what went into the development of specific aspects of the site. For example, on a technical level it may be necessary to know that a site uses JavaScript for client-side form validation so that JavaScript compatibility may be tested. The HTML specification conformed to should be indicated so that pages can be validated. On a design level, the screen size and color support designed for should be noted so visuals can be checked. Lastly, performance requirements such as download speed, simultaneous numbers of users, and execution speed of programmed elements should be documented. Lastly, what the site should do should be indicated so that the proper actions can be tested for. Given the requirements for the site, which are probably already documented in a design document, a test plan could be written to account for each testable feature of the site. This design document could then be distilled into a test procedure that could be given to a tester. Do not be tempted to have developers or other parties who know intimately the details of the system be the only testers. Such testers tend to miss obvious mistakes because they are "too close" to the site. From the tester's point of view, the site should be somewhat of a black box that they must make sure works. Testers should also be encouraged to go outside the test procedure and attempt to push or break the site.

Functionality Testing

Functionality tests are performed to make sure that the assertions made in the design document are conformed to and the site works as it should. Functionality testing includes unit testing, integration testing, browser and configuration testing, and delivery testing.

Unit Testing

The first phase of functionality testing is called unit testing. *Unit testing* focuses on testing only a small section or even page of a site by itself. The idea is to test each component, page, or section of the site separately and then integrate them together once they pass the unit test. Unit testing for a static HTML Web page might simply include a visual test that the page looks correct, a print test to make sure it prints properly, and HTML validation to ensure the correctness of the HTML markup. HTML validation can be handled by many sites (validator.w3.org) or tools. Link checking can also be performed at this stage but often much of the link checking must wait until the various units of the Web site are integrated.

Unit testing for an interactive page is slightly more complicated. Think about a page with forms. For the page to be considered correct, data tests must be performed to make sure the results are specified in the design document. For example, if the design document specifies that a form field should accept only positive numbers, this should be tested for. Testing does not just include making sure the field accepts positive numbers. It also deals with cases such as negative numbers or letters that obviously fall outside the base cases. Functional testing of Web pages can often be automated through the use of playback tools that record keystrokes or mouse clicks. This may be extremely important when trying to test a site that has thousands of pages. However, manual checking is preferable whenever possible.

Integration Testing

Integration testing involves testing the site after all the individual parts have been integrated. During integration testing it is especially important to make sure that consistency is achieved. Often individual pages or site pieces work and look fine, but when they are linked into a larger site subtle differences creep in. For example, font sizes, error alerts, or layout may be slightly different from page to page. Integration testing makes sure that the whole site works together. A key portion of integration testing is ensuring that all links in the site work. While manual traversal of the site is important to make sure links work and the navigation makes sense, it can be error-prone. Link checking tools are widely available, so there is generally no excuse for a broken link on launch. Don't avoid manual browsing of a site just because links can be checked. For example, navigation jumping around a page is obvious when a human browses the site. What is meant here is the positioning of the navigation on screen, notice how buttons appear to jump when moving from page to page. Tools just won't pick up such problems.

Browser Testing

One very important aspect of functionality testing is browser testing. *Browser testing* is performed to make sure that the site works properly under a particular set of browsers. As described earlier, testing sites on different browsers is problematic because it may require numerous configurations. There are literally hundreds of different browsers, but the payoff from making a site work under a specific uncommon browser is generally minor. The primary focus should be testing under browsers that are likely for the site. For many sites this will be the two major browsers, Netscape Navigator and Internet Explorer. On occasion, however, other browsers may be very important in certain situations. WebTV and AOL might be important for a consumer-oriented site. Lynx might be important for a library site with heavy ASCII terminal use. Some companies may even have legacy or odd browsers in place for users on mainframes or low-end systems. Even if the site requires testing only on Netscape Navigator and Internet Explorer, just how many versions of these are there? As of the time of this writing, both browsers have undergone four major releases (1.X, 2.X, 3.X, and 4.X)—and there are still various beta versions still floating around. There are also multiple platforms for each browser, including Macintosh (68000 and PowerPC), Windows 3.1, Windows95, Windows NT, OS/2®, and various flavors of UNIX including AIX®, Linux, SunOS®, Solaris®, and IRIX®.

Developers first need to realize that browsers are not perfect despite their functional goal of being able to render supposedly standards-based Web technologies. Most developers understand that different browsers support different technologies. For example, frames are supported by many browsers—but not by all. Certain HTML elements like <MARQUEE>, <LAYER>, <SPACER> and others are also unique to particular browsers. Even when browsers support technologies such as Java or JavaScript, bugs and subtle differences creep in between versions. JavaScript code and Java applets can be shown to be syntactically correct and still crash or operate improperly under certain browser configurations. Browser compatibility must be well considered, and a base platform should be set to design for. The base platform should have been considered during the requirements and specification phases of the project. If there is ever a question about the support of a particular browser feature, sites like BrowserCaps (www.browsercaps.com) can provide information about browser feature compatibility—at least at the HTML level. It is unreasonable to support all historically available browsers, especially considering the potential bugs they may introduce. If the site was well designed and user profiling is used as discussed in Chapter 7, testing for extreme browser cases should result in the site producing a page that warns the user of degraded or unacceptable compatibility.

Browser testing should not only encompass pages loading properly and interactive elements working, but assure that extreme cases are handled. Users should be allowed to change default browser settings such as font size, security settings, image loading, colors, and any other commonly set preferences to see if the site conforms to common use. Browser testing should also include basic browser use like bookmarking, printing, and resizing. A test called the snap test, where pages are dramatically resized, is important to see how page layout is affected under extreme conditions. It is especially important to test sites when common features like JavaScript, Java, and CSS support have been disabled at the browser level. If a site that relies on such technologies does not notice the reduction of support or does not degrade gracefully, it has failed this test. With a baseline set of browsers and tests defined, a test matrix for accounting for different issues can be devised as part of test plans. A sample filled in Web site browser test matrix is shown in Figure 8-1.

	Basic Layout	Basic Technology	Extreme Layout • Snap Test • No images • High Res • Low Res	Print Test	Feature Reduction • JavaScript Off • Java Off
Netscape 2.X					
Macintosh PowerPC	PASS	Java Failed	Cosmetic error on Low Res	PASS	PASS
Win 3.1	PASS	Java Failed	PASS	PASS	PASS
Win 95	PASS	PASS	PASS	PASS	PASS
Win NT	PASS	PASS	PASS	PASS	PASS
Solaris	FAIL	PASS	PASS	PASS	PASS
Netscape 3.X					
Macintosh PowerPC	PASS	JavaScript Failed	PASS	PASS	PASS
Win 3.1	PASS	PASS	PASS	PASS	PASS
Win 95	PASS	PASS	PASS	PASS	PASS
Win NT	PASS	PASS	PASS	PASS	PASS
Solaris	FAIL	JavaScipt Failed	PASS	PASS	PASS
Netscape 4.X					
Macintosh PowerPC	PASS	CSS Problems	PASS	PASS	PASS
Win 3.1	PASS	PASS	PASS	PASS	PASS

(Continued)

Win 95	PASS	CSS Problems	PASS	PASS	PASS
Win NT	PASS	CSS Problems	PASS	PASS	PASS
Solaris	PASS	PASS	PASS	PASS	PASS
Explorer 3.X					
Macintosh PowerPC	PASS	JavaScript Failed	Redraw problem	PASS	PASS
Win 3.1	PASS	CSS Problems	PASS	PASS	PASS
Win 95	PASS	CSS Problems	PASS	PASS	PASS
Win NT	PASS	CSS Problems	PASS	PASS	PASS
Explorer 4.X					
Macintosh PowerPC	PASS	PASS	PASS	PASS	PASS
Win 3.1	PASS	PASS	PASS	PASS	PASS
Win 95	PASS	PASS	PASS	PASS	PASS
Win NT	PASS	PASS	PASS	PASS	PASS
WebTV					
Classic	FAIL	PASS	Cosmetic issues	N/A	PASS
Enhanced	FAIL	PASS	Cosmetic issues	N/A	PASS

Figure 8–1. Example Web Site Browser Test Matrix.

Depending on the complexity of the site, browser testing may require a large battery of tests—particularly when plug-ins or other add-on features are used. Commerce-enabled sites would want to pay particular attention to security testing.

261

Configuration Testing

While browser testing deals with the majority of problems that arise between different platforms viewing the Web site, there are potentially other limitations that must be tested for. As discussed in Chapter 3, the end user environment is more complicated than simply what browser the user has. System aspects such as processor power, disk speed, and operating system issues may affect Web site use dramatically. System performance is one major consideration during configuration testing. For example, a site using client-side scripting for animation and timing may find that a particular minimum system memory and processor requirement is required to insure adequate playback. The design document should have considered what the base platform was and testing should be performed to make sure that the site works on the base platform. Testing on less powerful machines is also useful to determine how the site degrades. Testing on more powerful systems will ensure that timing issues work properly for the lucky few with the latest and greatest technology. Oddly enough, too much power has been a problem in a few instances. Some entertainment Web sites have Java applets for games, which once loaded, run far too fast on high-end equipment to be enjoyable. While speed of execution is important, it is often the speed of delivery that is the problem. This must be tested for as well.

Delivery Testing

Delivery testing involves testing the delivery of the Web site or application to the user. Delivery testing involves testing the network and server aspects of the site. This is a very important test as the network and server may significantly influence the user's perception of the site. Chapter 3 discusses the medium and conditions of the Web and the differences between the environment of the Internet versus the often more controlled or managed environments found on an intranet or extranet. During the delivery-testing phase, the environment must be revisited. It should have been addressed or thought of in implementation, but this is often not always the case; the development environment of Web sites does not often accurately mimic the actual environment in which they are deployed. For example, developers often create sites on internal or staging servers and migrate them to the real server as a final step in site delivery and then proceed to test. The hosting environment is not accounted for in internal testing. Accordingly, specifications and development should address this; testing should revisit it.

Delivery testing should address network delivery speed as well as server performance. Testing should account for end-user perception of page loading using different connection speeds. Other environmental issues, such as loss of state due to cookie file destruction or sudden disconnect, may also be important in programmed sites and may be considered part of delivery testing. The end user experience, both common and uncommon, should be tested or simulated as well as possible. This may include modem-based tests and stopwatch timing of page loads. Load should be simulated to show how a site will actually operate under a true production environment. Already many tools are available to simulate site load and benchmark server performance. Because of the lack of control over the end-user environment, load and performance testing will only ferret out fundamental problems. There may always be those users who find site performance unacceptable because of the way they connect to the Internet. Performance and network conditions can vary across the Internet and on private networks. Nonetheless, the system test as a whole should include some manner of testing for user perception. The difficulty of understanding how a user perceives the site often extends beyond user speed perceptions into user expectations based on previous browsing experience. Delivery testing attempts to simulate what a Web site will actually be like in use. However, there is no substitute for actually having users access a site, either in a controlled environment such as a usability lab or during a controlled or uncontrolled beta test.

Content Testing

Beyond functionality testing such as browser checks, it is important to check if content is in place and correct before release. Sites may need to be proofread for accuracy, grammar, and spelling. It may be very critical to carefully proofread sites where accuracy of information is important. For example, financial figures in annual reports on a corporate Web site for a publicly-traded company need to be completely accurate, as investors may make decisions based on this information. Reading the text contained within graphics for correctness is also important, as this information cannot be read by a spell checker. There are also issues of proper usage and the spelling of names of companies, products, and services. Copyright inclusion and legal disclaimers are also important and should be checked. Depending on the type of site, particularly external Web sites, there may be potential for legal exposure. A lawyer may have to review a site for liability issues. Images must also be checked to make sure they are clear and colors appear to reproduce correctly. Ownership issues of images should also be double-checked to make sure that any content may be used in the Web medium. For example, many developers wrongly guess that any stock photography used in a firm's print material can be freely reproduced on Web sites. In reality there are often extra fees depending on the medium of use. Other forms of media, like sound and video, would have similar legal checking requirements.

Rigorous checking of content should not be new to Web developers with a print background. In print media, many checks are made before going to press, including film checks, blue-line checks, and proof checks. Often, developers are lulled into the false sense that such degrees of checking aren't necessary for Web sites since they can be easily changed. This is a dangerous approach, considering that huge typos may not be spotted for weeks after a site is launched. While some users will proof-check your site for you, don't count on users bothering to tell you about the huge errors; they might just simply leave. It is the tester's job to find these errors, not the user's. One key test during the content-testing phase that is often overlooked is print testing. Make sure to print out every page of a site to ensure that it is correct on paper. Remember, because of onscreen reading difficulties, many users may opt not to read online, but print pages instead. How the user is going to use the content is just as important as what the content is and what the user might think should always be the focus of any Web site testing procedure.

User Test: Usability and Beta Testing

Thorough system testing by developers does not account for actual user activity on a Web site. User testing and feedback can only be obtained through studies of user activity. Traditional software approaches to this have involved the use of testing rooms where users are observed or videotaped while they use an application. This approach may not be for most Web sites. However, low cost usability testing, including having someone who isn't familiar with a site use it and comment, may provide many of the benefits of rigorous usability testing without the expense. Be careful not to confuse a usability test with a beta test. When releasing a site for limited availability to a core group of users, the use of the site may not mimic true use. Beta testing may be more intense or critical than real world use if a viewer is trying to find bugs; it may be much less if the user is simply trying the site out to get a sense of it. A beta test is a great way to get a first impression, but don't be tempted to release a site simply to get feedback to fix problems. Remember that a beta test of a seriously broken site may leave a negative impression or convince users not to use the site in the future. Don't make beta periods too long. The site must ship, and experience shows that long beta periods often lead to diminishing returns in the receipt of information about bugs or features users don't like or don't understand. The bugs and feature requests can be documented and then dealt with. Remember, there is plenty of time for more feedback during the maintenance phase as discussed in Chapter 9. It may even be possible to employ site tracking software that tracks user movement throughout sites to study patterns of usage. These types of studies could address any number of things based on site requirements. For example, the activity of users entering sites at different points and how well they navigate throughout a site could be used to test the effectiveness of a navigation scheme.

The Result of Testing

The point of testing is to uncover problems with a site. Invariably, bugs will be found and new features suggested. As testing proceeds, any bugs uncovered should be tracked and potentially dealt with. A bug tracking system is generally necessary for large projects so that bug fixes can be monitored. Bug information should be carried on into future test plans and testing phases to eliminate possible redundancy in testing and problem correction efforts. Once a bug is fixed, the page or module where the bug was found must be retested. Re-testing of corrected aspects of a system is generally termed *regression testing*. Developers should be careful to always retest after making fixes, since any changes may introduce new bugs.

While it would seem that any bugs found should be corrected before release, it often is not possible to do so. Remember, time is often a critical issue for Web sites. Testing may bring up difficult decisions. Continuing to fix every bug that appears and add every new feature suggested can delay site delivery dates—potentially indefinitely. The site must ship, so decisions must be made. When a bug is encountered there are three choices of how to deal with it. The first is to fix the bug either directly or through some work-around. The second choice is to redesign the site to avoid the bug. This choice may result in drastic cutting in a site to eliminate buggy sections. The last choice is to ignore the bug and ship the site. While ignoring problems may be the easiest choice, at least in the short term, it can lead to bigger problems down the line, and risks alienating the visitors who visit the site and find everything broken or under construction. Judging by the number of sites with "under construction" statements and broken links, this advice is often ignored. To determine the best course of action, bugs must be prioritized based upon factors such as severity or occurrence rate. Those bugs that are significant, such as system crashes or incorrect functionality, generally must be dealt with. Others may wait until the maintenance phase to be corrected.

Summary

The testing phase should yield an improved site that is relatively free of defects and ready to be delivered. By recognizing a greater degree of testing in Web sites and using some methodology and planning, the testing process should produce results that can be used effectively in site development. Various tests at the browser and system level should be conducted. The degree of testing will vary depending on site requirements. It is vital to conduct tests during all phases of a site's development; saving testing until the last moment can lead to disaster. The most important consideration for testing is real-world use, which considers the environment of the Web as well as user expectations. From the user's point of view, what appears to be a bug or a poor design choice is just as bad as a real defect. Once defects are uncovered by internal testing or user testing, they must be tracked, evaluated, and fixed, assuming the schedule permits. Once site defects are at an acceptable level a site can be released, and new features and bugs will be dealt with during a future maintenance testing period.

Recommended Reading

Apple Computer, Inc., Haykin, R., ed., *Multimedia Demystified*, Apple-New Media Library, Random House, New York, NY, 1994.

Linthicum, D., *David Linthicum's Guide to Client/Server and Intranet Development*, John Wiley & Sons, New York, NY, 1997.

Nielsen, J., *Usability Engineering*, AP Professional, Boston, MA, 1993.

Chapter 9

Post-Development: Promotion and Maintenance

After extensive testing, the site is ready to be launched for the intended audience. While the initial site development may have seemed trying, post-launch maintenance and enhancement can be equally demanding. The life-cycle of a Web site is *not* simply develop, launch, and maintain. First, the site must be used. Promoting the site can help users find the site and use any new features developed. In addition to promotion and general upkeep, a site must be enhanced and further developed to suit the changing needs of its developers and users. However, in order to determine what this audience wants, some sort of feedback is required. The real-world use of a site will determine what changes are appropriate. Through user feedback, problems will be discovered and new features will be requested. Feedback can be obtained directly via user input or indirectly in the form of statistics. The waterfall method works well for initial site development. Maintenance and evolutionary development typically follow the spiral model discussed in Chapter 2. Depending on the scope of the modifications, more significant changes might be better handled by the structured approach of the waterfall method.

Promotion and How People Find Sites and Information

Although the maintenance and growth of a site are the main focus of this chapter, it is important to acknowledge the reality of the need for promotion. In the practical sense, Web promotion addresses how users actually find the information or functionality they are seeking, whether it is at a new site or within a known one. Most Web developers and marketing professionals agree that promotion is appropriate for consumer-oriented public Web sites. It is also interesting to see how promotion relates to other types of sites and how people find the information for which they are looking.

Promotion for Intranets and Extranets

Even though intranets and extranets are not geared to the general public, promoting these sites *is* very important. To ensure the success of a Web project, the site's intended audiences must be made aware of its availability. For an intranet site, promotion might involve sending e-mails to the staff or holding training classes to make employees aware of the functionality offered by the intranet. If an existing intranet is in place, it may be possible to leverage its popularity to promote new sites. Cross-linking by placing a link to a department page on the main corporate intranet Web site is a good way to build traffic. Lastly, setting up users' browsers to start on the corporate page is probably the best way to encourage people to at least look at the internal site.

Extranet sites are typically built with a specific audience in mind to increase communication between a company and its partners, distributors, or customers. As a communication mechanism, an extranet can really only be successful if there is participation on both ends. Users of an extranet site may be made aware of the site via e-mail, training classes, or other non-Web forms of communication. Web-based promotion of extranets is often limited by their private nature. Mentioning an order-tracking extranet system on a public corporate Web site might seem like a good way to alert partners to the existence of a new facility, but it also encourages other parties, like competitors or just the curious, to "knock on the door." As extranets bridge the gap between the trusted audience of an intranet and the potentially unsafe public, care must be taken in their promotion.

Generally, promotion of intranet sites or even extranet sites is relatively easy because the audience is a known quantity. However, informing users about a site is not the same thing as encouraging them to use it. Sometimes an internal Web site application is used to replace an existing system. Convincing users to start or continue using a new Web-based method may not be automatic. To gain "buy-in" from management and users, proof of benefit as well as continued promotion may be necessary.

Promotion for Public Web Sites

For major Web sites geared toward the general public, word-of-mouth and print, television, or radio advertisements seem to be the main conduits for promotion. In addition, attraction by reputation provides another means of getting people to visit a site. If people are aware of and interested in a business or company with a *real-world* presence, there is a good possibility that they will attempt to access the company's *online* presence.

A corporate Web site with a niche audience might be best promoted by including the URL of the Web site on company materials such as marketing literature, print advertisements, and business cards. Promotional efforts for a corporate Web site should leverage existing marketing materials because they already target the appropriate users. Perhaps promoting the site to existing customers will introduce them to value-added benefits offered by the Web site and provide another means for the company to do business. The site might also be used to provide additional information to prospective customers and in that way, improve the likelihood the prospect may do business with the firm.

In addition to leveraging existing marketing efforts, horizontal linking can be an effective method of promoting a corporate Web site. In most industries, print directories and online publications provide lists of relevant industry links. Where feasible, it makes sense to put a reference to a corporate site where a prospective customer might already be browsing on the Web. For example, a person searching for information on a specific type of electrical component probably frequents online electrical engineering sites. Placing a link or advertisement at such a site can improve the likelihood of a prequalified visit. Of course, placing a link at a related site may not be free. In addition, determining which related site to obtain a link from is just as difficult as choosing a magazine in which to advertise. Remember that users of the Web are not always purely browsing. They often task-browse, looking around trying to accomplish a specific goal. Don't expect random users to simply stumble onto sites and find something to do. Respect users and make sure to help a user accomplish a task or fulfill a goal.

Searching

Beyond promoting the site to ensure that the appropriate people know that it exists, it is important to make sure that people can find the site if they look for it, and locate what they need once they get there. If users know to visit sites but are not made aware of the information or features that interest them, they may eventually stop using those sites. Features like "What's New" sections, internal search tools, and automatic notifications of changes may help encourage use, as discussed in the previous section, but it may take more hand-holding and training to get users to actually use a site or visit new sections. A heavy emphasis is often placed on the use of search engines and directories for users to initially discover a site. While there is some truth to the fact that end users may rely on search queries to find information, the quality of such searches is suspect; it is currently very difficult to guarantee ideal placement in search results.

▪ Problems with Web Searching

Searching the Web is difficult mainly because there is little structure in Web documents. Imagine a search query for the phrase "Florida orange juice." Different search engines will return very different results, as shown in Figure 9-1. But how were the results generated? The basic idea is that a program, often called a robot, spider, or crawler, traverses the Web and attempts to create an index of the documents found. However, determining what a particular document is about is somewhat difficult. The indexing program may look at the title of the document, the number of times that a particular word appears, or any metainformation as indicated by the HTML element <META>. Unfortunately, this is a very inexact approach. A document may contain the words "Florida," "orange," and "juice" but not be about this topic. This hints at the inherent problem of search engines.

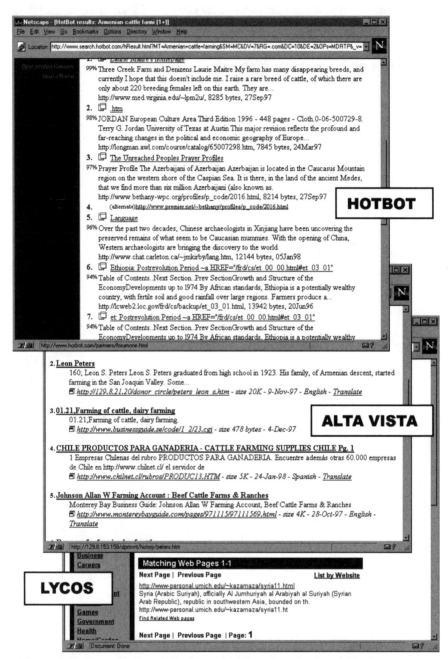

Figure 9–1. Example Search Rankings for Three Popular Search Engines.

While search engines may use different heuristics such as the frequency or proximity of words to determine what a page is about, without the interference of human intelligence, these approaches often fail. Think about two documents: one discusses the baseball team, the San Diego Padres, and the other recounts the history of San Diego, which includes a discussion of the padres and priests who founded the missions in the area. If a user enters a query for "San Diego Padres," both would be returned. Adding the word baseball should improve the quality of the search, but there are still problems. Even if all the documents about the San Diego Padres baseball team are returned, there is a question of quality. Shouldn't the official Padres Web site come high in the query result? Human intervention could improve the quality of the search result by ranking the results, but it is unreasonable to think that a large document space like the Web could be manually indexed. Adding structure to documents could improve the searching process dramatically.

Meta Information

Meta information is "information about information." Information on the Web often involves many pieces of associated descriptive information which is not always explicitly represented in the resource itself. Examples of descriptive meta information include the creator of a document, the document's subject, the publisher, the creation date, and even the title. When used properly, descriptive meta information has many benefits. It can make information easier to locate by providing search tools with more detailed indexing information and rating information to protect minors from viewing indecent content, as well as a variety of other things.

HTML's primary support for meta information is through the <META> element, which allows authors to add arbitrary forms of meta data. Although there are many different classes of meta data, there are some well-understood values that have meaning to Web search tools. Specifically, *keywords* and *description* are the two that are important in relation to search tools and how a site is indexed.

The description should be a short summary of the company or Web site (see example below). Some search engines will use the META description as the short summary they return when listing the site in search results. Often, the summary of sites without META description information consists of the first few lines of text on the Web site, which may not provide an accurate or coherent description.

Keywords can be included to provide specific words for indexing by search engines. Keywords specified in the META information should be based on the words that a person trying to find your site might enter into a search engine. For example, a Web page about the San Diego Padres baseball team might use the following meta information:

```
<META NAME="description" CONTENT="San Diego Padres Baseball Team
home page">

<META NAME="keywords" CONTENT="San Diego, Padres, Baseball,
Qualcomm Stadium, MLB, Major League Baseball, National League">
```

Information included in the <META> element can affect how a site appears in a list of results from a search tool. It would seem that meta information provides the mechanism to add structured data to a page. However, there are significant problems. Because everyone wants their site to appear as the first result of a search query, people try to defeat search engine indexing algorithms by seeding their pages with extra words (often made to match background colors) or loading the <META> elements with numerous keywords. Some sites go so far as to use unrelated words, commonly typed words, or even names of competitors to improve their chance for page views. Such "spider baiting" makes Web cataloging very difficult. A phone book mentality is strong in those who believe in search-engine-based marketing. Notice how many firms want to be first in the list of services in the phone book, and use names like AAA-1 Pest Control. Many people seem to think the Web works the same way. However, there is a problem with this idea on the Web—it's a world wide directory. Given its scope, there could be hundreds if not thousands of firms all vying to be first in a global search for a particular service. The benefit provided to the potential customer as companies fight for first place, combined with the overwhelming number of search results, shows that marketing by today's search methods won't work much longer. A standardized format for meta data, as well as a naming authority to help categorize information, would go a long way to improving search results. On the Internet at large, it will be difficult to reach a consensus on how meta information should be used. However, within an organization or group of organizations, the outlook is more favorable.

Adopting a corporate meta information and information structuring policy is an important step in improving the long-term maintainability of a large information space. Because private organizations will not have to compete with all the other documents in Web space, they should take advantage of the ability to control the indexing of documents. The first step is to adopt a unique naming scheme for documents. Do not assume that a URL is unique enough to describe a document. For example, what happens when the same document lives in more than one place on the network? Just as a book has an ISBN number, a unique document identifier should be bound to each Web page where applicable. (Note: The use of dynamic documents complicates the use of document identifiers.) Other important meta information might include title, author, department, creation date, expiration date, keywords, summary, and so on. It may be possible to use the HTML <META> element or even a corporate XML (Extensible Markup Language) vocabulary to structure data. The technology used and actual structure of the meta information is important, but often the biggest problem is enforcing the document structure. Within organizations or even within trade groups, it may be possible to encourage particular document structuring styles. Unfortunately, widespread adoption of meta data is often a slow process; internal politics may be far more of a problem than technology. Content structure and organization should be considered one of the significant problems facing the Web. Promotion and realistic use of search engines and directories will help users find and hopefully use a site. However, once people start to visit and use a site, problems will be detected and changes suggested.

Maintenance

Web sites can be thought of as "living entities" that require some form of maintenance, though the degree of maintenance may vary significantly from site to site. Maintenance can be generally described as any development activity performed to modify or fix the Web site after it has been completed or reached some milestone, such as its first major release. Software maintenance and, correspondingly, Web site maintenance should be further classified by the reason for performing the maintenance into the following forms: perfective, adaptive, preventive, and corrective [(1) Gorla 91]. *Corrective maintenance* is performed to fix bugs and design deviations in an existing system. *Preventive maintenance* is done in order to avoid future bugs or maintenance. *Adaptive maintenance* is performed when a system's environment changes, such as when a new browser is released and the system must be modified in order to function properly within that environment. *Perfective maintenance* is used to introduce enhancements such as new functionality or increased efficiency to the system. Remember that, in the case of a Web site, the site also includes content features as well as application features, so we need to introduce the idea of *content maintenance*. Content maintenance, which deals with keeping site content fresh and correct, includes perfective and corrective maintenance. Web projects also includes *delivery maintenance*, which is concerned with the hosting of a site on a server and delivery of a site across a network.

Maintenance Costs

Software maintenance can be extremely costly to perform. Maintenance can take up to 50 percent of an organization's total programming effort and account for up to 70 percent of a software product's lifetime costs [(2) Lientz and Swanson 80]. Casual observation suggests that Web site maintenance cost issues are no different. In general, system maintenance is often costly because of the frequency with which it must be performed and because it is a difficult and error-prone task. Studies indicate that changes to an existing program (maintenance) are three times as error-prone as writing new code [(3) Landsbaum and Glass 92]. Web site designers should attempt to reduce future maintenance costs through proper technology choice, use of structured design, and implementation of consistent markup and coding styles. However, maintenance costs are also related to many nontechnical factors such as site familiarity, developer skill, communication, and documentation, as shown in Figure 9-2.

Nontechnical	Technical
Site Familiarity	Programming Language
Developer Quality	Markup Language
Communication	Page/Site Structure
Documentation	Coding/Markup Style

Figure 9–2. Factors Influencing Maintenance Costs.

Structure—of programs, pages, and sites—is the most influential technical aspect of a Web site affecting maintenance costs. Unanticipated changes introduced over time result in structural degradation of sites. Observations indicate that, as a program's structure degrades, the costs of making changes to the system increase exponentially with the system's age [(4) Belady and Lehman 76]. As Web sites age, such cost characteristics are likely to be the same. For the moment, many Web sites are redesigned from scratch when they become difficult to maintain or new features are desired. As sites and costs increase, more incremental changes will become the norm. Reducing the cost and difficulty of such future changes should be a chief concern of Web site developers.

The key to reducing the costs of maintenance is to limit the impact of changes. Easily making changes to a site requires a regular structure that provides the ability to change one page or program component without undesirably affecting another component. Such a structural form makes the maintenance process easier by allowing the maintainer to focus only on the component to be fixed. To obtain such a structure, the design phase must have determined a decomposition of the site into pieces that are relatively independent from each other. As discussed in Chapter 6, segmenting the site and its programming elements is the basic idea behind programming methodologies such as modular decomposition. Besides trying to limit the impact of changes, there should be a focused attempt to isolate the portions of the site that are anticipated to change often. Web sites are often highly dynamic, which adds a new problem to traditional software maintenance.

Performing Maintenance

When discussing maintenance, many questions arise. The frequency of updates will affect how maintenance is carried out. Who will be making the changes and how they will be made are also important issues. Maintenance does not only consist of simple text and graphics changes to the Web site. Rather, it refers to the evolutionary growth of the Web site and covers a continuum ranging from minor bug fixes and content changes to major site overhauls. Regardless of scope, some type of methodology and management must be employed. Because of the urgency of many of the problems that may plague Web sites, maintenance is well suited to the spiral model of development. The spiral model provides a methodology for quickly addressing and resolving individual problems. For major maintenance tasks such as a graphical redesign or the addition of a section, some elements of the waterfall method used in the site's initial development may be more appropriate. For purely static sites, maintenance might consist of periodically checking to make sure that the information is current and that links to external sites are still valid. For time-sensitive content sites, daily or even hourly updates may be necessary. Technically complex sites with database or commerce functionality may require constant maintenance in the form of monitoring server activity and performance. In addition to anticipated maintenance, sites also encounter unexpected issues, such as bugs, server problems, or spontaneous feature additions that require maintenance.

Content Maintenance

Content maintenance is what people typically think of when Web site maintenance is discussed. It consists of gathering the content and then making the updates to the site. Maintenance in this sense was discussed briefly in the Requirements Analysis and Specification phase, where the site was classified as either static or dynamic. As mentioned in Chapter 5, one of the considerations for developing a database-driven site was for facilitating maintenance. Thus, to some extent, the methods of content maintenance for the site are already predetermined. However, there are still issues to be decided. As Web site content maintenance requirements become more of an issue or focal point within an organization, it may become necessary to integrate Web site updates into workflow or existing business processes.

In order to maintain the content of a Web site in a timely manner, responsibility for the updates must be assigned. Changes and content updates must be considered in terms of *what* needs to be updated, *who* controls the updating and *how* frequently updates are made. The process that is employed, whether manual, automated, or a combination of both, must address these factors. If the Web site was developed in-house, it seems likely that content maintenance will be performed in-house as well. However, because of the potential cost and problems of managing site maintenance, many firms opt to completely outsource the maintenance of the Web site. Though content collection is still the responsibility of the client, the coding and posting is off-loaded to the outside firm. Assuming the vendor is responsive and detail-oriented, this can be a time- and money-saving solution. However, some organizations may find themselves at the mercy of the vendor. They may wait weeks for changes to appear on the Web site and risk the integrity of the content. Regardless of the approach, given the critical nature of maintenance, staff issues or outside contracts should be considered before a site launches.

Once maintenance starts, a strict process should be established to determine who will perform the updates or request for updates, and when the updates should occur. Some companies elect to funnel all information through one primary "Webmaster." This process can slow the publication of the information to the Web. Giving content modification control to many individuals can also cause problems. If many people will be modifying the site, procedures, rules, and facilities must be implemented. Some Web server software or publishing tools have evolved to accommodate workgroup development and content management needs in terms of access control, revision control, and publishing process management. Simple rules, such as rolling in changes only once a week or once a day, can vastly improve the maintenance process. However, the most important maintenance rule is to **never work on a live site**. Far too often, the production site is the only existing version of the site, and changes are made to it live. This often results in broken links and pages changing while a user visits the site. All sites should be mirrored in the form of *a staging site*. Changes can be made and tested on the staging site; then the maintenance can be added to the production site in a controlled fashion. The staging server also has a secondary purpose of providing a full backup of the site just in case something goes wrong on the server. Other approaches, as discussed in Chapter 7, involve Web document publishing conventions such as adding comments to changed files, and naming files a certain way to indicate version or modification dates. Even with established templates and guidelines, it is inevitable that document authors will inject their own standards, causing the site's structure to degrade. Furthermore, though individual people or departments may *create* the pages, certain environments may necessitate the approval and posting of those pages to the Web site by a single person or team responsible for content management. By building accountability and a standards check into the process, the Web site quality deterioration process is at least slowed, if not eliminated completely.

Content Maintenance Systems

Often, an assessment of the process by which content is developed and published makes clear the need for a system to manage updates to the Web site. Usually, a clear set of processes or practices is evident. For instance, in news-oriented sites, a particular work-flow can be described. The center of activity is the online publication that is delivered with updated content to users at a certain frequency. Because of the quick turnover rate of the content, document authors must have a simple way to post their articles online. There may be editors who coordinate the posting and review, manage, and enter content in the appropriate sections. Obviously, this type of environment would be extremely difficult to manage by hand or with static HTML documents. A system that facilitates work-flow by maintaining content and controlling the formatting and publication of articles via the Web site is very useful.

Content maintenance systems typically involve a database back-end and a defined set of templates that control the presentation of the content that is flowed into them. They may also incorporate different levels of access and publication control. The power of such systems enables document authors to be concerned about content rather than the technical aspects of Web publishing. The degree of automation and the scope of such a system can vary. Smaller scale subsystems can be developed to maintain the content for certain sections of Web sites. Factors such as the frequency of updates and the regularity of the data will determine the appropriateness of the solution. Certain portions of corporate Web sites such as press releases, event calendars, job postings, organization chart listings, catalog data, and other forms of structured or time-sensitive data are well suited to this type of content maintenance application.

In addition to the many shrink-wrap tools and packages that address these needs to some degree, custom system can be created in-house or by an outside Web developer. The applications developed can range from very simple to extremely complicated. An example of a custom site maintenance is shown in Figure 9-3.

While site maintenance tools seem to automate only the inclusion of information or production of HTML pages, the real value is often far greater than what is seen on first glance. The value that is brought to a company can often be measured by how well an existing business process, such as the publication and distribution of press releases, can be engineered and automated on the Web. Because the Web has become such a focal point of corporate information and knowledge, this progression seems natural. Traditional business consulting firms and business process automation software vendors have begun to recognize the importance of developing Web-based solutions.

Functionality Maintenance: Corrective, Adaptive, and Perfective

While content maintenance is relatively predictable, functionality maintenance, particularly corrective maintenance, is often more like crisis management—problems arise and then must be dealt with. The "bugs" of a Web site are often thought to consist mostly of broken links. The discovery of such problems can be reduced using tools like site mappers, sweepers, or other analysis tools that chart the structure, links, and vital aspects of a site. Among other things, these tools can detect broken or unresponsive links, missing ALT attributes, and incorrectly sized images. In addition, the byte-size of pages is calculated, which can be useful in keeping the site download-friendly. Other testing tools can be used to attempt to break systems by feeding in various test cases to forms or other interactive elements.

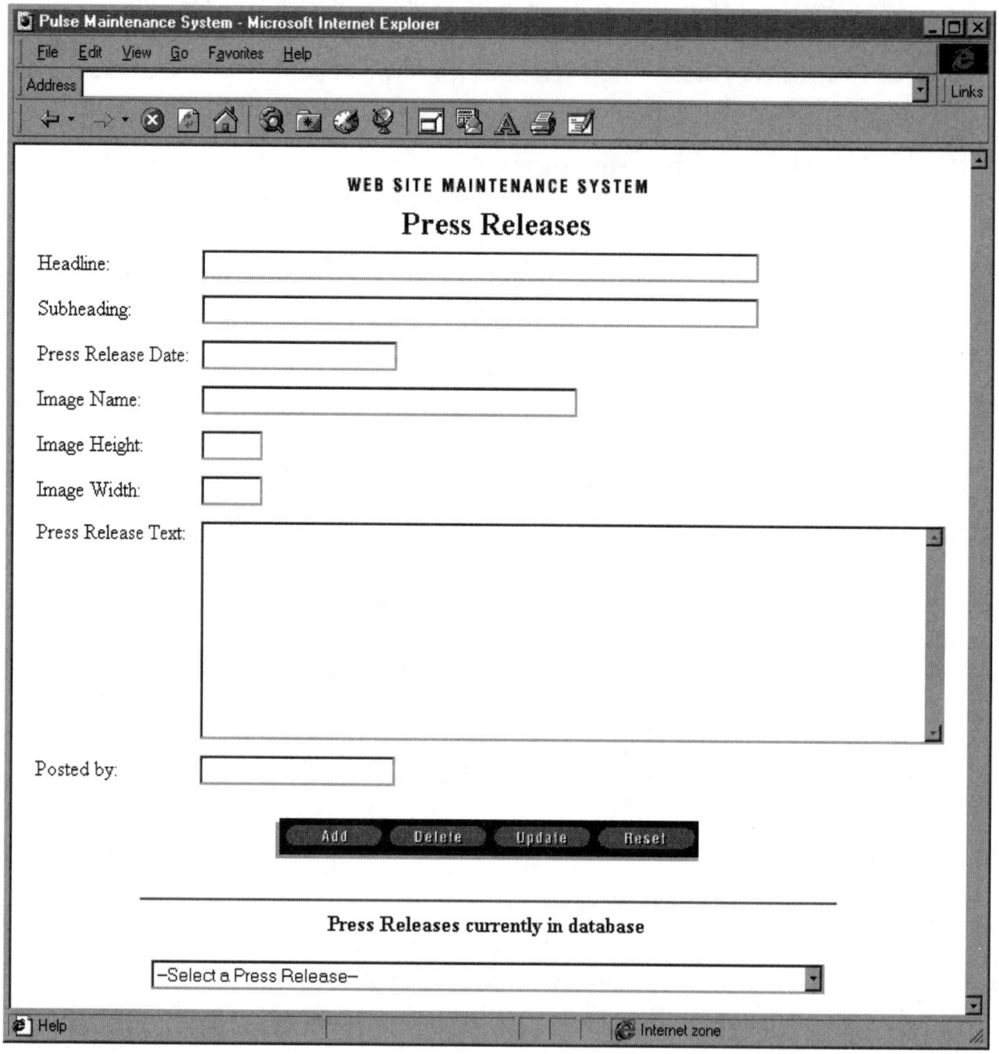

Figure 9–3. Example Site Maintenance System.

Though detection tools are helpful, it seems that users, not tools, overwhelmingly point out the need for functionality maintenance, otherwise known as "bug fixes." Though the problems are not always related to a bug in the code, but to a bug in the browser, it is still the Web developer's responsibility to make it work. Users will blame the developer even if the browser is at fault. These types of environmental changes introduce a major difference between Web site maintenance and software maintenance. Adaptive maintenance is inevitable, especially when considering the rapid development mindset of Web site building, the variety of client environments, and the constant change of browsers. This amount of adaptive maintenance required for a Web site is much greater than for traditional software, given the rate of change on the Internet. Because environment changes are hard to predict, future maintenance costs even when a Web site is well designed may be hard to determine.

As Web sites become more application-oriented, the number and variety of bugs tend to increase. Functionality problems may include applications that don't work correctly, or certain cases that cause crashes or bad output. Maintenance to fix site bugs and design flaws is termed corrective maintenance, and can often be thought of as equivalent to software patches. Depending on the severity of the error and its impact on the user, dealing with the problem often becomes an urgent matter. Unfortunately, due to the accelerated nature of time on the Web, the urgency of fixing problems is more on the order of hours than days or weeks. Consequently, the methodical planning of a software engineering methodology like the waterfall model may only get in the way. However, the spiral model of development lends itself well to these type of "fix on failure" situations.

Regardless of who or what is to blame, bugs that hinder the functionality of a Web site must be promptly addressed. Unfortunately, it may be impossible to address all bugs immediately. Using the spiral model, issues can be prioritized and then individually addressed and resolved. If the situation becomes so bad that serious bugs exist in many places and a significant number of pages fail, process models will not help. If there is a critical problem that will take more than a few minutes to rectify, a Web site or home page should be replaced with a placeholder indicating that that site is undergoing maintenance and will be available shortly. It is better to have one page that works than an entire site that doesn't. Furthermore, it is important to recognize the difference between bug fixes and feature additions, otherwise termed perfective maintenance. As discussed later in the chapter, extensions to a Web site are often encouraged by users and changes in site purpose. While the spiral model works well for minor crisis-oriented functionality maintenance, more major feature and functionality modifications should be addressed with the modified waterfall method used to build the initial site.

Delivery Maintenance

Even if a site is perfect both in its programming and its content, it is important to address delivery issues to ensure that an optimal delivery environment is maintained. If a site's traffic increases dramatically, it may be necessary to increase bandwidth or add servers to adequately support the site usage. For example, a public Web site hosted on a company's internal server may start to create an unacceptable drain on the company's network as the site's usage increases. As a result, the company might choose to outsource the hosting of the Web site. Alternatively, they may consider network upgrades or advanced techniques such as site mirroring or distributed hosting to accommodate the bandwidth required for the site. Bandwidth is not the only factor that affects the delivery of the site. Hardware and operating system upgrades may also be warranted. In addition, new versions of server software or middleware might be necessary to improve the site's performance or allow functionality to be added in the future. As mentioned throughout this book, it is important not to underestimate or overlook the delivery of the site from the user's perspective. Problems with delivery are often just as serious as poor visual design or functionality bugs.

Using Feedback to Grow or Modify a Web Site

While maintenance such as adding new features or correcting bugs may be initiated by the site design team, in practice maintenance is often encouraged by feedback, both direct and indirect, from the users and other interested parties. Sources of direct feedback include management, Web developers, interested individuals within the company, and users. Indirect feedback consists of monitoring a site's traffic with statistical analysis of the server log files.

Direct Feedback

No Web site will meet all requirements for all users. Users may notice bugs or suggest changes or improvements to a Web site. Site developers should encourage users to give feedback about the site through the use of comment response forms and surveys. In some cases, an audit or study should be performed to determine what users want. However, developers should be cautioned that not every demand for change or improvement can or should be met. Some users will make unrealistic requests and, just as the initial development phase proceeded by carefully determining feasibility, so should on-going maintenance.

Inevitably, most Web projects will have an individual, be it a vocal user or a manager, who doesn't have a good understanding about the Web and issues with Web sites, but continues to provide his or her unsolicited and generally nonconstructive comments. The use of trendy new technology or a desire to overload the home page with links will probably be suggested. The best way to deal with people like this is not to dismiss them, but to attempt to educate them as quickly as possible. Try to appeal to outside sources such as usability studies and articles from "experts" to avoid getting into a political battle. If it is possible to convert the person, he or she may become a powerful ally. Alternatively, this person may continue to cause disruptions and discourage others from using the site. Even if a site is well designed, a lack of use due to any reason—promotional or political—will inevitably result in failure.

Comments from users should not be viewed negatively. Instead, consider them as a positive opportunity and free usability testing. The management, designers, and developers of a Web site do not have the same perspective as the users. Consequently, they can only imagine and anticipate what those users might want. Feedback is important both for general maintenance changes and for determining enhancements to the site via requests for additional features. For example, if an overwhelming number of users of a Web site are requesting similar functionality, such as electronic commerce, it seems obvious that management should look into the feasibility of providing it. Similarly, users of an intranet or extranet might request the integration of the intranet with the existing inventory control system. Regardless, without a method to submit comments through e-mail, staff meetings, or some other medium, user feedback will go unheard.

In addition to providing a generic email address for free-form responses, it can be helpful to create a form with specific questions to encourage user feedback. For example, the company management might have several ideas for the next phase of the Web site, including threaded discussion groups, the use of online order status checking and enhanced search capabilities. A questionnaire can be helpful in determining if management has correctly anticipated the desires of the user. Querying the same company's staff to determine how the intranet could facilitate their daily tasks is important for the success of the site. With an extranet, the goal of the site is to serve the customer better. Consequently, an extranet survey might ask the user what would make this site even more useful. It is imperative to have some mechanism for collecting feedback from users. With user input regarding feature requests, future enhancements for the Web site can be planned. Users might even report that the Web site is currently meeting all of their needs.

Feedback is also possible by observing people using the site. While user comments can provide some sense of how people use a Web site, actually watching over someone's shoulder or from behind glass can reveal the areas with which users have trouble or where they hesitate. In general, such feedback only addresses the usability of a Web site, and not what it does or what content it may lack. Usability studies are often part of the testing process and were discussed in Chapter 8.

Management will also give feedback about a site. However, sometimes this feedback may be based more on what others are doing. For instance, if a company's main rival has a site that is very flashy, management might start to think that their own company's site pales in comparison, though it is in accordance with their existing corporate look-and-feel. Technology-wise, management may make similar demands for new features, based on the latest trends. While both types of suggestions may seem off-base to a Web developer, remember that management sets the goals that enable developers to create a site that fulfills a need. Revisiting the goals for the Web site can be helpful in this situation.

Web developers, either internal or external, can help provide a reality check for the real needs and goals of a site. With a strong technical understanding of what is involved in building a Web site, developers can attempt to convey the issues to management. In a sense, the developers provide ongoing concept exploration and feasibility analysis for the ideas proposed by management. In addition, Web developers often will propose ideas for the Web site to management. Knowledge of what is being done on other sites and in the industry can help incite ideas. However, do not rely solely on the suggestions of developers to maintain or fix sites. Users should be the final arbiters of what makes sense. Developers should be used to propose new ideas, which can then be tested or confirmed through user feedback.

Indirect Feedback: Statistics

In addition to directly gathering information, monitoring the traffic of the site is an important method of obtaining feedback. Indirect feedback comes from obtaining and analyzing statistical information captured by a Web server. The information is usually available as text files but is sometimes linked directly to a database. There is confusion over what type of information Web log files *contain* versus what type of information can be *interpreted* or *extrapolated* from software applications that analyze such information. For example, the number of users accessing a site is not a statistic natively logged by Web servers. There is further confusion as to the terminology used when talking about Web statistics. In some cases, there is no general consensus as to the correct way to reference concepts. Web site developers often speak of site success in terms such as number of visitors, hits, page views, etc. However, it is important to determine what really is being measured as well as the information upon which these values are based.

Web Site Statistics Terminology

First, it is important to understand site statistics terminology. Management often uses such information in the form of reports to determine site success or return on investment. Indeed, such information can be used to determine what portions of a site are being used, repeatedly used, or underused, etc. Interpreted correctly, this type of feedback can be valuable for developing a plan of action for site improvement or correction. It may be determined that certain sections are not attracting as much traffic as expected or desired. Further investigation might reveal that the users are only linking to the section from a limited number of pages/places and that additional linking is in order.

However, Web developers and management must be careful not to think of success simply in quantitative terms. Web site statistics should be considered in the proper context to derive meaning and value that can be useful for additional site maintenance and development. Just because a site is generating a lot of traffic does not necessarily mean it is a success. A good way to ensure that statistics are being interpreted properly is by using statements such as the following:

"The Product Section of the site with new information on such and such a product was viewed 1,000 times from 300 unique visitors during a period of two weeks. From this we can ascertain, _____."

From management's point of view, this kind of information is clearly more relevant than simply knowing the number of hits or visitors. As mentioned, the terminology used is often confusing and should be clarified up-front within organizations to establish a common frame of reference; statistical reporting software often contains its own terminology. For discussion purposes, we will provide some generally agreed upon definitions used in Web site statistics.

A *hit* is defined as a request for a particular object. Any page on a Web site may be composed of numerous objects. For a default Web index page with five images, the number of hits generated may be as high as seven. The HTML page itself would count as one hit and the images would account for 5. In some situations a Web server may also be having to redirect a request to another server or fix a URL that is missing a trailing slash. This redirection can also be considered a hit and may be logged.

A *view* indicates the number of times a particular page is brought up in a user's browser regardless of HTTP requests or who that viewer is. The term "visit" indicates the actual visitation of a particular user to a site in a unique time-frame. A user may view many pages and produce numerous hits, but count as only one visit. The term "unique visitor" is used to indicate a particular user. One way to measure unique visitors is through user authentication via log-ins or with cookies, which are small bits of information which can be issued to users and stored on their local hard drive for future retrieval and use, such as tracking visitations. Additional Web server software can be used to create and log information such as a Session ID that is later used by analysis programs to determine session intervals. However, if we use only an IP address or domain name to resolve a visitor's identity, we may find that the same IP address/domain name actually corresponds to different people. This is particularly troublesome in environments that use a proxy server or that have dynamic IP address allocation, as is the case with a dial-up terminal server.

■ Summary of Web Logs

In addition to understanding the terminology used, it is also important to understand the different types of logs. There are two basic logs available on all Web servers— the access log and the error log. Beyond these two basic logs, often there is a referrer log and an agent log. The access log contains detailed information about every request made to the Web server, indicating what object was requested and when. The format of the log is typically in what is called *common log* format. The basic structure of a common log format entry is:

Host-Field Ident AuthUser Time-Stamp HTTP-Request Status-Code Bytes-Transferred

An example from a real access log is shown in Figure 9-4.

```
131.116.213.114 - - [11/Mar/1997:01:15:36 -0800] "GET /workshop/
intervunj.html HTTP/1.0" 404 633

131.116.213.114 - - [11/Mar/1997:01:15:46 -0800] "GET
/workshop/intervu.html HTTP/1.0" 200 1683

131.116.213.114 - - [11/Mar/1997:01:15:48 -0800] "GET
/workshop/images/header.gif HTTP/1.0" 200 2048
```

Figure 9–4. Log File Entries.

Just looking at this, it is evident that the raw information from log files is not terribly useful. Logs will show the machine requesting the information, the time of the request, the file/object requested, the resulting HTTP status code information, and the actual number of bytes transferred for that particular object. Information such as the type of browser being used (user agent) as well as what link was followed to reach the page may also be included in the file. This information may be part of the main access log if a combined log format is used or part of separate log files like the referrer and user agent log. An error log is also generally available that indicates errors the server has encountered, particularly internal errors and configuration errors. The log simply contains a time stamp with the day, month, year, time and the error message. The actual errors in the file range from messages about the server starting up, reading new configurations, being unable to find files, unauthorized access requests, and so on. In conjunction with the 404 errors in the access log, it is possible to easily isolate broken links and other problems with the Web site.

Interpreting a Log File: Log Analysis Software

Regardless of the log format, information on *what* objects are being requested and *when* they are retrieved is available from all Web servers. Using log analysis software, more useful and meaningful information about the site activity can be extracted from the log(s). The software reports typically convey information such as the unique number of addresses making requests or the breakdown of activity in meaningful time-frames. Reports may also show information such as the unique number of URLs or the sections being accessed on a site. Sophisticated analysis may also reveal how users move through the site and even approximately how long they linger on particular pages. Statistics reports can be used to determine the actual amount of data transferred or traffic that is occurring, which is useful in determining both ongoing bandwidth requirements and whether they are being met adequately by the current server.

There are many different classes of statistical analysis packages available, and prices vary from free to tens of thousands of dollars. Currently, there is a vast market for auditing companies and real-time site tracking services. Some organizations might require a dedicated person to manage the statistics and understand the log information. For others, a package, potentially one that comes with the server, will probably produce adequate results.

Summary

After the initial site development is complete, there is still a great deal of work left to do. Even the most well-designed and implemented site will fail if nobody uses it. Promotion can help ensure that the proper people know about the site, but getting people to use a site on a continual basis may be difficult. Users are particularly frustrated when it is difficult to find new or updated information. Searching the Web at large, as well as localized sites can be difficult. The search problem is mainly due to the fact that there is little structure to Web documents. The Web is currently a completely open publishing environment. Any user can create any document he or she wants, about any topic, and in just about any form. Meta information can help provide some meaning for a document's role in a global or local information space. This is especially true in an intranet or extranet setting where the search space is limited and the document authors have full control over the indexing of their documents.

Once users are visiting a site, some sense of the site's usefulness and success can be determined by user feedback, both direct and indirect. While user comments provide specific suggestions, statistics can also be used to determine trends in the site's use. After determining problems, changes, and extensions, it is possible to begin the maintenance process. How maintenance should be performed and by whom should be well considered. When maintenance is poorly planned, the site can quickly degrade. Site maintenance tools can help, but the same challenges faced in software maintenance certainly apply to Web sites. The methodology of the maintenance process may be much different from the initial development of a site. Because there are often many unanticipated, urgent changes that arise, the spiral model of addressing important tasks first and then reevaluating the situation makes more sense than the relatively slow waterfall process that may be used on a large well-defined project. However, when a major change is made to the site, the modified waterfall model may still be appropriate.

References

1. Gorla, N. "Techniques for Application Software Maintenance," in *Information and Software Technology*, vol. 33, no. 1, pp. 65–73, January–February 1991.

2. Lientz, B., and Swanson, E. *Software Maintenance Management: A Study of the Maintenance of Computer Application Software in 487 Data Processing Organizations*, Addison-Wesley, Reading, Mass., 1980.

3. Landsbaum, J.B., and Glass, R.L. *Measuring & Motivating Maintenance Programmers*, Prentice Hall, Englewood Cliffs, New Jersey, 1992.

4. Belady, L.A.,and Lehman M.M. "A Model of Large Program Development," in *IBM Systems Journal*, vol. 1, no. 3, pp. 225–252, 1976. Reprinted in Lehman, M.M., Belady, L.A., eds, "Program Evolution: Processes of Software Change", Ch. 8, *APIC Studies in Data Processing No. 27*, Academic Press, London, 1985.

5. Longstreet, D.H., ed. *Software Maintenance and Computers*, IEEE Computer Society Press, Los Alamitos, CA, 1990.

Chapter 10

▶ Beyond Web Site Engineering

Web site engineering principles can be used to help bring Web projects under control and minimize the risk of a project being delivered late or over budget. However, anyone who has ever actually run a Web project can attest to the fact that no methodology or level of planning will account for every problem that may occur. Given the chaotic nature of the Web and the impact that it is having on corporations, the degree of uncertainty is only exacerbated. Running a successful Web project means being able to deal with uncertainty and all the outside factors that may sabotage the most well-engineered site.

Real Life: That Which Can't Be Planned For

Books about running projects, whether software projects or construction projects, always attempt to present real-world examples of situations to be avoided. While we will certainly present a few of these problem situations here, it is impossible, even counterproductive, to enumerate all the possible caveats that may occur during a Web site project. Real world project management accepts that some events are just plain unpredictable. While some of the problems that occur on a Web project may be specific to an organization or manager, others are repeated over and over again. We will attempt to illustrate a few of the most common real life Web management problems that occur, and present a few ideas on how to deal with them.

When the Hype Is Over

Hype often drives Web projects. This is not unique to Web projects, but the number of hype-driven sites is significant enough to indicate that this is a common problem. In some sense, hype is good because it can get Web projects off the ground. A little excitement is a great motivator. Hype gets people to attend the Web planning meetings. Hype often helps move projects along, even facilitating the prompt allocation of funds. Hype can get volunteers to help build the site. Often, a person generally termed the *Web Evangelist* is at the center of the hype maelstrom, stirring up the excitement. The background of the evangelist ranges from a summer intern to the CEO of the company; the only requirement for the position seems to be that he or she thinks the Web is the greatest thing ever. For the Web manager, the evangelist is a great person to enlist in keeping Web projects alive. However, it is important to keep the Web evangelist in check and prevent the creation of unrealistic expectations for Web projects. Hype has a downside, and the evangelist never seems to be around once accountability becomes an issue.

While hype is a good motivator to start projects, it is often short-lived and fails to carry the project through to completion. It often seems like every department is willing to provide content for the Web site at the preliminary meeting. However, continued support doesn't always follow once the work involved is understood. This is particularly true when maintenance is involved. While collecting content from all departments for an initial site launch may be possible, continual content updates might be more difficult. Will the Web team have to go around weekly and encourage departments to update sections? Will people even listen to the Web team's request once they are busy and not as interested in the Web site? What will happen when the Web team volunteers are asked to return to their regular job duties within the organization? Who will keep the site up then? Don't get carried away in the hype. Hype is good, but it always ends, even if the site is wildly successful. Once the Web isn't new, business issues or boredom may set in and the Web team will no longer be the center of the corporate structure. This isn't the signal for the Web manager to jump ship. On the contrary, it is time to really go to work.

Veto From Above

The "veto from above" is a common problem with Web projects, particularly those that don't involve senior management at an early stage. What happens in these projects is that near the release date, the site is delayed by a senior executive, generally due to some look-and-feel or conceptual problem that should have been dealt with much earlier. To avoid this, project managers may attempt to involve management from the start. Because of the novelty of Web sites, however, there is often a desire for nearly everyone in an organization to get involved. Realistically, not every person who may use or have an opinion about the Web site can or should be made aware of all the issues before release. With a dozen senior level executives on the final review committee, there is certain to be something that somebody doesn't like. To make matters worse, senior management often lacks a full understanding of all the issues or a complete history of the project. Consequently, their last minute criticism is way out of bounds. Little can be done in advance to avoid the delays due to "vetoes from above," particularly when there are many levels between the actual project manager and the reviewers. Getting everyone involved in a project just isn't practical. Outside Web developers must make sure to protect themselves from pre-release vetoes with special contracts and project termination fees. The good news is that while there may always be the occasional unexpected management veto, as the novelty of Web sites subsides, the number of times high level management wants to personally inspect every page of the site should diminish.

Attack of the Outside Experts

One of the problems in Web site design is the assumption of the quality of opinions from outside "experts." Web site construction—from simple brochurelike sites to high-end database-driven networked applications—is an exploding industry. The number of people calling themselves Web developers is enormous, but the variation in the skills of these developers is just as enormous. Project managers should try to educate management about Web sites and instill a sense of what it takes to build one lest they open themselves up to an attack from an outside "expert." Outside experts tend to have a vested interest in telling the decision makers that a site is slow, buggy, overpriced, or just plain poorly designed, particularly when they are angling for work. Occasionally, these often unsubstantiated claims can run a project off course, especially when management hears that the Web project could have been completed for a fraction of the current cost. While the opinions of outside experts can be valuable and keep a project inline, there should be a focus on how to *fix* a project, *not* place blame. When dealing with an outside expert attack, ask for suggestions and recommendations, not criticism, and be sure to check their credentials. Many times, the "expert" Web developer is a person with little formal training who has built a few Web pages with a WYSIWYG page tool. While his or her opinions may be valid, it is curious to note that, in other industries, such random barbs would be ignored. It is unlikely that a studio boss in the movie industry would halt the production of a film because he heard the negative opinions of a home moviemaker whose only experience was filming his child's soccer games on the weekend. Yet, in the Web industry, projects can be derailed by people with similar levels of experience in Web development. The only way to minimize or avoid this type of project sabotage is to educate management and increase the possibility that they will be able to accurately rate outside opinions. Of course on the other hand there is certainly the possibility that the outside expert is truly an expert, but there may still be problems. Never questioning the advice of a consultant may lead to trouble particularly when an ego or hidden agenda is involved. Like all outside opinions, a second one never hurts and always remember that those who pay for the advice have the right to ignore it.

Web Egos

Software engineering experts generally believe that people are key to a successful project [(1) McConnell 96, (2) Boehm 81]. Many have suggested that a really good developer can be up to ten times as productive as a mediocre one. On Web projects, there seems to be similar evidence that certain individuals excel at Web production while others with equal backgrounds perform poorly. A common example of the difference between a good and bad Web developer is a lack of attention to detail. It seems that often highly skilled Web designers find things like spelling or realistic directory structures to be beneath them. While the site may look or work great, the project suffers from lack of polish and hard work may go unnoticed because of a typo or errant broken link. Obviously, seeding a project team with Web superstars can really help a Web site. However, there is often a downside to high-producing Web professionals that is common among high-producing software engineers, but maybe not as common—Web egos.

Web Dictators

Because of the emphasis on the Web within a corporation, Web development has created some monstrous egos and attracted individuals who crave attention. Occasionally, a star developer will attempt to wrestle control of a project away from management and start taking titles such as "Webmaster" or "-mistress," "Web Czar," or "Web Guru" a little too seriously. On some occasions, the key developer may hold a site hostage, requiring all changes to be personally inspected before appearing on the Web site. At this point, the overempowered Web developer or Web development group is basically insubordinate; it has set up its own small kingdom outside normal management channels. Why such nonsense is tolerated within a corporate structure is not clear, but it appears to be common, probably due to some belief that the Web is so new and difficult that only the superstar developers can possibly comprehend it.

Overcompensation

Another problem with Web superstars is their expected compensation. The news media often has promoted the idea that superstar developers get paid superstar salaries. While some developers are paid executive level salaries, many are not. The truth of the matter is that such exceptions occur in every industry. The game programmers that come up with a hit title earn enough to drive multiple sports cars. But how many game programmers don't make hit titles? Think about what the nonsuperstar programmers and Web developers really make. The "exception is the rule" attitude has many less-than-stellar Web developers demanding ridiculous wages, with some actually getting them. The rates charged by top Web design firms like Organic Online (www.organic.com) should not be used as the standard for what most Web developers earn. It is also interesting to compare dollars across industries. While there is no doubt that building Web sites is difficult, sometimes it is interesting to see how much HTML skills are valued compared to C++ programming with an engineering background.

When held hostage by Web developers who want ego money, project managers might consider letting the troublemakers go and training team members from within. While it may slow the project down, dealing with compensation-hungry Web developers may have serious consequences. Those who think that Web professionals always deserve huge salaries may stir up trouble in the development group, suggesting that all are underpaid and should demand more money or leave for freelance contracts. There is nothing wrong with Web professionals being paid well. However, it often seems that desired compensation matches the ego and not the skill. Managers are well advised to try to determine what motivates Web developers.

■ Ego Sites

Ego sites are those sites that are built to satisfy the ego of the developer. Given the artistic crossover with graphic design and multimedia, there seems to be a common desire for ego-driven Web developers to put their own creative stamp on projects. It is interesting to watch outside vendors actually convince a company with a 20-year-old brand identity to toss it in favor of their "personal" Web look. Conservative companies with wild-looking sites and well-regarded companies with amateurish sites often result when sites are built to meet an ego requirement rather than a business one. Occasionally, it is more the "not invented here" attitude rather than a business need that convinces firms to bring projects in-house once they learn a little HTML. When high-level executives decide they want to personally design and implement the site, the ego site can become a huge problem. Unfortunately, it is often difficult for underlings to tell the boss that the excessive use of animated GIFs really isn't that cool, and that he or she has better things to do than code HTML.

Ego-driven sites transcend look-and-feel, and rely heavily on technology. For example, a large cosmetics company site initially employed every Java, JavaScript, multimedia, and server-side trick in the book just to show off a few different shades of lipstick. The site was built to show off or to win awards, not to fulfill user needs. Ego-driven projects are not new. However, the hype of the Web in combination with the possibility of high compensation for spectacular sites make ego-driven sites a little too common on the Web. No further evidence of ego sites is needed than visitation counters, award icons, and mandatory links to credits pages with the names of outside vendors. Management needs to control ego sites and be realistic about vendors. Most companies generally don't allow commercials for outside designers or developers on their print literature, television spots, packaging, or other outsourced projects. Why should they let this practice go on with their Web site? In short, egos may be useful to motivate individual developers—but don't let an ego overwhelm a project.

■ Everyone As Webmaster

One team-oriented problem that often jeopardizes Web projects is every team member's desire to be a Webmaster. The Webmaster, in the form of an individual who knows everything about Web site building from graphic design to database design, is mostly a myth. Yet an astonishing number of graphic designers want to learn Java programming, and the same number of programmers want to learn graphic design [(3) Powell 97]. While there is nothing wrong with a person wanting to explore other careers or interests, there often seems to be a lack of acknowledgment of one's core competence. Rare is the individual who is a gifted artist, elegant programmer, excellent writer, and diplomatic manager. While such people may exist, the rate of change of the Web industry makes it impossible to excel in all these areas. Team members should be made to feel that their individual contributions are important. Graphic designers should not be belittled by the programmers, and the programmers should not be told by the graphic designers to stay behind the scenes. A Web manager should acknowledge the backgrounds of individual participants and prevent a technical or virtual caste system from emerging.

Many projects cannot avoid this because of the background of the person in charge. When the Web manager's experience is based on the visual aspects, there is often an overemphasis on the visual nature of projects and a corresponding lack of support for or interest in the programming. Examples of this abound. For instance, high-end advertising agencies and graphic design firms burn through huge budgets for Web projects and leave nothing for the development of backend systems and databases. Even worse is when they try to do complex interactivity themselves and build programmed sites that aren't thoroughly tested, or are designed only to work under ideal conditions. Likewise, similar problems occur when the Web manager encourages the technical side of the project too much. A few computing professionals who build sites may forego any assistance with visuals. While the site may work, navigation may be confusing, and the lack of visuals or use of less-than-professional visuals may counteract any genius going on behind the scenes. The lack of quality visuals is especially dangerous when the site is initially evaluated by management or customers who may not immediately see the site's functionality. Technologists should remember that first impressions really count. Designers should remember that first impressions wear off and focus will shift to purpose and use. The ideal Web manager embraces the diversity of the staff and realizes that it is this diversity which makes Web sites successful.

Technology Shifts

One aspect of Web projects that is not a significant problem in software engineering is technology shifts. Web projects are very difficult because the technology changes so often. The software development community doesn't have to worry that the specification of C++ is going to change dramatically from one month to the next. On the other hand, in the short history of the Web, developers have already seen multiple versions of HTML, Java, and JavaScript emerge. Often, management may regard new Web technology as the mythical "silver bullet" described by Brooks [(4) Brooks 87] and adopt it midway during a project. Shifting technologies during the project causes major setbacks as developers attempt to absorb and adapt to the changes. Furthermore, many of the new Web technologies are often riddled with bugs, causing developers to struggle to develop work-arounds. Ego-oriented developers often feed on technology shifts and attempt to incorporate every new browser feature into their sites. Usually, the new technologies are added simply to show off and provide no tangible benefit. Frames, layers, Java applets, animation, scrolling tickers, and various JavaScript gimmicks have all enjoyed initial heavy site use, often only to be removed at a later date. Sometimes, they are eventually worked back into the site where appropriate.

In gimmick form, new technologies seem harmless enough. However, the costs of the new technologies are significant. First, they may distract developers from the important features of a site. Second, the development costs for new technologies generally initially outweigh those of known technologies. The developer has to learn the new technology before it can be used to improve the site. Of course, down the line, new technologies may afford significant savings. However, if the site is always being rebuilt with a new technology, it may never realize any cost reduction benefits.

Defending Web Projects

As Web hype dies down, a Web project often comes under criticism. If a Web project appears to be over budget or an outside expert suggests that the site didn't do what it was supposed to do, Web managers may have to defend the project or may even face losing their jobs. Defending well-thought-out Web projects isn't necessarily difficult if it can be shown that the site has some effect on the bottom line. Unfortunately, it isn't always possible to show benefit because a measurement of success hasn't been established. Even worse, a Web developer may be held responsible because the people who initially evangelized the site have long since moved on to other projects or are above the developer in the management structure. While all types of projects are subject to questioning, it seems more common with the Web projects because of their relative newness. Just as easily as people fall in love with the Web, they seem to question its usefulness. This shouldn't come as a surprise; it is the logical reaction to excessive hype.

Before a site can be defended, its purpose must be evaluated. The critical nature of site planning is evident when it comes to defending why the site was built in the first place. A clear purpose can be used to avoid future defense because it can help achieve management buy-in and educate people about what the site will eventually do. Unfortunately, sites which are not well planned often require a purpose to be retrofitted onto them after launch. This lack of well-defined purpose is somewhat unique to the Web. It is probably due to the novelty factor surrounding Web sites, as well as the fear that corporations need a Web presence to remain competitive. The Web Site Engineering process described throughout this book has focused on heavy planning during initial site development to avoid having to graft on a purpose later. Future iterations in a Web project may have less well-defined purposes in order to react to changing business needs. However, some risks can be taken once need has been established. In many ways, the analogy of a Web site as a house applies. Without a base purpose as the foundation for a Web site, it is not wise to add further features, particularly those that aren't well understood.

The less clear the need for a Web site feature, the greater the risk to the Web developer. This is especially true if management loses faith in a project and begins to question the purpose of the site.

Measurements

The best way to defend a Web project is to show the benefit of the site in the form of some measurement. As discussed in Chapter 9, statistics can be used to show the value of a site. However, site measurements are often not well thought out. A site's success is not necessarily determined by the number of people who visit it, but rather by whether the site's goals were met. Don't be fooled into trying to use the common measurement of success like visits, as it may not work in your favor. For example, an educational site we worked on was considered a failure by outside viewers because it only had a few hundred visits a month. Yet with $300,000 or more in revenues generated in a year from a $12,000 initial investment, management eventually hired full-time staff to keep the site going. Another site we worked on reached tremendous numbers of individuals and won an award, but generated little tangible benefit for the site's owners because their purpose and business plan wasn't well thought out. In fact, the site cost more than $5000 a month in hosting alone due to site traffic, but initially generated absolutely no measurable revenue. Oddly, while measurements were useful in showing the benefits or problems with the two example projects, each client's appreciation and long-term retention did not correlate with the site's success. Measurements that are helpful for defending a site from its detractors are those that show the usefulness of the site. If a return on investment can be shown, most managers will support a site regardless of any complaint from an outside expert about look-and-feel or technology used. However, while measurements are useful in helping to defend against complaints, politics and bad management decisions will continue to exist both inside and outside the Web industry.

Politics

Politics will often take a Web project manager by surprise. Even if a project is completed under budget and on time, politics may get in the way and doom the project. For example, if a marketing department leads a Web project team, the MIS department may later attempt to derail the project because they feel it is part of their territory. The reverse works as well with an MIS-developed corporate site being shot down by marketing.

Disruption of Corporate Structure

The Web has disrupted corporate structure. In the past, the Marketing Communications (also known as "MarCom") group of a corporation has been the primary point of contact from a company to the public beyond any form of technical support or sales. Developers and internal support staff for information systems (MIS) generally had little contact with the public and did not interact greatly with the marketing department. With the dawn of the Web, this line between marketing and technology has begun to disintegrate. Marketing departments that are building Web sites have to acknowledge that they need technical people to help create working systems. MIS groups that are building sites have to acknowledge that MarCom generally understands what customers want better than they do. Both groups have to work together, and the corporate structure must accommodate a new path of communication between groups that are generally staffed by very different types of people. Often, the two groups can't work together and attempt to circumvent each other by outsourcing services.

Outsourcing for the Wrong Reasons

Often, marketing departments will call on an external vendor to build a Web site's technology because they can't or won't talk to internal developers. The Web vendor often acts as a surrogate MIS department, helping the marketing group hook into databases and build systems for the Web. Conflict may eventually arise when internal MIS staff members feel slighted because they weren't consulted or used. It really doesn't matter who the outside vendor is: problems will arise if the MIS/MarCom split isn't resolved. If the outside vendor is very good, the MIS group tends to feel threatened. If the outside vendor is incompetent, the MIS group will criticize the marketing department's poor decision. The Web critics in MIS groups are a vocal bunch and will often rightfully derail Web projects. Unfortunately, they often lack the time to take on the Web project they inherit from the marketing group or the outside vendor. If MIS drops the ball after taking a project away from a marketing group, it potentially increases the animosity between the two groups. To avoid a rift between the marketing and information services departments, there should be a representative from both involved in every Web project, even when it is outsourced.

Web development outsourcing should only occur for the right reasons—specifically, because it is cheaper than doing it in-house, because there isn't enough staff to do it in-house, or because there isn't the required talent to do it in house. Web development is expensive and may require the talents of many individuals. When considering the cost of even one full-time dedicated staff member to run a Web project, a budget of $100,000/year for an outsourced vendor is actually reasonable. Don't be fooled by the volunteerism of the Web hype phase. If employees from all over the company are using time to work on the Web site, there is still a cost involved. One large defense contractor stated during a Web budget and bid meeting that their site cost $3,000/year. This was the cost of their Web server and did not consider any development costs. Inspection of the site revealed that there were over 1,000 pages and at least a dozen individuals working on the site. Many of these individuals were senior scientists who were hand tagging newsletter updates despite the astronomical value of their time. Outsourcing makes sense when it is too expensive to do everything in-house. Outsourcing also makes sense when management won't add new employees but adds a Web site to a department's responsibility.

Web Sites Affect Organizations

As discussed in the previous sections, the Web can shake up the corporate structure. The rift that often occurs between MIS and marketing departments is only one example of the shock waves caused by the Web. As a Web site becomes a mechanism for selling a product, supporting customers, recruiting employees, communicating with investors, and a variety of other tasks, the boundaries between departments in an organization blur. If a Web site is to be used throughout a business, the sole Webmaster or even marketing department can't be in charge of the whole thing. They lack the understanding of all aspects of the business. Senior management must step in when the corporate Web site matures to the level that it is more than a brochure or marketing vehicle. The Web site, particularly when it is in the form of a corporate intranet, may become the information backbone of the company and can be considered part of the overhead of the firm. Typically, managers in charge of operations and information systems will eventually inherit overall responsibility for the corporate Web direction. If not, they may find their role in the company diminished in favor of the person who runs the site. The reliance on a corporate Web site shifts the balance of power in favor of those who control the information within the company.

Intranet Communication and Empowerment

When intranet or extranet Web sites are built, the effect on a corporation can be tremendous. Posting information on intranets can significantly increase the flow of communication within a company. However, along with this new information comes change. Employees may feel empowered by access to a Web site and may become disruptive because of their newfound publishing power. There have been numerous examples of employees using Web sites to promote their own ideas both within and outside a company. The effects on a corporation of an employee promoting less than acceptable political, moral, or religious views can be disastrous for corporate image and may cost clients. Web managers need to rein in developers who don't understand the significance of the content they place on Web sites both internally and externally.

Some Web professionals may claim that we are encouraging censorship by management. Not at all. The empowerment brought by the Web is valuable and should be encouraged, but there needs to be some common sense. Why should a corporation pay an individual to promote, internally or externally, views that are not related to the business? Most employees would not assume that they could use company funds and time to start a print magazine. Obviously, the boss would notice the high postage bills and heavy use of the photocopy machine. Is it only because management may not notice similar efforts

307

on the Web that employees feel it is their right to start a personal site on company public and private Web servers? Managers are faced with a new challenge of keeping Web developers under control lest they turn Web projects into pet projects that may not necessarily represent company views.

Even when employees act appropriately, publishing both internally and externally may bring more management challenges. In some sense, a corporate intranet can provide a voice to those who have not had one. Just as e-mail messages often include things that are not generally said face to face, so do Web pages. Corporate intranets, particularly in very large organizations, may include statements about the "powers that be" that are less than acceptable. Such information broadcast around the company may be very destabilizing. Management should act quickly to determine why such messages are being posted and to ensure that the posting ends. In some sense, a corporate intranet may open up a dialog between disgruntled employees and management that may be far removed from the front lines. In other ways, an intranet can act as a bull horn for the radical fringe in a corporation and cause damage. Corporate communication policies are more important than ever because of the speed and reach of the Web.

Extranets Bring Customers Closer

Just as an intranet or public Web site development project may blur the lines between departments within a business, an extranet may begin to blur the line between a corporation and its partners and customers. Extranets allow customers and other trusted parties a "peek behind the corporate veil." In the past, most customers, as well as trusted partners like distributors, had very little access to information about how a company worked internally. In many ways, being able to hide how the business ran encouraged less than ideal internal solutions. Software systems built for internal staff lacked the polish of professional software development. The attitude was, why put the extra effort into internal software products if they're only for internal customers; they'll understand, right? Even if they didn't, the MIS department knew they really couldn't be fired by another department very easily. However, now that external customers are beginning to have access to the internal systems, they must have the same quality standards as any other corporate contact with the outside world. When done properly, bringing the customer closer to the organization through a custom extranet creates a stronger relationship between the organization and its partners. Web developers must face the fact that the quality of their work may affect the company's bottom line.

Web Sites May Reveal Business Problems

Because a Web site may fundamentally change the way a company does business by encouraging more communication, both internally and externally, it also tends to reveal inherent problems within the business. For example, Web sites are generally content-driven, and gathering the content for a Web site is a challenging task. While performing this task, it often becomes evident that the documents are not centrally controlled in an organization; there may be crossover between information that appears on a public Web site, an intranet, a corporate CD-ROM, and print documentation. Many corporations do not control documents well and, as a result, knowledge is lost. Inefficiency may occur because information must be repurposed from one media to another as it is exchanged in a company. Often, a Web site may become the focal point of a firm's knowledge resources and serve as a repository for documents. In this sense, the Web reveals the problem of document management that is often overlooked in companies. Whether the Web site should be the document repository or not is an open question, but the benefits of thinking about information more abstractly is obvious as shown by Figure 10-1.

If anything, a Web site proves that information is an asset of any organization that should be tracked and controlled. Besides revealing documentation problems, a Web site may expose problems in business processes like work or document flow. For example, when automating a job recruiting system it may become evident that certain aspects of the hiring process are no longer required, such as manually distributing resumes to hiring managers. Other aspects, like quality filtering, may become important as the volume of applications increases. The changes that may result from automating a business function can be significant and may result in a shift of job duties. Because it often spurs the reevaluation of work flow, the Web goes hand in hand with process reengineering. However, Web developers are warned not to let this go to their

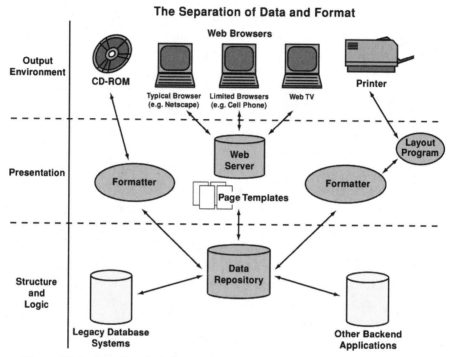

The Separation of Data and Format

Figure 10–1. Benefits of Abstract Information Storage.

heads. Reworking the business practices of another department is not the right of the developer. Serious political battles will surely result for those developers who take such tasks upon themselves.

Staying In Bounds

The key point to realize about Web development is that it provides plenty of opportunity for the developer to go out of bounds. Whether it is the marketing department trying their hand at applications development, a Web developer trying to re-engineer the sales process, or the MIS department trying to set look-and-feel for the corporation, there are plenty of chances to overstep lines of responsibility and ownership. Web site engineering principles say nothing about how to deal with the politics and problems that result if a Web site drastically affects an organization's practice. They simply acknowledge that such issues may arise. Web developers are well advised to keep perspective on their role in an organization. While the hype of a Web project can quickly propel them to fabulous success, it can just as quickly bring them down if mistakes are made. What may appear, from a developer's perspective, to fall under the responsibility of a Web team may not be how management views the situation. So until a consensus is reached as to what Web development includes, Web professionals should try to understand business issues ranging from marketing to site purpose and measurements, if only to protect themselves. In some cases, they may have to provide substitute decision making if management takes no interest or relinquishes ownership of the Web site. However, do not assume that such knowledge or decision making forever empowers the developer to go outside any existing structure in the organization. Eventually, management may want to control projects or may notice Web developers going around existing chains of command. Going out of bounds puts both project and manager at risk.

Summary

Web site development is difficult. Web sites involve a mixture between print publishing and software development, between marketing and computing, between internal communications and external relations, and between art and technology. While it is difficult to make generalizations about all Web sites, one thing can be said: They are important to organizations and may affect the corporate "bottom line." Because of their growing importance and complexity, there is a need for more formal methods. Software engineering provides processes that are useful in developing Web sites. However, the difficult nature of Web sites and the lack of familiarity with site development suggests that developers should try more basic methods and development practices first. This book has discussed how software engineering principles can be applied to Web site development. However, even perfect use of all theory will not guarantee site success. The real world is ripe with pitfalls and the Web project manager must watch out for a variety of problems ranging from internal politics to industry hype. Yet these risks are not unique to the Web—all projects have risk, though the newness of the Web may make running a Web project seem more difficult than it is. In short, the current environment of the Web, in conjunction with the dramatic effect that Web sites have on business, makes Web development both a risky and a rewarding endeavor.

References

1. McConnell, S., *Rapid Development*, Microsoft Press, Redmond, WA, 1996.

2. Boehm, B., *Software Engineering Economics*, Prentice Hall, Englewood Cliffs, NJ, 1981.

3. Powell, T., Personal observations of student enrollment traits in University of California, San Diego, Extension Web Development classes for years 1995–1997.

4. Brooks, F., "No Silver Bullet: Essence and Accidents of Software Engineering," *Computer*, 10-18, April 1987.

Index

N

O

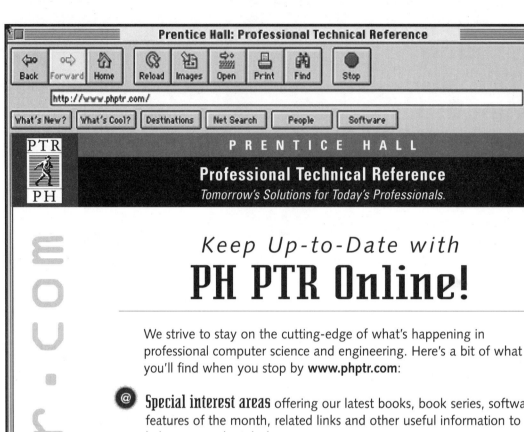